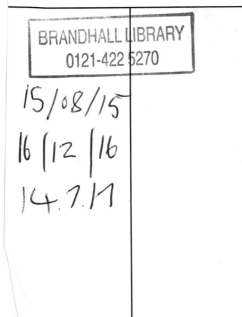

Police, Crime & 999

the true story of a front line officer

John Donoghue

Matador
Unit 9 Priory Business Park,
Wistow Road
Kibworth Beauchamp
Leicester LE8 0LQ, UK
Tel: (+44) 116 279 2299
Fax: (+44) 116 279 2277
Email: books@troubador.co.uk
Web: www.troubador.co.uk/matador

ISBN 978 1848766 853

British Library Cataloguing in Publication Data.
A catalogue record for this book is available from the British Library.

Printed and bound by TJ International, Padstow, Cornwall, UK

Typeset in 11pt StempelGaramond by Troubador Publishing Ltd, Leicester, UK

Matador is an imprint of Troubador Publishing Ltd

For Bethan

ACKNOWLEDGEMENTS

This may sound like a bad Oscar speech, but I have some people to thank.

Firstly, I want to thank all my friends and colleagues in the police, particularly on E shift, without whom I'd have no material to write about. I've been told by the hierarchy not to mention any names, but when you read on, you'll know who you are, except, that is, if you are deeply offended by your portrayal, in which case you've made a mistake and it's meant to be someone else... probably. Anyway, I have enjoyed working with you all. Well, most of you (it's a joke!).

Next, there are the kind group of people who, despite having better things to do, devoted their valuable time to help me with the draft manuscript. This help has taken the form of wearing pencils down to a nub correcting my many errors, photocopying endless drafts at their workplace instead of mine, advising what anecdotes I'd better leave out to avoid the risk of a disciplinary (and not taking offence when I ignored them), offering constant encouragement and occasionally, just occasionally, giving me a biscuit.

I can name these people, and so I will. Thanks to Sharon, Diane, Maggie, Nancy, Glynda, Lysa, Elizabeth and Jemima. I am indebted to you all. Not financially though, I just want to make that clear.

Then, there is the highly talented Rich Endean aka The Creative Agent. I actually am indebted to him financially.

Finally, I'm well aware that, generally, people only read the acknowledgements to find out if they are in them. So, if you've read this far and not had a mention already, then consider yourself mentioned now as I thank you, dear reader, for picking up this book; you now hold in your hands my tales from the sharp end of the Fuzz. If you are in the police yourself, I'm sure that many of the incidents, escapades and bizarre calls won't come as any surprise to you. If you aren't though, be prepared to find out what really happens behind the scenes in the police as all is revealed before your astonished face. That's not meant to sound conceited, by the way, it just sounded a bit comical when I wrote it.

I hope you enjoy the book.

John Donoghue

www.policecrime999.com

INTRODUCTION

Someone once said that a policeman's lot is not a happy one, however, I beg to differ. Despite all the drunkenness and cruelty, crime and disorder, the job has the potential to be fun – a lot of fun.

There is a tale of two police officers who went to the house of an elderly lady to take a statement from her. She made them both a cup of tea and ushered them into the front room where they all sat, discussing the purpose of their call. As they talked, the door was nudged open and a German Shepherd dog pottered into the middle of the room. The dog looked around and then proceeded to squat down and, with his back legs all a-quiver, deposited a fresh steaming turd on the lounge room carpet. The police officers exchanged sideways glances but didn't say anything. After all, it was the woman's house and everyone has different standards – it wasn't up to them to admonish the hound. They looked over at the house owner but she just acted as if nothing had happened. Instead, she avoided looking at the dirty beast and his doings, picked up her cup of tea, took a sip and continued to politely chat to the officers. Meanwhile, the dog, having completed his ablutions, sauntered back out of the room.

Twenty minutes later and ready to leave, the officers' curiosity had finally got the better of them. As they thanked the lady for the tea, one of them felt compelled to enquire why she hadn't said anything when her dog had come into the room and pooped on the floor.

"*My* dog?" replied the old woman. "I thought he was *your* dog!"

*

I have served my Queen and Country in the military, been both a sailor and a soldier, and travelled the world from the Gulf of Mexico to the Arabian Sea. I've seen the majesty of the Northern Lights, experienced a desert night sky fall and roll the whole day over, been frozen in the Arctic and almost got heat stroke in Africa. I've suffered sleep deprivation in Germany, dehydration in Djibouti, been shot at in Puerto Rico and kicked in the Urals. But nowhere, nowhere I tell you, have I ever come across a dog entering a room, having a shit, and no one saying a word!

Like most men my age, I was forty. Since leaving the Armed Forces I had spent the last few years as a manager for a large international security consortium. It may sound like a shady organisation straight out of a James Bond movie; staffed by Pussy Galore and presided over by Dr Evil plotting world domination but, believe me, it wasn't.

If I use phrases such as 'quarterly budget review' and 'sales growth forecast', you'll get an idea how action packed and exhilarating my days had now become. As the rest of the world had celebrated the arrival of the twenty-first century, I just realised I was stuck in a job I hated. I was bored and needed some excitement in my life again. Whilst some men might have an affair with a Latvian lap dancer, learn to play the guitar, get a pair of aviator sunglasses or buy a fancy motorcycle, after hearing about the pooping German Shepherd, I knew there was just one answer to my own personal dilemma. Join the police!

I put my notice in, handed back the keys to my company car, got a girl round to flog my semi and cancelled my subscription to 'Networking and Deadline Quarterly (incorporating Downsize monthly magazine)'.

So it was that a year later I found myself on parade as the newest (and possibly oldest) recruit to the forces of law and order, swearing the oath of allegiance, being presented with my warrant card and being sworn into the office of Constable (so named in order to amuse children and drunks the world over).

I would also be known to some as a 'Bobby' after Sir Robert Peel, who first invented the idea of a uniformed service to police the streets back in 1829. Some might even call us the Bill after (and I'm guessing here) someone named William who helped Peel set up the Force in the first place. It seems perfectly reasonably to speculate that as William got older, people then felt justified in calling us the Old Bill. His other mates who assisted in the initial establishment of the service were presumably named Fuzz, Filth, Pig, Rozzer, Five-O, Babylon and Black Bastard.

After the obligatory two years pounding the beat on foot, I eventually took the month long police driving course. Four weeks were spent driving at breakneck speeds across the highways and byways of Britain, around the skid pan at headquarters and on blue light runs through the busy rush-hour traffic. When we weren't blue lighting, we had to obey the 30 mph limit, but out of town we had a training exemption from any speed regulations and were encouraged to push the car to its limits ...and we did. We'd drive for breakfast in the Lake District, take afternoon tea in the Highlands of Scotland and then speed down South to get chips for supper. It was a totally different driving technique compared to what I'd been used to – driving to the 'system' – and most of the time I thought I'd never get the hang of it. On some runs, I'd even be required to provide a running commentary as I drove: what hazards were ahead, observations on the road conditions, my intended overtakes, if it was my turn to buy tea - and I'd end each high speed drive soaked in sweat and with a headache from the concentration. Eventually though, it all came together, and at the end of the course I was confirmed as a police driver.

I don't know why I was so pleased. In reality, it just meant that I could get to jobs quicker and, consequently, have a bigger workload – yet, I was. In fact, I was delighted. Becoming a police driver is a watershed moment in any officer's career.

It meant I could now drive a marked police car commonly known as a 'Panda'. The name originally comes from the seventies when police forces bought a number of black cars and an equal number of white cars. To make them stand out from ordinary civilian vehicles (and to save a small fortune on painting), the bonnets, doors and boot were all taken off and swapped with the vehicles of the opposite colour. Hey presto – a police car! So what if it also happened to look like a giant panda? The modern day police cars may no longer be black and white, but the nickname lives on ...and now I was in charge of one.

I was no longer a beat bobby; I was now a 'Panda Commander' – or more officially, a shift response officer. As the name implies, we are the uniformed officers that initially respond to all incidents ranging from fights and thefts right through to rapes and murders. We then either keep the crime and investigate it, or if it's a protracted investigation or really serious crime, take the basic details of the job and then pass it onto CID or other specialist units to progress.

I was duly posted to the town of Sandford, which is where our story really begins.

Although it's a real enough town, Sandford isn't its real name, of course. My experience from my former escapades in print has made me realise that in this age of litigation and people punching you in the face if they are upset, certain names have to be changed to protect the guilty (mind you, as there are no pictures or fuzzy felt in the book, I don't think many of my 'customers' will actually steal and read the book ...except if they are wanting a thick beer mat or something to balance that wobbly table leg).

The original Sandford was a replica town used for police training, where police recruits could engage in simulations of routine police activities, dealing with anything from traffic accidents and hooligans through to burglaries and robberies. The criminals, victims and bystanders were portrayed by the civilians from the neighbouring towns ...sometimes just a tad too well. There is actually a real Sandford in Devon and I just hope that they don't suffer the same high degree of social disorder as its training namesake. Nowadays, Sandford is used in most text book scenarios for the police. Sandford was also the main setting for the fantastic police action film *Hot Fuzz*, and if you are really into trivia, a young boy in the film *28 Days Later* also says he comes from there. Anyway, welcome to this particular Sandford.

My colleagues' names have also been changed for similar reasons. For example, the person I refer to as 'Whitey' later in the book is really called Brad. Oh, shit!

Sandford is an average sort of town. It could be any town, it could be your town. It's not the best of towns, but neither is it the worst of towns (actually, maybe I've given too much away there, as it's fairly obvious now from that statement that Sandford is neither Winchester nor South Normanton). In police radio talk, Sandford is known as Kilo 1.

To the east of Sandford, there is a collection of small villages, known by the collective name of Kilo 2. These are what I would call Jekyll and Hyde villages – lovely, quiet, charming, picturesque places by day, which go over to the devil on weekend nights, when the bored youths and dissolute drunks assume control of the streets.

To the west is an industrial town known as Kilo 3. I say 'industrial town' but a lot of the heavy industry has now gone and Kilo 3 seems to have been reborn as the takeaway capital of the area. It's not the greatest place to live I'll concede, with a fair degree of crime but at least it's consistent: crime by day, crime by night.

(Unofficially there is also a Kilo 4. It's actually the Tesco store in Sandford. It just sounds a little bit more legitimate saying you are attending an incident in Kilo 4, rather than letting the bosses hear that you are popping to the supermarket canteen for your breakfast.)

I joined the officers on E shift, who, in no particular order are:

Barry: Shift Sergeant – oracle and font of all knowledge (about World War II that is).

George: Everyone has forgotten his proper name, but he thinks he looks like George Clooney so the name stuck ...although we think he looks more like George C Looney. Also known as 'The Gasman' because he services old boilers.

Ron: Ex RAF, and also, we suspect, veteran of the Bermuda triangle exhibition 2000 – 1997. Ron doesn't let the abuse from Sandford's criminals get to him, as he believes they are sub-human and, therefore, don't count. Sometimes I think he's onto something there.

Bob aka Eyeore: Former Zimbabwean Police. If things are going just a little bit too well, you can rely on Bob to find the downside to any situation. Come to him with your glass half full, leave with it half empty.

Steve aka Geezer: Ex Met Police. Our tame cockney.

Lloyd: Ex metal worker. Off sick for quite a while after he was bitten by a monkey or something. Monkey is recovering well.

Gwen: Former secretary. Smells nice and the only person on

shift who you can talk to properly and who won't point at you and laugh if you reveal you actually have 'feelings'.

Ben: Rugby player ...doesn't really suffer from insanity ...seems to enjoy it.

Chad: Law graduate. Rumour has it he has more brains than a fairground beef burger.

Daisy: Custody Sergeant – looks like Davros, sitting behind a big desk in custody – but with better legs (that's a guess).

Bunny: The girl who sits in the custody area, normally reading a book. Not sure what she does – suspect she may be the civilian detention/custody officer.

And there was me: Early forties, divorced, now living in a small village in the countryside with my dog, Barney. I may have been the oldest on the shift, but despite looking like a hound, the new career change had reinvigorated me, and I felt like a pup.

These were to be my travelling companions during my first year at Sandford; a year in which I was to discover the highs and lows of policing. A year that saw me, amongst other things, arresting porn stars, fighting with the abominable snowman, meeting swearing babies, chasing the naughtiest dog in the world, searching for Dracula's tomb by moonlight ...and laughing till my stomach muscles ached.

If this was a low budget American monster film from the 60's, it would probably have a poster which reads:

There are Cops and Robbers.
There are Heroes and Villains.
Marvel at the stupidity of some of the people
who ring the 999 system.

Thrill at the bizarre world that the bad guys live in ...and discover why they wear two pairs of socks.

But it's not a movie; it's the twenty first century and we are British, so to put it in good old plain English, this is the tale of twelve months in the life of a newly qualified Panda Commander at his first posting. The events, incidents and anecdotes are told in chronological order over the next twenty one chapters as they happened to both me and the shift, and, believe it or not, they are all true.

Starting at the 999 calls:

Male caller: "I can hear shouting coming from the house on the corner."

Control: "Have you an address?"

Male caller: "No, just a shirt and trousers. Why? What sort of f***king pervert are you?"

(Note to reader: calls to 999 are free, not £1.50 a minute as this call may suggest.)

Right through to the interviews:

Interviewer: "And what was the first thing your husband said to you when you woke up that morning?"

Answer: "Where am I Rebecca?"

Interviewer: "And why did you then assault him?"

Answer: "Because my name is Louise."

And finally through into the court room:

Solicitor: 'You say that you attempted to commit suicide on the day that you were arrested?'

Defendant: 'Yes I did.'

Solicitor: 'Did you succeed?'

Defendant: 'No.'

I've also been told to add that all the opinions expressed are my own and not endorsed by any Constabulary. Shame really.

These are the true tales from a year in the life of a front line police response officer, and this is what happened next...

CHAPTER ONE:

Response

January. My first day in Sandford and I was up in the police station canteen with George. Behind me, the traffic cops were quietly playing cards. They seem to spend a lot of time up there, but credit where credit is due, they do an excellent job. To the best of my knowledge, no one has broken into the kitchens for the past five years.

As I looked out of the window, supping my tea, I could see a solitary rabbit sitting on the school playing fields opposite. He just sat there, stock still, as if he was in a trance, nothing troubling him in his little, stress-free life. He was probably mulling over whether to go and dig up a carrot from the farmer's field for his tea, or maybe pop home instead and make some more baby rabbits with Mrs Rabbit. Well, either that or he had myxomatosis.

All was peaceful, all was serene, all was well with the world.

Suddenly, I was shocked back into reality as my police radio crackled into life.

"Kilo 1 mobile from Control – immediate response detail. Domestic in progress."

Shit! An immediate! Fast response – this was an emergency!

We both sat bolt upright. We instantaneously cast aside what we were doing and raced out to our panda car, leaving abandoned cups of steaming tea, half-eaten sandwiches and less than half read newspapers. From the speed of our departure, you'd have thought that someone across town had announced they were giving away free cakes. We left the canteen looking like a scene from the Marie Celeste ...well, except for the traffic cops still playing cards quietly at the back.

Our police vehicle uttered a series of broken whoops as it tentatively poked its nose out of the station yard before diving in amongst the busy rush hour traffic.

"Kilo 1 mobile en route."

Domestics are unpredictable. They occupy that vast grey area between falling in love and eventually hating each other and, as police, we can get involved and dip in at all points in between. And sadly sometimes we find that they are not just that unfortunate place where the words you should never say, meet those things you can never take back. Every so often it's not just a pointed finger that is raised at the one they love, and sometimes those cruel, callous, cracks are not just verbal. You just can never know what you will find – domestic violence accounts for almost a quarter of violent crime in this country, with an incident being reported every minute to the police. It's not only love, trust, laughter and belief that die during those countless counterattacks. On average, two people are killed each week by their current or ex-partners in domestics. It seems that terror, like charity, begins at home. We needed to get there fast.

With headlights flashing, blue lights cutting up the evening twilight and sirens assaulting the senses, George charged the car down the white lines in the centre of the highway, taking the commanding position on the road. Cars and vans tucked themselves into the kerb, clearing a path for us like Moses parting the Red Sea. We made good speed as we raced through the gridlocked traffic. Time is of the essence, seconds can cost lives. Suddenly, a purple car pulled out right in front of us, testing the quality of our inertia seatbelts. Tosser!

You get that on blue light runs. One driver who is not paying attention, who bizarrely thinks that the cars in front of him are just cowering into the kerbside for the sole purpose of letting him through. He overtakes, and pulls out directly in front of the emergency services vehicle.

Whilst it's dangerous to blue light, driving at high speed through traffic, always waiting for some idiot to do something stupid, it's much more dangerous to be the second emergency vehicle racing to an incident. Whilst most drivers do actually pay attention and pull over to let the screaming police car through, many don't expect another one to be following behind, and as they pull out in the wake left by the initial car, they find themselves directly in the path of the next speeding vehicle.

Police drivers train intensively to prepare for dangerous blue light runs like this. Concentrate on the drive – put out of your mind what you're going to, what you might find, anything that could distract you – concentrate on the drive!

George added an angry horn to the cacophony of sirens, squealing brakes, strobing blues and flashing headlights. I could see the purple car driver glance up at his rear view mirror. Maybe the 'ECILOP' printed on the bonnet could do what the disco lights and deafening sounds couldn't. I could see him in his mirror looking back at us, and hoped he couldn't lip read.

He stole a few more car lengths before he eventually pulled back into the edge to let us past. Goodness knows what was happening at the domestic. This idiot was costing us precious time. We raced on to the junction with Carlington Way.

As George flung the car around the roundabout, I gripped the seat tightly, thirsty for a deep breath, the drums sounding off in my chest, and I felt reassuringly for my baton and pepper spray.

We were heading for an estate on the edge of town. The Communications Centre updated us with what scant information was available – they had received an incomplete 999 call from a hysterical woman. There had been the sound of smashing in the background as the woman had simultaneously been shouting and bawling at both the call taker and a male in her home. Then the phone had gone dead.

An immediate call has a maximum response time of ten minutes. This includes the time taken by the call taker getting the initial details, the inevitable short delay whilst it is passed to the dispatcher who allocates available units, and then the time taken by the individual unit to work out where the address is and the most efficient route across town to get from A to B through the inevitable traffic congestion. Time is never on our side.

We were now on an open stretch of road and George opened up the accelerator to make up for our interrupted progress earlier.

A few minutes later and we were there. With a screech of brakes the vehicle juddered to a halt outside the address – "Kilo 1 mobile on scene."

George was out within seconds and I quickly followed, racking my baton as I went.

We kicked open the garden gate and ran up the short path, past the damp sofa and requisite broken push-bike. This was the Black Estate. The council estates in Sandford are named after the colour of the bricks they were built from. There is the Red Estate, a Yellow Estate, and this was the highly imaginative Black Estate.

The door was open, we went straight in. "POLICE!" we both shouted in unison as we stormed into the lounge, only to be greeted by a bemused looking male, wearing a thousand wash grey singlet that was straining over his ample form. I quickly looked around. It was difficult to see if there were signs of a struggle or if it was just a failure to tidy up.

By now we were joined by a female who shouted, "Look what he's done to me!" before disappearing back into the kitchen.

I only managed to get a quick look, but by all accounts he seemed to have made her dress her equally ample form in a tight, pink lycra outfit, making her resemble of all things, an egg on legs. The bastard!

Glancing over at the mantle-piece, I could see a sun bleached photo of a baby dressed up as a toilet roll cover; what sort of crazy madman were we dealing with here for goodness sake?

I stayed with the evil psychopath, whilst George went through to see the woman to get her side of the story.

The main thing in domestics is to separate both parties straight away. Whilst many won't talk freely about what happened in front of their partner, you can normally get people to open up when they are on their own. Whilst singlet man slouched back down in his armchair, I surveyed the surroundings.

The householders didn't appear to be that keen on recycling as the room seemed to contain everything they had ever owned. They were clearly very keen on tigers as various framed prints and dusty ornaments attested. Red Indians too; there were various busts of Sitting Bull, Geronimo and other Indian dignitaries sitting under a dream catcher, which also appeared to double as a cobweb catcher. Maybe it was the maid's day off. A shelf of porcelain dolls with grubby faces looked scarily down at the cruddy Indians. A couple of glass dolphins, joined together by a long cobweb, sat on the fireplace next to a grimy glass orb attached to a wizard with a broad brimmed hat who, in turn, stood next to a dragon with little, jewel eyes. All these items, I suspect, made by that highly acclaimed Chinese designer, Chee Po Tat.

"She's very spiritual, you know," volunteered the male when he caught me looking.

"Really?" I replied.

The pair obviously had a few dogs judging by the carpet – both must be moulting and, judging by the smell, at least one of them was wet. The ensemble was completed by a large leather-look armchair, an enormous sofa, a rug with various types of DNA on it, several empty discarded tins of Carlsberg and Stella, and the biggest television set I had ever seen in my life. My expression must have given away my disbelief at the state they were living in and, if by way of mitigation, the singlet guy jerked a sandwich filled fist in the direction of the enormous screen in the corner of the room.

"The telly doesn't watch itself, you know," he mumbled. How true. Pure words of wisdom.

I asked Mr Singlet what had happened.

"Nuttin," came the reply as he squirmed in the armchair, leaning his whole body to the right in order to catch the full glory of the omnibus edition of EastEnders on his gargantuan plasma. Clearly, I was spoiling his depressing enjoyment. Before I could get any more information out of him, George had returned from his chat with Lycra egg woman.

"We're going," he grunted at me.

On the way out, I had more time to admire the bomb site that was once a front garden, which I could now see was also adorned with a centrepiece – the ever popular Cortina on bricks.

We got back into the vehicle in silence. My colleague didn't appear too talkative. I was sad to say that neither Mr Singlet or Mrs Egg bothered to come to wave us off. How rude.

George drove back at a much more sedate pace. We had got halfway back to the station before I deemed it was safe or, indeed, prudent, to ask him what had happened.

"Don't ask," he replied and then proceeded to tell me all anyway.

It transpired that Mrs Egg had been cooking dinner when she discovered Mr Singlet making himself a sandwich. I don't know about you but it does seem a little bit naughty after she's gone to all that effort. Naughty yes but hardly a crime and certainly not enough to warrant a 999 call. Yet that's what she had done. That's why we had left our own dinner, charged through rush hour traffic, disrupted commuters on their way home – all for a cheeky sandwich.

The smash heard by the call taker had apparently been Mrs Egg throwing Mr Singlet's dinner plate onto the floor. When she shouted, 'Look what he's done to me!' she had been alluding to the fact that he had allowed her to slave away, cooking his dinner, whilst he led his carefree life watching the telly. I guess she had chosen to wear that outfit herself.

George had tried to tell her that this wasn't really a police matter – that we had risked our lives, as well as the lives of others, racing to her house for nothing. Someone, somewhere, could really be in need of our help. Someone, somewhere, could be in the middle of a real emergency ... but we wouldn't have been able to assist them because we were here instead – because of a piece of ham between two slices of bread. He added that she was lucky that he wasn't going to book her for wasting police time.

However, instead of ruminating on what was said, she shot back indignantly with the classic "I pay your wages."

As George explained to me, you only ever get that from those people who are unemployed. It's the law abiding and hard working people of Sandford who *actually* pay our wages through their taxes. However, we very rarely get to see them, precisely because they *are* law abiding and hard working. Instead we spend ninety per cent of our time running around after the ones who don't actually contribute one penny to the pot.

In time, I discovered the other popular retorts from law breakers/drunkards in Sandford are:

"My cousin is a barrister."

"My uncle is your Superintendent."

And the perennial favourite, "Do you know who I am?" to which my preferred response is "Clearly not, and I'll need your address as well."

The next day Gwen and I raced to another immediate response in true 'Dukes of Hazzard' style, although my colleague has asked me to stress that she was not wearing her Daisy Duke cut offs on this occasion. On our arrival, we were disappointed to subsequently discover that the caller just wanted us to put her curtains up. It seems that some people have their own definition of what constitutes a 'domestic emergency'. I am not ashamed to say, dear reader, that I refused. If it had been a poorly old dear, I might have considered helping out, but since it was an abusive, drunken harpy, I politely declined.

"But you're the Police!" the female shouted indignantly at us as we got back into the panda car, shaking our heads in disbelief. That's right I thought, we are the police – not interior decorators. I sometimes wonder where some people get their impression of what the police are actually there to do. I always thought it was to fight crime. As we pulled away, I mentally counted down: 'Five, four, three, two, one' and then, right on cue, a shrill voice filled the air, quoting that other old favourite, "I'll get you sacked!"

Well, they say that things come in threes, and half an hour later another bizarre 999 call was added to the litany of shame.

The job had been passed to me simply as 'burglar in dog snatch'. That's a funny place to hide, I mused.

Sadly, it turned out to be nothing half as exciting. Ten minutes later and Gwen and I were sat discussing an alleged stolen dog in the smoky front room of a house in Kilo 3. I had cleared a space for us on the sofa amongst the bric-a-brac, bin bags full of laundry and the artificial fibre optic Christmas tree that had yet to be put back into storage. The chain-smoking householder had kindly enlightened me when she saw me clocking it, informing me that it was 'one of those cystic fibrosis trees'. Elsewhere, two small children were sat crossed legged on the floor, glued to the TV, watching some kind of out-takes programme that seemed entirely inappropriate for their age group. It looked as if it was called something along the lines of 'when checkout girls bend over' judging by the snippets I could snatch through the smoky haze.

I could barely hear the mother as she tried to explain over the din from the telly, why she had seen fit to call us out. It seems to be a modern phenomenon in the Yellow, Red and Black Estates of Sandford – the TV goes on when they get up and it only goes off when they go to bed. Come hell or high water ... guests or police visits, it stays on. They might reluctantly turn the volume down if requested, but even that's not guaranteed.

Meanwhile, back at the smoky abode, I got out my pocket book to note down the lowlights of this dismal tale. Occasionally, the goggle box kids would turn round to add some comment to the adult conversation that was going on behind them, or else utter some expletive descriptive about their mother's former partner. Meanwhile, a naked baby was snacking on the last remnants of a packet of Dorritos that were scattered across the filthy carpet. After a while, he crawled over to show me his toy – a lighter. Lovely!

Piecing together the disjointed story, I managed to come up with the following chain of events: it was their dog; that is it belonged to her and her ex-partner – he had then moved out when he found the Dorrito baby wasn't his and took Mutley away with him ...or something like that. She loved the hound and was heartbroken. However, she continued, if we persuaded him to give her a tenner for some lager, her broken heart would mend.

This was a civil law matter. It was a dispute between two individuals. Nothing to do with the police and it certainly wasn't 999 material. I was here on false pretences, thinking some sort of heinous dog theft was in progress. As a police officer, I deal in criminal law – thefts, assaults, robberies etc. It's the highly paid solicitors who tackle (at great expense) civil litigation. I certainly wasn't going to be the mediator between ex-husband and wife. Do I look like Solomon?

"It's a mess," I commented. As soon as the words left my mouth, I wondered if she thought I meant the situation or the state of the house. I didn't want to appear rude. I was here to help after all, but I was growing increasingly exasperated.

"Yes, it is," she replied. Well, that answer covered either question equally well.

I put on a pensive look, initially designed solely to impress girls with glasses, but now used to buy me some time as I tried to rationalise to myself how I was going to sum up the difference between civil and criminal legal conventions to her in twenty words or less. I was toying with the idea of touching my earpiece, tilting my head to the side as if listening intently, and then informing Gwen that we had another urgent call to attend, in order to save me from such pedantic semantics when uproar suddenly ensued.

With a tremendous bang, the door from the kitchen suddenly burst open and a small child with an empty cereal packet over his head ran into the room, promptly tripped over the baby and flew headlong into the television set, knocking it off its stand and causing it to crash onto the floor in a pile of broken glass, fizzing wires and expletives. Cue howling baby, manic laughter from cereal boy, shouts of indignation from the goggle box twins and, having jumped to her feet, a frankly unbelievable outburst from the mother.

"I've already telt you about that once, you fucking idiot! If you do it again, I'll let the paedophile man get you!"

Simultaneously, Gwen and I shot each other a glance. My colleague then did an impression of someone sucking a lemon whilst I involuntarily made one of those faces that middle aged men pull when they are miming to an Eric Clapton guitar solo.

As I've pounded the beat, I've often seen mothers nodding towards me and informing their toddlers that if they don't stop crying, the policeman will come over and tell them off (and then wonder why the child gets confused the next day when they are told 'if you are ever lost, ask a policeman for help'), but I've never heard anyone anywhere, ever threaten their offspring with a child molester in order to keep them on the straight and narrow. I couldn't have been more surprised if the Easter Bunny had suddenly appeared and punched me square in the face.

As I regaled the tales back at the nick, it was as if I had passed some sort of ritual initiation. Barry turned to me, patted me on the back and told me that I had only seen the tip of the iceberg when it came to the bizarre calls that the police have to attend, but it's that variety that makes it one of the best jobs you can ever have. Our position gives us a unique insight into other people's lives, he continued, allowing us to glimpse through the peephole into their souls, albeit momentarily. It's like being on a slow train as it passes through a busy town; brief vignettes of extraordinary life that are played out before us. We may only have bit parts in their ever unfolding drama, but the actions we take can affect the outcome of the performance – for better or for worse – either a tragedy or comedy of errors.

Ron's view was slightly different, and he summed it up a little more succinctly, but maybe a little less eloquently with, "Welcome to life in the shit lane."

A Gallic shrug accompanied by, "Welcome to Sandford Constabulary," was Bob's maudlin contribution to the party.

And that's how I discovered that a 999 call may not always be what it initially seems.

We may respond with all haste, scattering the good people of Sandford in all directions in our quest to hit our target times, only for the caller to treat us as an unwanted nuisance or demand some service that certainly wasn't taught at police training school when we do arrive.

But it's not just 999 calls made in relation to absent dogs, interior design and catering catastrophes ...some know very well that the call isn't urgent but they just can't be bothered to walk down to the station to report an incident, or sometimes our customers will call 999 just because they haven't any credit left on their mobile phone and they know that emergency calls are free. Some callers, and I know that you may find this difficult to believe, actually use a technique that we like to call 'telling porkie pies' in order to get a quicker police/fire/ambulance response. Indeed, not all calls are 'as reported'.

There are over thirty million calls to the emergency services every year in the UK. I guess they can't all be top notch. Just by the law of averages, there are going to be some howlers in there.

Sometimes though, you just wonder if the caller has been connected through to the right emergency service in the first place.

Caller: "I want to complain. I can't sleep."

Control: "How can I help?"

Caller: "The boy next door has been banging his balls against my wall for the past few hours."

Control: "This is the police you've got through to. Did you want an ambulance?"

Other times it's just hard to understand what's going on.

Caller: "I want to report that the boy next door has ruined our Ivy."

Control: "How old is your daughter? Is she under sixteen?"

Caller, sounding very perplexed: "We haven't got a daughter. What are you on about? Are you going to send out someone or not? He's pulling the roots up now!"

And sometimes the calls are just out of this world.

Caller: "I'd like to report a large glowing sphere that has been floating over the hill for the last hour."

Half an hour later.

Control: "Kilo 1 mobile, did you manage to check out the suspicious object?"

Kilo 1 Mobile: "Yes – it's the moon."

CHAPTER TWO:

Here Come The Fuzz

"Here come the fuzz," we heard them chorus, as Geezer and I made our way through the evening dusk towards a group of youths, or to be more precise, twenty or so Chavs (also known as Charvers on Sundays). You may have a different name for them in your town, and they may sport differing attire, but I'm sure you will recognise this particular anthropological sub-culture.

The call had come in about a rowdy group, drinking in the street and generally intimidating anyone who ventured near them. Geezer and I parked up and walked into the pedestrianised town centre to where the youths were engaged in their favourite activity which appeared to be 'just hanging around'.

It may help at this juncture if I introduce you to this tribe as, to put it in Home Office speak, the Chav is a key consumer of the service that the police offer here in Sandford. A third of all crime is committed by persons between the ages of sixteen to twenty four and over sixty percent of crime happens after dark. If you were to draw a Venn diagram right now, you'd see that as the police, we tend to overlap a fair bit with those two sectors.

The Chav is a strange sort of creature. The male of the species is often fond of wearing sportswear, and from the number of them meandering aimlessly around the town centre on a Saturday night, you could be forgiven for thinking that you had suddenly been transported to the Olympic village. To my knowledge, however, none of these specimens has ever partaken in any sporting activities. Unlike your standard athlete, the Chav will also have his trouser leg tucked into sock (so when he drops the items he is shoplifting down his trousers, they don't all just drop out of the bottom). Usually with large ears and a frown, they have a distinctive pasty colouring and the body of a pliable string bean. Male Chavs see branded baseball caps as a status symbol and wear them at every opportunity. Often seen texting because they have mostly given up on speech, they tend to spend a lot of their time pondering on which ring tone to download next. Not noted for their educational prowess, they probably think that the sequel to 'The Diary of Anne Frank' is 'Anne Frank – The Edge of Reason'.

The female of the species, often known as a Chavette or feckless tramp, share the same lack of basic education, although to be fair, they do excel in the pregnancy tests. Unfortunately, after that initial high, things go rapidly downhill from there, and scores are not nearly so good thereafter for their level of childcare. There must be something in the air in Sandford to cause so many teenage pregnancies. Probably their legs.

Mind you, it would be wrong of me to generalise. Not all of the town's Chavettes are so easy. Gwen swears that outside Tesco a few weeks ago she overheard the following conversation between two Chavettes about a new Chav boyfriend:

Chavette 1: He took me behind the kebab shop and we had a snog, like. Then he put his hand down me trackies, like.

Chavette 2: He nivva! What did you do, like?

Chavette 1: I smacked him round the heed, like and telt him, 'Where's your fookin' manners, like? It's tits first!'

Anyway, where was I? Oh yes, Chavettes. They have a propensity for stilettos and large, hooped earrings (who cares if your ear lobes are down by your tits by the time you're twenty five? It's years away!) Orange in hue, they are often seen with a tight forehead due to their hair being pulled back harshly into a severe ponytail, which is commonly known as a 'Croydon Facelift' (named, respectively, after its place of origin).

Their usual haunt is the town centre where Chavs, mostly too young to get into pubs, hang around the 'offie', waiting to persuade (aka intimidate) someone to go in and get their sweet sweet tasting alcohol for them. Meanwhile, Chavettes can also be seen chewing on their fingernails, eating pasties and pushing a pram. Inside the pram is a baby, usually sporting big stud earrings (whatever you do, don't let God see or else we could be in for another big flood or something). Baby is either sucking on a dummy, holding an unfeasibly pink and oversized sausage roll or chomping its way through a packet of pickled onion flavoured Monster Munch the size of its own head.

It is highly likely that eight years on, this baby will have been transformed into a six stone dead weight. He will now be sullenly sitting in a buggy with a blank expression on his oversized face, being navigated around the aisles in Tesco by his now skinny, bag-head mum, who, whilst skilfully avoiding any contact with the fresh fruit and veg sections, is about to develop a hernia at any minute from pushing this monster. This monster, by the way, will still be perfectly happy to be treated as a baby, sucking on his 'doo-dee', even though he's almost old enough to vote.

Mind you, the hummy mummy may be quite happy to keep him in this mode of transport to which he has become accustomed as buggies and pushchairs are excellent for hiding your pilfered goods in.

The female of the species are drawn towards bright lights, Lambrini and extra strength cider that hasn't actually ever seen an apple. Males can also be spotted in deserted supermarket car parks showing off their pimped-up Novas, looking at the pictures in 'Max Power' and 'Nuts' magazines and comparing alibis.

George told me how he had once spotted a souped-up Chav mobile driving erratically around the local estate. After stopping the vehicle, he went and spoke to the driver. A quick glance at the documentation indicated that all was not in order.

"Can you get in the back of the vehicle, please?" George asked the Chav before walking back to his patrol car and commencing some checks on the radio. A few minutes later and the Chav hadn't yet made his way over to the police car. A few more minutes passed and still nothing. Eventually, George had had enough and went back to the Chav mobile. However, on looking in, the speedy boy racer appeared to have gone. Surely not, thought George. 'I didn't see any doors open. He couldn't have disappeared anywhere, I didn't see anyone running away.' As my colleague stood in silence, retracing his steps and wondering what to do next, a small voice broke the silence.

"I'm here."

Somehow our compliant Chav had climbed over the oversized headrests, navigated past the padded seatbelt covers and managed to slide himself betwixt the massive drum and bass speakers on the back seat.

"Back seat of *my* vehicle, dummy," growled George before turning and stifling a snigger.

Elsewhere, if you are interested enough, the species can be studied at close quarters on the Trisha, Jerry Springer or Jeremy Kyle shows. It is now generally accepted that such shows should be included as an additional option available to callers to the police reporting the 'he texted me and called me a divvy / well, she texted me and called me a radgie / only 'cos he called me a doylem first' scenarios. The shows could then provide a valuable service to society, allowing the divvy and radgie to air their pointless grievances to their heart's content in front of an army of happy daytime TV watching doylems ...and let the police get on with some proper work instead.

For those not familiar with the 'word on the street yo man' parlance, with the aid of the Urban Dictionary, allow me to elaborate:

Divvy: Idiot/fool/waster. Originates from the dole which is *div*ided amongst the unemployed. (See what they did there 'eh, 'eh?)

'You divvy, you got sacked from the pig farm six months ago and you're still on the jigger.'

Jigger: Derived from Giro or the Giro-cheque used to pay out dole money to the unemployed.

Radgie: Person allergic to books, education, any witty remark or words with more than two syllables (has the same effect on them as Kryptonite does to Superman). Often become agitated or violent if intelligence is flaunted in front of them.

'The group of radgies attacked the old man.'

Doylem: An idiot. Person who thinks someone who is described as 'erudite' is a type of glue. Derived from Mrs Doyle who was a twat (according to the Chav nation anyway ...I quite liked her. Maybe the humour was a bit above them).

'You sir, are a doylem.'

For further reading, see Dickhead / Skanker / Fucktard / Spaz / Chemo / Kerry Katona.

Other Chav trivia not worth knowing is that their favourite colour is gold, they usually have a tracksuit 'for best' – for that romantic dinner at Pizza Hut or the occasional court appearance – and that they call their thirty year old grandmother 'Nan'.

That best tracksuit, by the way, may possibly still have the cord in it. The others probably don't as cords are required to be removed or cut out of tracksuits before the said Chav is put into a police cell (in case they use it to hang themselves). Of course, I'm making the big assumption here that most Chavs will end up in police custody at some time or another – actually, it's not much of an assumption at all really.

Once in custody, you'll discover that the male Chav often wears two pairs of tracksuit bottoms (so he can quickly change his appearance after he has been out shoplifting) and often wears several pairs of socks (well, fair play, how easy do you think it is to steal exactly the right sized pair of trainers?).

Favourite sayings whilst in custody include:

"I'm not saying nowt till I see me solicitor."

"What the fook you on about?" when you point out that what they have just said is in fact a double negative.

"The student deserved it, he was being clever." Insert your own punch line here.

And finally, when asked by the magistrate, "What gear were you in, when your car crashed through the park gates?" their standard response is, "Burberry top, Kappa trackies and Nike trainers." (It is a commonly held belief by my colleagues back at the nick, that Kappa actually sponsor the youth of Sandford).

Sometimes though, our Chav is capable of true, faked remorse if they think it will benefit them as I found out recently when I brought one of the clan into custody.

I had outlined the circumstances why I had arrested our friend to the Sergeant (it was actually for public order – or more appropriately, public disorder). The Custody Sergeant asked the Chavster if he wanted to make any comment in relation to what I had said.

"Yes," replied the arrested one, doing his best dispirited shuffle and choking back the crocodile tears for the benefit of the custody camera. "I'm sorry that when I addressed the officer, I used the F word, the B word and the K word."

"The K word?" enquired a perplexed Sergeant.

"I think it's a spelling thing," I quietly clarified.

Mind you, our Chav in custody wasn't the brightest crayon in the box. I'd go so far as to say that with an IQ roughly equivalent to that of a slack handful of monkey nut husks, he couldn't pour piss out of a boot even if the instructions were written on the heel. In fact, he was the type of person that you'd find difficult to describe without using hand gestures.

My rationale for this outrageous attack on his good character is based on events a month earlier. I had been in the fields on the outskirts of the town on a Friday night, confiscating alcohol from the underage kids in a forlorn effort to prevent their drunken antics later on. From amongst the gathering of fifty to sixty youths, I had cause to speak to our lad because of his drunken swearing. I'd taken his name and address, done a quick check on his details via Comms and then told him to calm down and to clear off home.

However, our miscreant decided on one last hurrah before leaving, and turned to another boy, and for no discernible reason, nutted him. As I started my way over to arrest him, our offender started to run off into the dark night. Now, don't get me wrong – I love a chase. There is nothing more exciting than hearing, "I've got a runner!" shouted over the radio. Police from all over will then drop what they're doing and join in the hunt for the runaway criminal. Police you've never seen before will appear: neighbourhood police, dog section, traffic ...hell, I've even seen CID join in the search.

In this case though, I just watched our idiot disappear into the pitch black, tripping and stumbling over the uneven ground as he ran. I slowly walked after him, following him with my torch. His eyes reflected in the light as he glanced back to see where I was. I could then hear a muffled expletive as he ran into a tree. I could see him pick himself up and then run on. Next, I could hear the splash as he jumped down into the beck. As I sauntered over and reached the edge, I looked down and fifteen feet below I could see our evildoer wading through the water before dragging himself up the opposite bank, using the thorn bushes for handholds. When he got back to the top, he looked back and then proceeded to launch himself over a thick hawthorn hedge in his bid to escape. As he pulled his body over the top, I thought it was only fair to enlighten him as to why I hadn't put myself through the same ordeal.

"I know where you live – you just told me," I called after him, and quietly got onto the radio to ask a colleague to wait round at the address that our runner had so kindly given me only minutes earlier.

Five minutes later and our master criminal was in police detention, complete with a self-inflicted bloody nose, sprained ankle, one trainer missing, sans mobile phone, arms and hands scratched to buggery, full of thorns and sopping wet.

Apparently, when asked by the Custody Sergeant who the officer was who had chased him in the field, he had replied that he couldn't see his face as it was dark, "but I'd remember his fucking laugh again anywhere!"

Meanwhile, back to me, Geezer, and the group of delightful Chavs in the town. We told the crowd to disperse and started pouring out the confiscated alcohol.

"Why are you so fat, copper?" one of the miscreants jibed at Geezer.

Big mistake. You can call Geezer a lot of things, but don't ever, ever call him fat. He can get very sensitive about things like that. For that matter, don't ask him if he dyes his hair either, but I digress.

I looked over at Geezer. I could see him mulling things over in his head. I could almost hear the cogs whirling away as he planned his response.

I can normally think of some great one liners ...usually about three minutes after it's all over with.

"So why are you so fat, copper?" the miscreant repeated.

"Because each time I shag your mum, she gives me a biscuit" – go on, use the line Geezer. You know you want to!

Instead, he said nothing and just raised himself up to his full height and pulled out his torch. The mob fell silent as they sensed that they had struck a nerve, and that maybe the

Maglite wasn't drawn on this occasion purely for illumination purposes. However, as Geezer was slowly shining it amongst the throng of faces to identify the object of his wrath, the moment was broken by the shrill call of the greater spotted Chav bird.

"You black bastards!"

Somewhere a wine glass shattered and all the dogs within a twenty metre radius pricked up their ears.

Geezer looked around in surprise.

"That's us," I informed him. "We're the black bastards apparently. Something to do with the colour of our uniforms."

"Hey, let's have some sort of continuity here," he replied. "I thought we were supposed to be the thin *blue* line."

I found the Chavette responsible and informed her to pack it in, "before you say something I'll regret, and in turn, I then say something you'll regret."

"Like what?" intoned our potty-mouthed young lady, readjusting her faux Burberry thong.

"Like *you're nicked,*" I replied.

"You can't arrest me if you haven't got your hat on," interrupted another of the tribe. "My uncle told me and he should know – he's inside for five years."

Chavs always like to think that they have a superior knowledge of the law than a warranted Constable. In reality of course, the sum of their knowledge of the law is actually equivalent to that of a baboon's ring piece.

I shaded my eyes as I looked at her – the light from the lamp post glinting off her tangerine forehead. I imagined the conversation between our Chavette and her mum – "*Now this is your new Uncle Wayne. Be nicer to him than you were to your other six previous uncles. Wayne has a lot of pseudo-intellectual legal nonsense to tell you.*"

"Hmmm, maybe the fact that he's inside is actually an indication that he *didn't* know the law?" I suggested. My comment was met with a blank, bovine stare.

Hat or no hat, if we see you wrong-doing, we can arrest you. I don't know for sure, but I'd like to think that her uncle found this out when he was wearing a stocking over his head, a stripy jumper and standing next to a smoking safe, stuffing ten pound notes into a bag marked 'swag'. When the police pull up, uncle initially panics and then visibly relaxes and has a little giggle to himself when he sees that the bobbies haven't got their hats on. Panic once again takes over as the emotion of choice when the cuffs are slapped on regardless.

The trouble is a lot of us suffer from 'source amnesia'. We forget where we learnt a fact – and in our muddled brains, a 'fact' picked up from a chat down the pub can, in time, gain as much credulity as a fact gleaned from The Encyclopaedia Britannica.

Other common misconceptions are that a truck driver can urinate on the side of the road, as long as one hand is on the truck (I don't actually recall that being detailed in the pages of the Road and Traffic Act 1977), a pregnant woman is allowed to 'go toilet' in a policeman's helmet (where the hell did that come from?) and finally, that the aforementioned Chavette looked 'well tidy' whilst wearing a gold coloured articulated clown around her scrawny neck (no, she did not).

By this time, I'd had enough of this nonsense and I singled out the leader of the herd and took him to one side to have a quiet word. He returned to the group, whispered something to them, and then slowly they all started to slink off into the darkness.

"What did you say to him?" asked Geezer.

I mumbled to him that I had mentioned to the boy something about the long arm of the law, anti-social behaviour, personal responsibility and all that sort of stuff. What I didn't tell him was that I had actually told chief Chav that I had seen him out in a nearby town a few days earlier having a meal with his mum and dad, at which time he had been a perfect example of a devoted son, chatting politely and even cutting up the sausages for his baby brother. If they didn't all go home now, I'd let his friends know what a nice lad he really was.

No, I'd keep that just to myself for now and instead bask in the somewhat dubious glory of being labelled 'The Chav Whisperer'.

CHAPTER THREE:

Death

"She just sat back in the leather chair, got herself comfortable, quietly drifted into a deep sleep and then peacefully passed away."

Barry was telling us about the first sudden death he had attended. "Of course, the dentist shat himself," he added.

Everybody remembers their first sudden death. Not their own you understand – the sudden death of somebody else. As police officers, we have to attend all deaths that are ...well ...sudden. By that I mean not naturally pre-planned, or to put it another way, where the deceased hasn't been 'under the doctor' for the last few weeks of their life. Our role is to attend and assess whether there is any foul play involved. If we think there is, we hand the job over to CID, and if we think there isn't, we hand the job over to the funeral director. In essence, it's as simple as that.

We can be called to a sudden death in all manner of locations, and sometimes when we arrive the relatives are at the scene and sometimes they are not. Either way has its pros and cons – you just never know how people will react.

It can sometimes be upsetting for the distressed relatives as you explain the procedure: why the police are involved in the first place, why we are checking the body for signs of trauma, why we need to take statements from who found the body, why we need details of the deceased's medical history, what happens next, etc.

On the other hand, with relatives on scene to identify the body, you are saved the unpleasant task of looking through all the dead person's personal possessions, delving in their wallet or purse, or raking through the drawers in their house trying to find anything that would confirm the deceased's identity. Rooting around a dead man's house isn't one of my favourite pastimes. There is something distinctly eerie about it, especially when the dead person is still lying in their bed, relaxed in their favourite armchair, sitting on the toilet or some other odd pose.

Identity confirmed, then comes the task of checking the body for anything suspicious. It would be very embarrassing to send the body off with the funeral director only for them to find a knife sticking out of his back when he got to the other end, so a full external examination of the body is required.

Then a wristband is attached with the deceased's name and date of birth. If a pretty paramedic is present, you maybe even allow yourself a pathetic joke about free drinks all holiday to lighten the mood a little, if not you quickly put it on and hope that whatever the person died of isn't contagious.

On the plus side for all you members of the general public out there, we also definitely make sure that the person is actually dead before we allow them to be carted off in a black bag. In most cases, the paramedics have already been called to anyone who is found to be looking, to all intents and purposes, expired. However, I've had a couple of calls to nursing homes where things haven't exactly gone to plan. I should have guessed that things weren't going to go to plan when my initial funny fell on deaf ears.

"Good morning, officer," said the attractive administrator, opening the door. "Would you like to see the body now?"

"Well, normally I'd take you out for a few drinks first," I replied, only to be greeted with a puzzled expression.

After being led into the bedroom where our alleged cadaver was, I asked her for the doctor or paramedic's report stating cause of death.

"What do you mean? We've not bothered the ambulance or the doctor. You can see he's dead," came the reply.

"I grant you, he looks dead to me, but I'm no expert. Maybe he's just in a deep coma or something."

This isn't as far fetched as you might think it is. In ye olde times, our ancestors realised they were occasionally being a bit hasty in the burial department, and were burying some people who were just in the aforementioned coma or some other state of unconsciousness. After several coffins were excavated and found to have scratches on the inside of the lid, morticians began the process of tying a string to the finger of the corpse, the string leading to a bell by the graveside. If the person in the coffin woke up, they simply pulled the string, ringing the bell. They then became a 'dead-ringer'. The person from the mortuary who was assigned the task of sitting at the new grave site to listen for the bell to ring, was said to be working 'the graveyard shift'. He would then dig up the unfortunate coffin dodger who was literally 'saved by the bell'.

At sea, there wasn't much chance of ringing a bell when you were sewn up in an old sail and tipped overboard. The practice there was for the sail maker to put his needle through the nose of the deceased as part of the last stitch, before despatching the body down to Davy Jones' Locker. This would shock any alleged corpse to sit up and revive from any catalepsy they might be suffering from.

End of history lesson: prepare to return to the present day.

My 'is he or isn't he dead' debate with the administrator at the nursing home continued.

"Well, the ambulance won't come out if we tell them the person is already a goner," she told me, "and it costs a fortune to get a doctor out. It all seems a bit of a waste of money when he's obviously passed away. Can't you just say he's dead?"

"No, I cannot!" came my retort.

In a home for the elderly, it appears that the cost of death is a significant part of the cost of living.

Whilst the orderly rang her head office, debating if they could save the budget, I occupied myself by having a conversation with one of the friendly-looking auxiliaries. There was a touch of the call centre about her – but she seemed quite flirty nonetheless. Mind you, to be honest, I think she was just glad to talk to anyone about anything that took her mind off her mundane duties at the home. Still, if the light was a bit dimmer, I could almost imagine that she had her own nurse's uniform, so I gladly chatted away. After a while, she was getting quite amorous, leaning up against the wall, drawing her finger down the front of my body armour.

"You boys, in your smart uniforms, with your handcuffs, having to deal with all sorts of ruffians, I don't know how you do it?" she purred.

"It has its ups and downs but, overall, it's good fun," I told her, and then, in a show of fake empathy, I replied, "your job must be hard though, having to wipe old women's bums all the time. How do you do that?"

"Front to back," came her straight faced reply.

Any flicker of a flame of possible romance was brutally stamped out in my mind there and then.

I spent another uncomfortable twenty minutes waiting, having to try and avoid any further dalliance between she and me, before a medical professional eventually turned up, and death was finally confirmed.

'Making sure the dead person is actually dead' may seem a small point, but it may actually be of great reassurance to anyone, like me, who remembers the scene from *Diamonds Are Forever* where James Bond wakes up in a coffin on the conveyer belt about to be cremated.

There is a theory that the body loses weight by twenty

one grams when it dies. The logical explanation, many believe, it that this is the weight of the human soul. When you die, your soul departs your body, hence the weight difference. About a hundred years ago, a Dr MacDougall carried out a series of bizarre experiments in which dying patients were placed on sensitive, industrial sized scales. Weights were then compared before and after death – the result was an average difference of twenty one grams – and a theory was born. Bizarrely enough, similar experiments were tried with dogs. However, they found no weight difference following death. Sorry Barney, my four legged friend, apparently you're soulless. There is no doggy heaven.

Back in the parade room, I was contemplating how I would be able to pack weighing scales into my kit when Ben piped up about the time he attended his first death, only to be greeted by three elderly, ashen faced pensioners sitting on the sofa. Naturally, finding a dead relative or receiving such grave news can have a devastating effect on anyone. The room was a typical old man's room – overly warm, with the pleasant smell of an old biscuit tin, pictures of grandchildren and loved ones on every available surface, dusty mirror above the electric bar fire, old TV in the corner, patterned carpet, pile of old newspapers on the floor, and a set of false teeth smiling away in a glass of water next to an old, tea-stained mug. The morning sun tried to battle through the closed curtains that no-one had any thought, or inclination, to open. It wasn't the sort of situation where you pulled back the drapes to allow the glorious sun in, and welcomed the brand new day. Instead, an old, bare, sixty watt light bulb burned dutifully away, hardly contributing any light to the proceedings. The room had a mellow sepia hue; a combination of diluted sunlight and, judging by the overfilled ashtray, the effects of decades of smoking.

Sitting down on the floral armchair, Ben explained he was sorry to meet them all under such tragic circumstances and that this was a formality that had to be followed. He could also inform the funeral director on their behalf if they wished and so on. Ben told me that he didn't really want to let on that this was his first time, and was careful to follow everything that he had been told in training. Get details of the deceased, recent medical history, next of kin information, details of medication etc. After all the information had been gathered, he realised he couldn't put off the inevitable – to go and see the body, check it for anything unusual and attach the identification wristband.

"Can I see Albert now please?" he asked. It's always a good practice to use the deceased's name rather than just asking for 'the body'.

"Why lad, this is Albert right here," the two pensioners chorused together, turning to face the most ashen faced pensioner sitting between them.

"I wondered why he hadn't said much," Ben confessed later. "In fact, to be more precise, he didn't say anything at all, although I swore he winked at me at the end."

Not to be outdone, George then regaled the time he arrived at the scene of another unfortunate report of a death. Relatives had found the deceased and called the job in. The ambulance was en route, but our friend had arrived there first.

Not one to be accused of not learning the lessons from Ben's experience, he established from the family members in attendance where the body was located – the bedroom. Walking straight through to the boudoir, he carried out his duties as per the book. Check for signs of life – none found (but obviously, wait for the ambulance staff or Doctor to formally confirm death), check body for anything suspicious – nothing found, attach identity wristband (no pretty paramedic – no holiday joke), exit the room, lock the bedroom door to secure the scene and wait with relatives in the lounge for the arrival of the medical practitioners. Feeling rather pleased with himself, not to say smug, he went back in to chat to the family as he filled in all the official documentation.

It can be surprising what reaction people have to death. Some clam up, some are inconsolable, others are quite chatty and almost everyone offers you a cup of tea. After the forty-five minute wait for the paramedics to arrive, George, the raconteur, was getting on famously with all and sundry. He was on first name terms with all the relatives and even flirting with the deceased's pretty twenty year old grand-daughter, who seemed in awe of his tales of bravery and excitement as a police officer: how he kept calm as those around were losing their heads, the blue light runs, the pub fights, the incidents and adventures during the caffeine fuelled nightshifts.

Finally, the ambulance turned up, and our relaxed and confident PC handed the key to one of the paramedics and motioned towards the bedroom door. As the medic disappeared inside, our hero stood up and put a reassuring hand on the young woman's shoulders. Within a minute the paramedic re-emerged, cleared his throat with a small cough and addressing the gathered group, whispered the words, "I'm afraid he's gone."

"No, no – he can't be! He was there on the bed when I locked the..." George's voice trailed away from pure panic to nothing, as he looked around at the relatives staring open mouthed at him. He suddenly felt very warm and could feel himself going very red as he realised what an idiot he'd been.

"Well, I'll be off now then," he told the assembled throng. "Maybe I might see you at another sudden death?" he added, directing his comments to the young girl.

"Maybe," she replied, more perplexed at his bizarre chat up technique than anything else.

"It's a date then."

"No, it is *not* a date."

I guess that relying on one of your potential girlfriend's family members to die, just to have an excuse to see her again, isn't the best way to start a relationship ...even for George.

As it was turning out to be 'death tale' time, Geezer

pulled up a chair and told us about the time he attended the report of an old woman that hadn't been seen for days. Having got no answer at the front door, he went around the back and eventually found a small window that was ajar. Carefully climbing in, he went into the lounge where, he said, he saw an elderly lady. She totally blanked him and walked straight past, through to the next room. He told me that he could feel the temperature drop as she walked by. With the hairs standing up on the back of his neck, he followed her into the bedroom. There she was again, but this time sitting up in bed, eyes closed, cold to the touch and clearly dead.

"I was shitting myself. I'm convinced I saw her ghost," he told us.

The worst was yet to come though, having to wait inside with her for the ambulance, and when it did arrive, realising that he couldn't let the paramedics in because the door was locked.

"Mr Brown was at the window," he told us (presumably Brown was the paramedic), "and I was stuck in the house with some spook. I eventually found the key, tightly gripped in her hand and I had to prise it out of her grasp to open up. I saw her ghost, I tell you. When she was taken out, the whole house warmed up again."

None of us believed him initially. Well, I mean to say, Geezer, climbing through a small window? However, the look on his face was enough to convince us that he spoketh the truth.

"That hour turnaround time waiting for the paramedics was the worst hour of my life. And I said turnaround ...it's got nothing to do with a reach around, before you ask."

As for me, my worries, when confronted with my first sudden death as a police officer were very different. My breath hung in the air on that cold February evening as I approached the driveway of the house. I tried to remember what I considered to be the one golden rule: however funny a face they may have pulled when they died, don't have a nervous laugh or giggle or you'll forever be labelled as the insensitive jerk who was laughing at the dead person.

Luckily, I was not alone. I was accompanied by Barry and Bob. As I ran through the order of questions I'd need to ask, I didn't look where I was walking, and stepped in the most enormous dog turd that then tried to cling tenaciously onto my boot. Awww, it was a yellow one, too.

"Barry, Barry ...stop ..."

I tried to get our Sergeant's attention but it was too late, he had already rung the bell. I could hear the chimes echoing in the grand hallway. Shit! I started to wipe the sides of my boot on the beautifully manicured lawn. "Bob, Bob ...get me a stick or something."

I had scraped the worst of it on the grass and the edge of the little picket fence, but there was still a fair amount of poo in the welts of the boot and ridges underneath.

Bob started to run about looking for a de-pooping stick, whilst I hopped on one leg trying to line up the bottom of my boot with the pointy bit on top of the fence.

"Behave you idiots, someone's coming," whispered Barry angrily, as the hall light came on.

"Sorry to hear about your loss," explained Barry as the door opened and we were ushered upstairs. Bugger! A cream carpet! As Barry and Bob followed the householder, I crept up behind, treading normally with my left foot, but only walking on the tiptoe of my right foot, as if I was auditioning for the role of Quasimodo, looking back after each step to ensure I hadn't left a turdy trail in my wake.

I don't know if you have ever seen a dead body, but after they have been expired for a while they develop a very waxy pallor, their colour resembling the hue of the inside of an old tea pot. If I hadn't known better, I would have been convinced that this was a training exercise with a Madame Tussaud's dummy. The gentleman in question was in bed in the 'granddad flat' that the owners had added onto this already grand and spacious house for their ageing relative. He had his own dayroom next to his bedroom, and as Barry sat on an armchair, and Bob sat on a dining chair that had been brought through, I quickly volunteered to stand behind both Barry and the chair, conveniently shielding the offending boot from view.

Barry took the details from the gentleman's daughter and son-in-law.

"I always thought he would live to be a hundred," she mused.

"Were you close?" Barry enquired sympathetically.

"Not far off – he was ninety seven," quipped the son-in-law.

"I think the officer meant were we a close family, Brian. Why don't you make yourself useful and go and make some tea?" rebuked the deceased's daughter, sending him scuttling off to the kitchen, before continuing with, "yes, we were officer. We had this flat built so he could live with us."

I should have been listening carefully and learning from Barry, the master of chat, but my thoughts were elsewhere. It was hot, incredibly hot in that little room, and it was causing some form of chemical reaction with the substance on the base of my boot, resulting in a strongly pungent odour that would have brought tears to the eyes of a clown. Goodness only knows what that mutt must have feasted on.

"I've never seen a dead body before." We were now re-joined by Brian carrying five mugs of tea on a tray. "I think the worst thing is the smell – I didn't really notice it before, but it really hits you when you walk back into the room."

Barry shot me a withering glance. I could see Bob's shoulders rise and fall as he looked away and buried his face in his paperwork – the bastard.

To say that the half hour spent at that house was one of the most uncomfortable times in my life, wouldn't be an overstatement. Things momentarily improved, and I felt the heat taken off me for a second when Bob got up and found that his handcuffs had clipped themselves around the arm of the chair, sending it, and his tea, flying. Aha, so there is a God.

I made best use of the confusion by excusing myself on the pretence of getting some fresh air and went and sat back in the van. Alone with my thoughts – and my smell. Next time it would be better. Next time.

CHAPTER FOUR:

Celebration

"Donoghue, you're going to a hanging," Barry informed me as I walked in for duty that morning.

It took me a few seconds to realise that I wasn't off to some spectator event, but rather attending a suicide. Well, I was hoping it was a suicide.

When I arrived the family was already there, gathered around the hanging man along with the paramedics who confirmed the victim was indeed dead (Yay!).

After the ambulance staff had departed, I shepherded the family into the next room, and then went and stood near the body. The male in question, Mr Marwood, had hanged himself with his belt from the top of the stairs. The scene needed to be preserved until both CID and CSI arrived – it was probably a suicide, but you can never be sure that it isn't a carefully staged murder. Everything has to be left until the area can be examined. This includes leaving the deceased hanging in position until the knot can be studied, the body examined, any suicide notes located, signs of forced entry to the building looked for, etc.

It was a sombre time. Now I know how the term 'deathly quiet' got its name. Next door, I could hear a few comforting hushed whispers, broken by the occasional muffled sob. For my part, I stood in silence by the limp body awaiting the arrival of my colleagues. The slow tick, tock of an old grandfather clock seemed to count down the time like a morbid metronome.

Slow tick.

Deathly silence ...then the inevitable tock.

Tick.

Then, tock.

Five past eight it read. I looked at my watch. Ten past eight.

The clock was running slow.

Tick.

Even a stopped clock is right twice a day.

Tock.

This clock would never tell the correct time.

Tick.

Unless it lost a minute a day.

Tock.

If it did, in about two years, it might be right again. For a second anyway. I'm not really that sure.

Tick.

Let's just say it'll be aeons before it's right again.

Tock.

All I do know is that there isn't much to do except to ponder on the imponderable when you are waiting ...and waiting.

Tick.

Like why do old people always insist on telling you how old they are?

Tock.

Are you supposed to say well done for not dying?

Tick.

For saving you the paperwork?

Tock.

A fly has just landed on Marwood's shoe.

Tick.

What a disrespectful little insect.

Tock.

A fly can taste through its feet. Not only cheeky but also a freak!

Tick.

God I'm bored.

Tock.

"Celebrate good times, come on!"

Suddenly, the tranquillity was shattered by Kool and the Gang.

"Celebrate good times, come on! Let's celebrate."

Shit! Where was that coming from?

"There's a party going on right here..."

No there's not! By now the family in the other room were up and about and asking through the door what was going on.

"A celebration to last throughout the years..."

I started to look around in panic. I'm as much a fan of Mr Kool's unique mix of jazz, R'n'B, funk and pop as the next man – but there's a time and a place for it.

"So bring your good time and your laughter too..."

And this was definitely not the time, nor the place.

"We're gonna celebrate this party with you."

They were knocking on the door now! Shit!

"Stay there!" I shouted back as if I was trying to conceal some dirty secret. It was the same type of 'stay there' you shout when you are on the computer and your girlfriend comes home unexpectedly. I just didn't want everyone clambering over the potential crime scene, searching for the elusive partymeister.

Just as suddenly as the party started, it stopped. All was silent again except for a few more muffled sobs adding to the mix.

Tick.

Muffled sob.

Tock.

Me, searching around for Mr Kool.

Tick.

Embarrassed cough.

Tock.

I recently read an article that asked the question '*When's the last time you heard Kool & The Gang's triumphal, anthemic, R&B smash "Celebration"? At your cousin's wedding last summer? After that stirring, last minute snatched victory at the stadium last Saturday? On your local oldies' station yesterday? On the soundtrack of your Toy Story 2 DVD?*'

I wonder how many people had replied '*At my first hanging.*'

A knock at the door. That must be the CID Sergeant and CSI bloke.

"Donoghue, you got things under control here?" The CID Sergeant strode in purposefully, closely followed by a man in a white paper suit. "It's a measure of a police officer how they handle their first suicide. I've heard some good things about you. I take it you've got it all sorted."

Please God. Not now.

"*Celebrate good times. Come On!*"

"What the fuck?" exclaimed the Sergeant.

You bastard God!

"*There's a party going on right here...*"

The sobs next door turned into wails.

"*A celebration to last throughout the years...*"

Shit! Where's it coming from?

"*So bring your good time and your laughter too...*"

"I'm not happy with this!" I'm not sure if that was the Sergeant or the family saying it. Probably both.

I could hear the relatives shouting through the door. Now they were banging. Banging on the bloody door.

"What's going on in there?"

I could see my prospects within the Constabulary disappearing before my very eyes. It had started on a low and gone downhill ever since.

"I'll complain to the Chief Constable, young man!" was

shouted from beyond the door.

Young man? Well maybe it wasn't all so bad.

Or maybe it was. I could just about visualise my career as a little paper boat slowly circling the plughole of life.

"We're gonna celebrate this party with you."

Not with me you're not, I muttered.

"My mate's got that ring-tone. A high water mark for the group, I'd say," said the nerdy CSI guy.

"YES!" I exclaimed. It suddenly dawned on me. "The phone! The phone!" I shouted excitedly pointing at the vibrating pocket of the corpse.

"OK, Tattoo. Calm down," replied the Sergeant. "Get the fucker out, and give it here ...and then see if you do a better job of getting someone to make us a cup of tea. And lighten up, too. We all make mistakes. Don't take yourself so seriously. Nobody else does."

I let the final line play out, and then got the phone out and gave it to the Sarge. I was still trying to work out whether he was being supportive of me or not. I then went to tell the family that there wasn't a party going on, and was it possible to have two cups of tea? None for me. I was off. Just time for the family to tell me one last time though what a wanker they thought I was. Brilliant.

However, despite my sorry experiences, I was mildly reassured, listening to my colleagues' tales that it wasn't only me who felt that sudden deaths were no cakewalk.

Mind you, even delivering the bad news to a relative is just as daunting – sometimes more so. Again, you can never second guess their reaction ...but I never thought I'd get this.

The Inspector had called Lloyd and myself over and given us the task. Old Mr Hucker, a well known local character, had recently moved with his wife into one of the old people's bungalows near the centre of town.

I say 'character', although some would use another C word to describe him.

I don't know if there is any official criteria required to

become 'a character', but Mr Hucker's application revolved around his obsession with dog doings. Other people's dog doings. Indeed, it can be said that Rudolph Hucker was, for the officers of Sandford, the person who put the 'turd' into 'Saturday'.

Every weekend, the office would get a call to attend the Hucker residence. Once there, Mr Hucker would point out all the irksome dog deposits in the street which he had now adorned with little flags, attached onto cocktail sticks, which he had carefully pushed into the turds.

The signs would read things such as:

'Black Labrador' or *'unidentified mongrel'* indicating that a Black Lab or mongrel had delivered the relevant brown parcel.

Another might have *'Lady from East Bridge Street'*, which did not actually mean that the lady from East Bridge Street had done the dirty, but rather that this was the next stage in his investigations, and that he had identified the owner of an offending dog. When I'd been on patrol, I'd seen a woman from that street taking her boxer dog called George out for a meander. Maybe our pooper snooper was fingering her?

For those specimens that had already perished due to the attritional forces of nature or had just been crushed to death underfoot, have no fear: Mr Hucker had recorded them for posterity on his Kodak instamatic. How they must have loved him down at the one hour developing counter at Boots.

He should have just walked my dog down the street. For some reason, eating other dogs' poop is a favourite pastime of Barney's. As much as I tell him off, he just can't resist hoovering them up. They say that one's man's rubbish is another dog's gold. Well, something like that. To Mr Hucker, they may be disgusting deposits, but to my hound, they are delicious delicacies. He'll pretend to ignore them, but it must be like walking down a street being tempted every couple of steps with pork pies, savoury eggs and chocolate éclairs.

There will be a pretence of ignoring them, but as soon as I'm looking away, those babies are his. My dog can resist anything but temptation ...especially if it is Mr Whippy shaped.

Things had come to a head though, when it was discovered that Hucker had been feeding the passing canines in the street with dog food laced with glitter in a bid to trace them to their home address. It was harmless to the pooches, but the idea was that the differing coloured glitter would pass safely through the said hounds, but then cleverly allow our sleuth to identify the jobbies of each individual culprit. There had been a dreadful stink about this sorry episode when it was exposed, although I do concede, the street did look very pretty for the next week or so as the jewel encrusted deposits glinted in the sun. I'm not sure if there is a connection or not, but shortly afterwards, Rudolph Hucker and wife moved out of the street and to the old people's bungalows.

Despite being well into his 80s, Mr Hucker still used to cycle to the shops on a daily basis to get his provisions, only now he cycled in from a different direction. This morning was one cycle ride too many, and he had a heart attack on the way. Death was confirmed by the paramedics who had arrived on scene minutes later. I wasn't looking forward to telling his wife.

"This is my number that you can ring if you need help," said the Inspector when he tasked us with delivering the news. I thought he was being really helpful which, I must admit, seemed a little out of character for him. I never really thought he liked me.

He got back into character though, when he added "...but if you do ring me, I'll regard it as a sign of weakness." Cheers.

Lloyd and I had pulled up at a block of pensioners' bungalows to deliver the bad news – to let an eighty odd year old woman know that she was now a widow. To inform her that her husband of fifty five years was now 21 grams lighter.

We were never taught how to break the sad news to the relatives when we were at training school. I guess it was left to our discretion. It's not something that you discuss until it's too late, until it's time to actually do it. It's traumatic enough for the husband/wife/father/mother of the recently deceased. I didn't want to compound things by making a mess of the death message.

Einstein had once said 'Keep it as simple as possible but no simpler'. I don't know what the crazy haired genius was on about at the time, but decided to take his advice when breaking the news. Maybe I'd leave the soul thing out for the time being.

I wasn't looking forward to it. Neither was Lloyd. However, I lost the game of paper, scissors, stone ...so it was down to me.

As we walked down the short path with our hats on as an extra mark of respect, an elderly, frail lady with a face like a tiny, wizened apple appeared at the door of the property.

"Hello, are you Mrs Hucker?" I enquired.

"Yes I am, love. Is it Rudolph?" She replied.

Yes, it is Rudolph, or it was Rudolph, to put it more precisely.

"I'm afraid ..." I was stopped short by Mrs Hucker who ushered us into her home.

"Oh I can guess. It's that bike isn't it? I always told him it would be the death of him. Still he's had a good run. Now, love, he was on the way to the video shop. Tell me, did he get *Dog Soldiers*?"

Dog Soldiers is an excellent film by the way and worth watching if you haven't already. In fact, a mate of Barry plays one of the soldiers in it. He's the one who says '*I hope I give you the shits*' when he is eaten by the werewolf. An inspired choice by the Huckers, but not exactly what I was expecting to hear from her under the circumstances.

"Well, I'm not sure, to be honest," I answered. "Do you want me to take you to the hospital?"

"Well, can you check, love? It'll save me a journey."

"I'm afraid I have checked Mrs Hucker, the medical staff have already confirmed that..." Again I was cut short by the widow Hucker.

"No, no ...the film. Did he get the film? Can you check his coat pocket?"

"Well, I don't really know," I replied insipidly. "I suppose I can ask."

"Yes please, love. Otherwise can you take me to the video shop ...it's just like him to drop dead and leave it all to me."

As I said, people can have different reactions.

As we drove back to the station, I was quite ill at ease with Mrs Hucker's attitude. However, being a bloke, I wasn't used to talking about feelings. Not many of my colleagues are. Not even tucking the subject in between the sports and weather. I know it's not good for me. I know I should be getting things out, discussing them, purging the demons from my soul ...but instead, like a lot of my workmates, I bottle it all up and bury those difficult thoughts, horrific experiences and bad memories. You can never bury them deep enough though, and sometimes when you are innocently digging around for something else in your subconscious, you uncover one of those things you thought you had put behind you. I really should learn to be more emotional, more sentimental, deal with issues effectively when they occur, but I just don't seem to have the ability to open up, I just can't seem to allow my guard to drop. Maybe it's been ingrained in me too long. I've been a sailor, a soldier and now a police officer. It just doesn't seem to be the done thing. I can't seem to let the facade drop. We're supposed to be the ones people depend on. Hell, we wear boots to work for goodness sake!

I guess that's where the black humour stems from. It's either make a joke about things or go back home and lie down in a darkened room listening to whale music.

As Barry approached me, I mentioned that I had just been

to see Mrs Hucker and that it had been a funny old visit.

"The Inspector mentioned to me that you were going to the old people's bungalows. How is Mr Hucker finding it there since he moved from Dog Poop Alley?"

Clearly, Barry wasn't up on the latest developments.

"He's like a fish out of water," I told him.

"What? Still feeling a bit unfamiliar with his new surroundings?"

"No. He's dead."

CHAPTER FIVE:

If Carlsberg Made
Shit Days ...

Sometimes your day just doesn't go to plan. Sometimes people say out of sadness comes joy. More often than not, I didn't have a clue what they were on about but that was before I joined the police ...

A call had come into the Communications Centre from one of the police driving instructors. On his way to work he had seen a small car parked in a lay-by. As he drove past, a smartly dressed young woman had emerged out of the bushes and ran to the car. She appeared agitated and distressed but what really grabbed his attention, he said, was that it looked as if she was naked from the waist down. He had turned his car around and drove up to park behind her vehicle to see if she was ok. She, meanwhile, was now sitting in the driver's seat with the door open. As he got out, she had suddenly become hysterical, screaming, "Don't come any closer! Leave me alone!" before slamming her door, revving her engine and disappearing in a cloud of exhaust fumes as she sped off into the distance. He had tried to follow, but she had too much of a head start on him and he had lost her in the rush hour traffic. He did, however, manage to get her vehicle registration.

At once, the vehicle details were put through the computer and an officer (me) was immediately dispatched to the home address of the registered owner of the car, whilst Lloyd was sent back to the lay-by to see if there was anything to indicate what had happened at the scene. This is what was classified a 'concern for safety'. There was no evidence of any crime as yet, but certainly something was up. We often get calls to check on a person to see if they are safe and well when, for example, a relation hasn't heard from an elderly relative, or we receive a report of someone who looks distraught and vulnerable walking in the street.

Who knows what might have occurred that would cause a half naked female to be wandering alone in a lay-by? She was also clearly very reluctant to talk to the driving instructor. He had been in a plain car so I guess she wouldn't have known he was police. Things just didn't add up. Had a sexual assault just happened? Had our colleague disturbed a suicide attempt? What else or, indeed, who else was in those bushes? It was up to me and Lloyd to try and piece the clues together and come up with an answer.

There are many mnemonics taught in training school to act as an aide-mémoire in different policing scenarios. Too many, in fact. I was finding I needed a mnemonic just to remember the different mnemonics. However, the one that I always used without fail was ABC.

Assume nothing.

Believe nothing.

Challenge everything.

It didn't make me the most popular person with the local vicar, but it always served me well at crime scenes.

I bore that in mind as I drove to the address – a new build house on an estate on the edge of town, no doubt full of aspiring professionals and young families. As I approached I could see that the car was parked haphazardly on the drive, the driver's door still open.

I knocked on the front door. No reply. I rang the bell. Nothing. I went and peered through the front window. I was sure I could see someone dart behind a chair when I looked in. Something wasn't quite right here. I went around the back and cupped my hands to my face to look in through the patio windows. Again, I could see movement. I got on the radio to Comms, asking them to look on their systems and find a land line for the address, and then to ring it.

"We've found a number, John. I'll try it now."

I could hear the ringing from within and a few seconds later the ringing stopped. There was someone definitely in there.

"She's answered," Comms informed me.

"Can you ask her to let me in?" I requested.

I made my way back to the front where the door opened slightly and a tearful female face appeared and quickly ushered me inside. Her hair, which had obviously started the day in a fashionable mess, was now damp and sticking to her forehead. She was barefoot, had a dressing gown wrapped tightly around her and was quietly shivering like a kite in a gentle breeze. I was shown into the front room and soon established that this was the female concerned. She had been driving across town and had subsequently parked in the lay-by as reported.

"It's just that my colleague was concerned as you seemed a little distressed."

Just then the radio signalled a private call. I informed the female that I'd need to take this before I could carry on our conversation. She appeared relieved.

"Are you state twelve?" asked the voice on the other end, meaning did I have my earpiece in so that no one else could hear our conversation.

"I am," I replied.

"It's Lloyd here. I've checked out the lay-by," he whispered urgently.

"Go on."

"We found a carrier bag there."

"Go on."

"With a skirt, pair of panties and stockings in there."

This was getting stranger by the moment.

"Go on, Lloyd," I urged.

"Well, I think I might know why your girl was a little distressed – and the half naked thing, too."

"And?" I was intrigued now. I could sense he was drawing this out on purpose, building up to some dramatic revelation. I glanced over at her. She looked like a bedraggled refugee, her head hung down as if in shame, just looking blankly at the floor. As Lloyd continued his overly dramatic pause, I glanced around at the photographs on the mantelpiece. She was clearly a confident and successful woman. Just what had happened that morning to turn her into a vacant wreck?

"C'mon Lloyd, tell me," I urged.

Another overly dramatic pause – he was milking this now – before he finally continued.

"Well, they were caked in shit. Looks like diarrhoea all over them... and I mean ALL OVER."

I looked up at the female and I could tell in her eyes that she knew what my colleague had just told me. She was mortified.

"I had a bit of a jippy tum this morning..." she started to explain.

Not even I could be that cruel.

"Don't worry. As long as you are alright," I reassured her, reaching out and touching her elbow.

I mentally repacked my ABC away for use at another time in a different situation. Sometimes, some things are better left unsaid. Let sleeping dogs lie.

I had so many questions, not the least of which was how had she managed to get from the car back into the house without anyone seeing her? However, I was too much of a gentleman to ask them now. I didn't want to tip her over the edge.

I thought about telling her the old urban myth about the guy, who, in similar circumstances, had soiled himself in town one day when he wasn't feeling too grand. He had waddled straight into the nearest clothes shop, selected the first pair of trousers he could see in his size, and then pushed through to the front of the queue to pay.

"Would you like to try them on?" the shop assistant had queried.

"No. I'll just take them," was his curt reply.

Waddling to the station, catching the train home, he headed for the toilets, locked the door, took off his soiled trousers and pants, threw them out of the window, and then opened up his shopping …only to discover that he had taken the wrong bag, and all that was in there was a ladies' pink lambswool cardigan.

I was going to tell her, but then thought better of it. In her delicate state, God knows what could happen if she started to laugh.

"We've got your clothes from the scene. Would you like the bag back?" I asked our female.

"No thanks," she replied. "Just give them to charity or whatever you do with them." Mind you, I think even the neediest person would balk at them in that state.

A few weeks later, and a different case. I was on routine patrol when another concern for safety call came in.

Neighbours and friends were concerned that they hadn't seen old Mrs Freader in a while. They had knocked on the door and rung the bell, but still got no response. It didn't sound good. I swung the car around and headed down to Dunbar Way.

I had heard about cases where some resident had died and the body wasn't found until days, even weeks later. In the old days, a build up of milk bottles on the porch would have quickly alerted the next door neighbours that something wasn't quite right, but with cartons from the supermarket and the general decline in community spirit, the demise of reclusive or lonely old people can sometimes go unnoticed for months. The bodies could be in an awful state of decay when they were eventually found, particularly if the deceased had passed away in front of the fire or in the bath.

It sounded though as if Mrs Freader's friends had acted relatively promptly, but even so, I approached the address with trepidation. Several residents of the street were already out, alerted to the possibility of some macabre discovery in their midst. I was greeted by the spokesperson, the local vicar, who brought me up to speed on developments.

Prudence Freader, it transpired, had worked in publishing all her life, retiring at the grand age of seventy, several years ago. Following the death of her husband, she now lived at home with just her books for company, not really troubling anyone and rarely venturing out, apart from the regular Wednesday coffee morning at the church, and the fortnightly meetings where she helped produce the local parish newsletter where, apparently, she was known for her eagle eye at spotting any mistakes. Moreover, she also knew the secret of guaranteeing that the newsletter was read – to ensure that all the people who get it, read it: make sure they are in it. Prudence, the Vicar added, also religiously attended the Sunday service. I don't know how else you could attend them.

Anyway, Prue hadn't turned up for mass at the weekend, and, this being Wednesday, it was also noted that she was missing from this morning's coffee engagement.

As I tried the door again, I feared the worst. I opened up the letter box and shouted through it. Nothing. There weren't any bluebottles about though, nor any smell, which is what I would have expected if the body had been lying there for some time. I climbed over the gate and made my way round to the back of the house. Cupping my hands against the glass, trying to find a gap in the net curtains, I could just make out the back of an armchair, and a hand on the armrest.

I knocked again, hammering on the glass. No response. I got on the radio.

"I'm at the concern for safety. I'm going to have to break in."

I thought I'd act before I was told to wait until they got hold of a locksmith. I didn't feel time was on my side. One swift kick and the back door went in. I stood in silence for a few seconds before cautiously entering the property.

It was a typical old person's house. I was momentarily taken back in time to my grandmother's home. The kitchen was clean and tidy, blue gingham tea towels neatly folded complementing the blue gingham tie back curtains. A proper teapot for a decent cuppa sitting on the work surface. Nothing so vulgar as teabags for this discerning tea drinker. I bet she even warmed the pot first like my Gran used to do. It even had its own little hat to keep it warm, too. It was probably a cup and saucer house – no mugs allowed here.

I went into the lounge. On a low table in the corner were some old battered board games still in their original boxes, lovingly preserved from when her children played with them and no doubt ready for when the grandchildren came round. Along with the chess set and compendium of games there was a John Bull printing set, Fuzzy Felt, a few boxes of Airfix toy soldiers and an old Jackie annual. By the condition of them, they didn't see much action from the grandchildren – nowadays more interested in their hand held computers, but at least Mrs Freader had good intentions.

The sofa and armchair both had antimacassars on, and I was transported back to my friend Stephen Carol's house. They had a room 'for best'. He was never allowed in there except for Christmas. Quite a few people had them ...twenty percent of the house they never used except for high days and holidays. We used to peek around the door and see the small pieces of cloth on the fabric to prevent it soiling. I had always wondered who they expected to call. They were obviously dirty buggers whoever they were.

Anyway, back to the incident in hand. I couldn't put off the obvious anymore. There was no time left to reminisce. I finally made my way over to where the body was located. She was there, slumped in her armchair, looking at peace with the world, eyes closed, a serene look on her face, all her worries far behind her now. It just all made me feel so heartbroken. This wasn't just a house – this was someone's home, full of love and fond memories. This wasn't just a dead body: it was someone's mother, a caring grandmother, a beloved member of the local community. After the initial adrenalin rush of booting the door in, I let myself stand in quiet contemplation for a while; our job can be so sad sometimes.

Still, she was eighty odd years old ...that's a good innings for anybody.

I got back on the radio.

"Could I have an ambulance around to this location to confirm ..."

"Oooh dear, what are you doing here?"

She spoke. The body spoke to me. Feck! I almost jumped out of my skin.

"Oh my God, Mrs Freader, you're alive!"

"Are you alright young man? You look as white as a sheet," the cadaver continued.

"We thought you were ..."

"Hang on, young man, let me get these out," she said as she took a pair of earphones out of her ears. "Now, what were you saying?"

"I was saying we thought you were dead, Mrs Freader. I've been banging away for ages trying to arouse you ..."

"Young man!" she interrupted smiling, "I do think you mean 'rouse'. Anyway, I'm far too old for a young whippersnapper like yourself," she added, winking at me. She was most certainly alive ...and kicking.

I went on to explain how the vicar was worried about her after her absence from church and had called us to investigate. In return, Prue winked at me and told me she reckoned that the vicar was only concerned about one less person paying into the collection. She seemed a wily old bird. It transpired that her eyes were eventually going after so much dutiful service, and she had now discovered talking books on compact disc, motioning to a veritable mountain of CDs piled on top of the bookshelf. Hence the ear phones, hence the contented look on her face, hence the lack of response to the banging.

"A good book is much better than those old gossips down at the coffee morning any day," she confided in me. "I'm re-discovering Henry Miller. 'Quiet Days in Clichy'. Have you read it?"

I most certainly have, you saucy old bird!

So, no dead old woman, no report to the coroner, no relatives to inform, just me, almost shitting myself when she came back to life. I never did get to ask her why she didn't jump out of her skin, too, when she saw me standing in front of her. Maybe she did, but she was more wrinkly, so there was more give in it and I hadn't noticed. Either way, a most satisfactory outcome …and I think I'll dig out my copy of 'Tropic of Cancer' when I get home, too.

Sometimes, you think the worst and it turns out fine. Other times it can be a little different.

Months later, I heard the cautionary tale of Ray Sondette, which, if he was alive today, I'm sure Henry Miller could entwine his story into an extravagant and prophetic romp.

Ray worked at the local airport. To all and sundry, he was a quiet, mild mannered man. One (or two) might even say he was a bit boring. However, under the surface, he was a different person altogether. It appears that Ray had been having an illicit and passionate affair with a co-worker, unbeknown to friends and family alike.

Ray's world was shattered though when Jean, the object of his desire, had broken off the relationship when she was transferred to a different airport. He had convinced himself that the unbearable lightness of Jean was his only reason for living.

Ray took it badly. As his calls and texts went unanswered, he became more and more despondent, and as weeks turned into months, he became more and more unpredictable.

One afternoon, he just snapped.

Driving into Sandford, he went to the nearest pub. There, he drank ...and drank ...and drank. In fact he drank until he had built up enough Dutch courage ...and then started to put his plan into action, not that it was much of a plan in the first place.

It went something like this: he would win Jean back. He would rekindle their relationship. He would relight her fire. He would stoke her charcoal burner, and various other bad metaphors. In short, he would mend his shattered world. Oh, and fan the embers of desire, I forgot that one.

Standing at the bar, he reached into his pocket where he felt something hard. Pulling it out, he discovered that he still had the key to her house. He felt like Gollum holding the ring. That's when the embryonic plan started to develop legs. Staggering out of the pub, he got into his car and drove across town to the street where she lived, and ultimately, to the place where they had shared their secretive trysts.

Reaching her home, he tried the key in the lock and let himself in. He shouted her name. No reply. No one was home. As he stood there wondering what to do next, the demons took over. More drink! Ray then went straight to the fridge and took out the two bottles of wine from within, sat at the kitchen table and waited ...and waited. He downed the first bottle, as he sat and thought of his wonderful Jean.

Then, the noise of a car on the gravel drive outside. What to do now? He looked around in a state of blind panic. Then everything suddenly slotted into position in his mind – there was no time to lose! He quickly started pulling his clothes off in a desperate attempt to get naked. His jacket was wriggled out of, shoes were kicked off and his shirt ripped open, buttons flying everywhere, as Ray tried to rid himself of every last vestige of clothing. As he heard the key in the lock, he just had time to take hold of the Semillon in one hand, two glasses in the other and run into the lounge. As the lounge door opened, Ray jumped stark, bollock naked onto the sofa, holding the bottle and glasses aloft, with a triumphant cry of "Ta Da!"

I don't know who was more surprised to be honest, Ray or the house's new owners.

Half an hour later Ray found himself in police custody on suspicion of burglary and drink driving.

A month later and I was crewed up with Ron. It was past midnight and we had parked up the panda to do some foot patrol in the local park. Over Christmas, there had been a spate of kidnappings there. Or more precisely, duck-nappings. Instead of the traditional turkey, a few locals had obviously thought that it would be a bit more adventurous to try a duck or two for their Christmas dinner and several of the pond's inhabitants had disappeared overnight. Someone had suggested that it might have been a cat burglar (ah, see what they did there!), but since the murderers had used a pedallo to get to the island where the ducks nested, I thought it was a good bet that a human hand was afoot. I know these cats can be cunning, but the idea of a couple of them pedalling away whilst another sat on the front directing them where they were going, was pushing it a bit. I checked the boathouse to make sure that all of the vessels were still chained up. Apparently, the one that looked like a big swan had been used for the dastardly deed. Goodness knows what had gone through the ducks' minds as the massive swan had made his duck-napping approach. Maybe it had gone down in duck folklore as their own version of the Trojan Horse?

A sign on the boathouse read: 'Vandals will be prosecuted'.

"What about the Visigoths?" I asked (the only people in history who could wear pigtails and still look hard).

Ron just looked at me and as a silence descended upon us,

I swear I could hear a lone church bell chiming in the distance. Where was Chad when I needed him? He'd have known what I was on about. He still probably wouldn't have laughed – but I'm sure there would have been some mutual respect for our shared knowledge of vaguely obscure historical minutiae. Luckily, I was saved further embarrassment by someone in the town doing mischief, as the radio barked into life.

"Kilo 1 mobile. Immediate response, 69 Foskett Way. Caller reports a group of males in the back garden."

As we ran back to the car, we were updated that the males had now forced the back door and were entering the house. Suddenly, the ducks were forgotten, as were hopefully any memories that Ron might still have had of my bad joke.

"We are literally two minutes away," I called back. We sped along through the deserted streets. No sirens – a silent approach was called for. We didn't want the intruders hearing us and making off.

We pulled up in Foskett Way and as we jumped out I pushed the 'at scene' button on my radio to let control know we were there. We were well within our target time.

"Shit – how do you get round the back?" I asked Ron.

Foskett Way was one of those long, meandering streets consisting of winding sections of terraces, broken occasionally by the odd tributary street leading off it. Finding the back of number 69 would be a nightmare and would certainly involve losing vital minutes as we drove around the side streets.

"We'll just have to try the front."

We dashed down the short path. Through a gap in the curtains I caught a glimpse of a middle aged man standing in the lounge. He seemed to be looking at the back of the house expectantly. I saw him physically jump as Ron hammered on the front door.

As Ron hammered again the male turned and ran upstairs. On the third hammering, a young female clad in a dressing gown, and doing a fair impression of a zombie came down the stairs. It took another knocking before she seemed to realise what was happening and came and answered the door.

Almost rudely, we pushed past her and ran into the house. I ran to the rear of the house whilst Ron started to question the female as to what had happened – where were the intruders – was she safe – who was the male?

"Nothing's happened. I was asleep. Broken in? Nobody's broken in. The man? That's my dad. I've no idea why he ran upstairs. What's going on? Who called you?"

"Ring the number back," I requested Control.

Control duly rang back the number where the call was made from and the house phone started ringing.

"You called us," said Ron. "Or someone in this house did."

"Ron, you'd better come and have a look at this," I interrupted, and shone my torch towards the back door.

There, hanging over the back door handle was what looked like a metal colander. Attached to it were some wires leading to a nearby socket.

I confided in Ron that if I wasn't mistaken, this was a home made device intended to electrocute the first bobby who arrived on scene and tried the handle on the back door. Luckily, we were only saved by our inefficiency at not being able to find the rear of the property.

The owner of the house had clearly tried to lure us to the death trap with a fictitious call of intruders kicking in his back door.

You see this kind of contraption on Cannabis farms, along with other booby traps, designed to incapacitate police search teams, but it wasn't really what I expected in a quiet, residential street on a Wednesday night.

We had clearly spoilt his fun when we had turned up at the front because of basic lack of a decent A-Z. The zombie looked on as her father was led away in handcuffs. In my book, trying to kill me is regarded as quite rude.

Not dead, but still not a great day.

That's what I needed ...a great day! A day that would end on an up note ...I needed something positive to happen ...I needed a 'feel good' day.

I was pondering on this during another nightshift later in the week. It was a chilly evening in late March; I was teamed up with Chad and we were patrolling the deserted streets of the town at stupid o'clock in the morning when I saw it ...my opportunity!

Outside the Old George public house, sitting on the kerb, like a despondent teabag, was an old fella, clearly the worse for wear. He was swaying from side to side and appeared to be humming away to himself. An old, drunk bloke – perfect!

Here was my opportunity to make myself feel better. Do a good deed, feel all warm inside and, in the process, banish memories of people trying to kill me. Three in one!

We stopped the vehicle and wandered over. I'd say he was in his sixties if he was a day. Clearly, he had over-imbued at the hostelry, the lucky devil! We could smell the alcohol before we had even got close. The last time I saw eyes like that, they were being sported by some sad monkey in an anti-vivisection poster. His hair was sticking up, he had a slightly dishevelled air about him and he was clutching a banana. I'm still on about the monkey here in case you were wondering. Our old guy, although sans yellow bendy fruit, was giving our simian a close run for his money in the dishevelled stakes.

"What's your name mate?" I asked.

"Rooooooooooooland," came the slurred response. He even spoke like I imagined a monkey would. I smiled.

"And what's your last name Roland?"

"Butttttttttttter."

"Roland Butter? Come on Roland, let's get you home. Up you get."

But Roland just looked at us and started mumbling

incoherently. So it was left to Chad and me to get Roland to his feet. He may have been an old guy, but he was a dead weight …he didn't even seem to be trying to help himself. We eventually got him to his feet but as soon as we let go, he just crumpled back down into a pile on the floor again. We both had a little laugh and tried again. This time we got him up and managed to lean him up against a lamp-post. As we relaxed our grip, he just slid down the pole into a heap on the ground.

"Come on, granddad. A little self-help here wouldn't go astray," urged Chad.

"Aye, get a grip. Put some effort in," I added.

I was starting to get a bit annoyed now …my initial feelings of goodwill were quickly evaporating, but I gritted my teeth and persevered.

"Let's just get him in the car," said Chad, "we can just drop him off home and be done with him."

After a few more minutes of unintelligible murmurings, I eventually managed to establish that our drunkard came from an address across town. With one almighty effort, we got him back on his feet and virtually dragged him to the police car as he just continued to mumble away. When we got to the car, I started to let go with one hand in order to open the door, but when our inebriate once again started slowly sliding towards the floor, we decided to slump him over the bonnet instead whilst we opened up. We left him there for a minute or so as we got our breath back.

"How the feck does anyone let themselves get in such a state?" we commented as we grabbed the barfly again and shoved him into the back of the car, bumping his head off the roof in the process.

We drove on in silence as our drinker moaned and groaned away in the back. Ten minutes later and we were at the address. We got out, took a deep breath, opened the back door and dragged our wino out and into the night air again. Another deep breath and we supported Roland, dragging him up the path, knocking the occasional flower pot over, before finally reaching the sanctuary of the porch.

I knocked on the door and a few minutes later a light went on upstairs ...then the landing ...and then the porch light. The door opened and a small, frail lady answered and looked out at us anxiously.

"Mrs Butter?" I enquired, "Is this yours?"

She looked over at her husband. "Oh yes it is ...Thank you, officers. I've been so worried."

"Well, he's back now ...I must say though, he's had a fair bit to drink!"

"He does like a wee drop," she replied, which seemed like a bit of an understatement, before adding the immortal words, "but what have you done with his wheelchair?"

CHAPTER SIX:

Drugs Raid

We kicked in his door at 5 am.

It may have been a rude awakening for him, but my day had started a good two and a half hours earlier. I calculated that I needed to go to bed at half past six the previous night to get my full eight hours sleep in, but since I didn't finish work until nine that evening, that plan was pretty much put paid to. Going to bed before your previous shift has finished is normally frowned upon.

When I did eventually get to bed, I had an interrupted sleep, scared I wouldn't wake up in time. I've also got birds nesting in the void between my bedroom ceiling and the loft. Now, you might reasonably expect our feathered friends to come in, have a bit of a chirp to catch up on the day, and then get their heads down. Everyone has to have a home somewhere, and I wouldn't particularly mind sharing mine with some starlings if they showed a little respect for their host. But no, do they buggery! They'll come in, feed the chicks, and then stomp around the place, fluttering their wings and having bird domestics, squawking away at all hours. I think they know perfectly well what they're doing. I've taken to wearing ear plugs at night to drown out their partying, but I couldn't even wear those for the little amount of potential kip I did try and get in case I missed my alarm clock going off. Spring isn't all bouncing lambs and hosts of golden daffodils, you know. Well, not for me anyway. Curse those pesky critters, it's not a bloody aviary up there!

When the alarm did eventually go off, I got up, showered, dressed and was putting on my boots when I realised I was actually still in bed and it was all a dream. Thank goodness I didn't dream I had a piss, too.

When the alarm eventually *really* did go off, I showered, dressed, and as I started putting my boots on, I thought to myself what if this was a dream, too? Despite pinching myself, I thought I'd wait until I got to work before I risked a number two.

I arrived at the police station, kitted up with my baton, pepper spray and cuffs, and got on the crew bus taking us down to the rendezvous point.

When we arrived, there were about eighty other officers milling about, with about thirty CID boys who were looking surprised to discover that there were two 3 o'clocks in the same day. Elsewhere, officers in full riot gear wandered round in their black romper suits with their big red keys – the battering rams to break the doors down – whilst Police attack dogs and drug sniffer dogs barked at each other, and armed response officers busied themselves cleaning their weapons.

I gave my name and number to the officer on the door and was directed to the canteen.

"Down the corridor and collect your bacon sandwich and coffee," I was told.

Food as well! Things were looking up.

"Word of advice," he added, "don't look the canteen woman directly in the eye or try and engage her in conversation." Evidently she wasn't a morning person.

I had come across her before at the self-defence school. She had a sullen expression on her face even then as she scooped up the meat pie and plonked it with a splosh onto my plate. 'Dark meat surprise' is what we used to call it. I would entertain myself during lunch by counting the number of tubes I could see in the 'beef'. There used to be a horse in the field behind the school. One afternoon I saw her there feeding the pony. I swear that the next day I arrived for the course, the horse had disappeared and pie was on the menu again.

I queued up for my bap, poured myself a coffee, and went back into the main hall for the briefing on the operation.

It was a drugs bust or, to put it more precisely, several drugs busts to be made simultaneously at ten different houses on the dot of five across the town. The trouble with drugs is that they're quite moreish, and people keep coming back for seconds ...and thirds – and when they can't pay for them, they start stealing to get things to sell in order to get more money to buy more drugs. It's a sort of drug fuelled merry-go-round. I even think that after partaking of such substances, you can actually believe that you *are* riding on a funny elephant or colourful hippo. Our job today was to spoil their fun.

A lot of intelligence goes into making sure that police target the right house, but errors can happen. Cannabis needs a lot of heat and light to grow. In cannabis factories, fluorescent bulbs are used to grow the drug which needs at least eight hours of daylight and temperatures of 59F (15C). The artificial lighting generates a bright white trace on infra-red cameras. If someone is growing cannabis plants in their loft, the heat from the lights can be picked up by the infra-red cameras on the police helicopter as it flies overhead. This intelligence can then be the basis on which to substantiate a raid. A Police Community Support Officer found herself being given the knock when the Force helicopter picked up large amounts of heat escaping through her roof. It turns out her only crime was poor insulation.

For every incident – spin, spin spin – there is an angle – spin, spin, spin.

'Advice on cutting down fuel bills' – another service offered by the Constabulary.

In Scotland, I read about a raid that had taken place after

someone mistook tomato plants for a cannabis grow. Since I didn't see any friendly advice given out after this job, I'll add my own: don't keep tomatoes in the fridge – they'll lose their taste.

Back to the drugs bust, and you never know what you can expect when you enter a house. Some can be booby trapped as in the colander death trap incident and often the householder has weapons in the house too. Baseball bats, knives and Samurai swords are a favourite, but firearms or crossbows are not uncommon, hence the armed officers on standby.

You need to get in as quickly as possible on a raid like this too. Any delay or warning could mean the drug dealer arming himself, destroying any evidence or even escaping.

Briefing completed and we were on the countdown to action stations.

By ten to five, all the teams were parked up near, but not too close, to their specific targets. Often drug dealers have more cameras surrounding their property than your average town centre.

I was in the arrest/search team – aka the strike team. A separate entry team was parked in front. These were the boys in black with the helmets, and the enforcer – aka the big red key – aka the aforementioned battering ram used to gain entry to the premises. The dogs and gun cars were on standby to attend whatever target location needed them.

I looked at my watch – the seconds were counting down to the hour.

"GO, GO, GO!"

As the radio barked out its command, our vehicles roared into the street. As I jumped out, the entry team were already swinging at the door with the battering ram. BANG! The first strike just smashed a hole in the PVC door. One of the team then got onto his back and lay on the floor, bracing his feet against the frame. BANG! The second strike sent the door flying off its hinges and into the hallway.

I clambered over the door with two colleagues following close behind, all of us shouting "POLICE!" at the top of our voices and making as much noise as possible. I quickly ran up the stairs towards the dealer's bedroom. I had been beaten to the punch though – the noise and commotion had already woken the owner who must have sprung out of bed and was now standing at the top of the stairs, clad in a pair of boxers and with a baseball bat in his hand. However, as he saw our numbers, he dropped it and raised his hands in the air.

"You should have knocked!" he implored, trying to come over all friendly.

"It'd be rude to wake you so early!" I replied.

I handcuffed him, did the necessary chat and sent him downstairs with one of my colleagues.

My job now was to search for any drugs, mobile phones, sim cards, bank statements, cash or books that may contain lists of suppliers and customers. Starting in the bedroom, I was pleasantly surprised to see the householder's foxy girlfriend sitting up in bed, rubbing her eyes. So there was a booby trap after all, but a nicer one than I could have possibly expected. I believe it was the comedian Michael McIntyre who said there were two things that you could justifiably wake a sleeping woman for without incurring her wrath. They are:

To let her know it's snowing outside.
To tell her a celebrity has just died.

I don't believe that 'raiding the property for drugs' feature in that list. No, I've checked and it didn't. Our non sleeping beauty though, seemed in fine form. Very fine form indeed. I said a brief hello, explained what we were all about and what was going to happen next.

A female officer then joined me as we started to look through everything ...and I mean everything.

You can imagine how small a space drugs can be hidden

in, so every possible hiding place was looked into. Imagine your bedroom; imagine everywhere you could possibly hide something if you didn't want it found. Now think of those places where you could hollow out and hide stuff, or take the batteries out and hide stuff, or empty the contents and hide stuff. Now be even more imaginative and sly, and think of where you would put something tiny if you never wanted it found. Think now of all those places and things that you wouldn't want strangers to look at. Well, we've got to look in all those places, and at all those things.

The homeowner's girlfriend, it turns out, was a beautician. She had a *lot* of shoes, a *lot* of underwear, a *lot* of clothes, a *lot* of make-up, and a fair few toys. Elsewhere in the house, colleagues were opening up every CD case, every DVD box, checking behind pictures, looking in the fridge, in the cistern, shaking open all the books ...in short, spending hours turning the place inside out.

"Excuse the mess," the girlfriend genuinely apologised, "you should have let us know that you were coming."

"Sort of defeats the object a bit," I replied. "But I'll bear it in mind next time."

She watched me as I searched through her clothes and belongings, occasionally interjecting with the odd remark like:

"Ooh, I wondered where I had put those!"

"I'm not a real nurse, you know – it's PVC."

"It's a neck massager. Honest!"

After about an hour of watching us search, she got up, made herself even more presentable, and offered us all a cup of tea. She wasn't a bad sort ...well, neither was the guy whose house it was, to be honest. I find I can get on with most offenders when they aren't up to their villainy. They all know it's just one big game of cops and robbers and we have a job to do. It's just the racists and bullies I can't stand. Not for the first time, I've struggled to arrest a volatile, vociferous hard case who has required several of us to lead him out in cuffs, and who has been all shouts and curses as we led him to the car, only for him to calm down and apologise as soon as he is in the police vehicle.

"Sorry about that, lads. You know what it's like. I have to keep up appearances in the street."

It's surprising how with many of your 'regular' career criminals, they don't seem to bear a grudge if they see you, either on or off duty in the street or shopping in the local supermarket. In fact, there is often a cheery smile from them and a pleasant greeting – 'Afternoon, PC Donoghue, how're you doing?' and they seem to genuinely mean it. Even your first timers can sometimes be just as pleasant.

"How do you know him?" all her friends asked, after one teenager offered me an amiable acknowledgement coupled with a coy smile when she saw me on patrol in the town.

"He locked me up for glassing my boyfriend," she confided in them. "But he was ever so nice."

I find if you treat people decently when you lock them up, they treat you with respect in return. Don't get me wrong, I don't want to be the villains' mate, but neither is there any point in antagonising people for the sake of it.

I was on a body watch a few months previous. Some travellers had threatened to come and steal the body of a teenager who had died. The boy had been the product of a fling between a nice, middle class woman and a gypsy. The male had wanted nothing to do with the woman or the baby, but now years later, on hearing about the death, he wanted to take the lad away for a traditional traveller's funeral, whatever that consisted of. Mother didn't want this, so a standoff ensued with the father threatening to bring a hundred travellers to snatch the body away.

Full riot vans had been on standby during the day whilst the mob was drinking at a local pub, but that night it was just me, on overtime, in a panda car, outside the funeral home.

"We'll drive by during the night if you want a pee break," the Sergeant had told me. Cheers.

Still, I was on double time. I had brought a flask, some

sandwiches, a Penguin biscuit, a banana, today's paper and a book. How difficult could this be?

After about three hours, the Sergeant pulled up alongside in his car.

"You got your radio on, Donoghue?"

"Yes, Sarge."

"I've been trying to call you for the last hour. You didn't reply. Thought I'd see if you were ok."

What? If you couldn't get me for an hour, why didn't you come to see if I was ok an hour ago? It's a bit late now! I could have been horribly murdered in that time. I wanted a pee by then anyway, so I didn't bother making a fuss and just took advantage of his dawdle over to nip back to the station.

One pee break later and I was sat on my own back at the funeral parlour working out what I would get with my overtime windfall. I had it spent five times over when I heard it.

I say 'it' but I mean 'them'. 'It' was a car horn, 'them' was about twenty car horns. Shit!

I got out of the car and stood with my back against the door of the funeral home as the cars pulled up, blocking my vehicle in. I guess this is where I earn my double time. I could have stayed in the vehicle, but they would have just dragged me out anyway – probably through the window. How undignified would that have sounded in my obituary? I tried to think of some witty last words to say before I was torn apart by the mob.

Witty last words? Poignant last words? Witty and poignant last words?

They are not easy to think of and don't just take my word for it.

A Dutch poet, who had devoted his life to lyrical musings and interesting verse, was probably quite disappointed to find his last words were "Yes, but not too many." His wife had asked him if she should bake some potatoes that evening. He had made his reply when getting out of the car just before he had a heart attack.

"There's nothing about my life that is an accident," said Marc Bolan of T-Rex shortly before his fatal car crash.

Norman Douglas (not sure who he is) had uttered "Get those fucking nuns away from me!" A riposte worthy of Father Jack himself.

Last words are just as hard to think of as trying to write something vaguely amusing on someone's leaving card or in a visitors book. "You write stuff ...you should be good at this," doesn't really help. I usually end up writing something that sounds a lot better in my head than it actually looks on paper. It's not easy trying to be funny. Ex-girlfriends say I did make them laugh in bed though. Hang on a sec! I wish I never told you that now. Anyway, back to last words.

When I was recovering from an operation and still high on prescription drugs, I did actually dream that I had died. It involved me and Megan Fox. We took the road out of the city, right across the desert to the misty mountains and through the purple valley. She took me to the water and clear crystal fountains and we lay beneath the trees and the flowers that no-one knows the names of. If I remember correctly, my last words on that occasion were something snappy like "Not *again* Megan Fox, that's ten times already. I'll die of exhaustion." (If any under sixteens are reading this, I was tired out because we were playing table tennis. Yeah, boys and girls, just game after game of ping pong. Nothing naughty going on at all. Miss Fox was thoroughly bushwhacked, too.) Actually, I wouldn't stand a chance with her even in my dreams. She apparently says, "I like the bad-boy types. The guy I'm attracted to is the guy in the club with all the tattoos and nail polish. He's usually the lead singer in a punk band and plays guitar." Well, he sounds like a cock to me.

Oh, what the hell, these meatheads weren't going to remember whatever I said anyway. Where was Kipling, Billy Bragg, Hawkins and Stanley, Mick Thomas or some other great writer or troubadour when I needed them?

Clearly drunk, the leader of the Traveller gang slowly staggered up the street towards me, supported by a couple of heavies either side of him. Usually, I find there is nothing funnier than a drunk bloke walking along, checking his footing as if he was 10,000 feet up ...well, except for a dog digging a hole, or maybe even someone falling hard on their arse. However, on this occasion, my sense of humour had deserted me. Well almost; imagine a shark wearing a funny hat and you have the same bizarre mix of menace and absurdity as the drunken Traveller. He was still going to kill me, but at least we'd all have a laugh about it afterwards.

I racked my extendable baton open, my finger hovering above the emergency button on my radio.

As the man staggered up to me, I recognised him as someone I had arrested for drink driving some months earlier. He stared at me as if trying to work out where he had seen me before. I gave him a nod of recognition and in a quiet voice mumbled, "We've got to stop meeting like this."

He burped as if in reply, put a picture of his son on the ground, burped again, and walked back to the car. Within moments the vehicles pulled away, leaving me standing alone in the street.

"Sarge," I radioed, "can I have another break?"

"Pee again?" he asked.

"No, poop this time."

Anyway, where was I? Oh yes, one big game of cops and robbers ...and cups of tea.

Later that same night, a criminal who lived nearby whom I had locked up recently and was now facing a two year sentence inside, came out to see me.

"Fancy a cup of tea?" he had asked. He sounded genuine. He didn't seem to hold a grudge that I had arrested and testified against him. He had obviously just thought of it as an occupational hazard. He had offered, and I was parched. I could just do with a brew now. Maybe he had just let bygones be bygones.

"Nah," I replied. "I'm fine thanks."

Yep, maybe he was just a nice guy after all, with a bona fide offer, but all the same, I didn't want to chance him rimming the cup with his genitals first. There is a world of difference between a cheery wave, and trusting a criminal with your drink. We are never going to be best pals.

He may appear straight, but deep down, he'll still be as crooked as a stick in water. Maybe I've just become too cynical. It probably wasn't Earl Grey anyway.

But I digress.

Back in the house where we were doing our search, I could see the drug-bust's girlfriend making the cuppa. There was no snatch of a glimpse of any dodgy moves and I had decided hers was probably safe. I swapped our cups around when she wasn't looking just to be extra careful anyway.

I wandered into the lounge with my tea where the detained dealer was sat on the settee in handcuffs. He spoke for the first time since we had initially arrested him.

"That was a mammoth search. I told you that you wouldn't find anything."

I thought about quipping that we weren't searching for prehistoric hairy elephants, but he had a rough enough start to the day so I just left it to the detective.

"Except we did," came the reply, "a big bag of pills. In the wagon with you."

As he was led away, his girlfriend asked who would mend the door. She was told that that was her boyfriend's responsibility. She asked if I wanted a biscuit. I agreed to wait back with her until she got someone round to board up the damage. It wasn't the best of areas and I didn't like the thought of someone just walking in off the street on my conscience.

"It's the world wide threat of terrorism that's driven him to dealing drugs, you know," she explained to me over the tea. "He used to say to me that in the good old days, you could just see an unattended bag and think *I'll have that*, but it's just too risky now with all those bombs about. You just can't make the money from theft like that nowadays. He said he needed to diversify."

"And who said a life of crime was easy?" I responded. Our crook obviously had his work cut out to earn enough money – his girlfriend looked high maintenance, but worth every penny too.

I've often wondered why villains have such good looking wives or girlfriends. The reply I often get back from the girls is that they are with the villain because 'they're dangerous'.

Dangerous? I'll give you dangerous. I once patted one of those dogs that you see tied up outside a newsagent. Once, I ordered a burger at one of those little vans parked at the fair. I've even mowed the lawn in flip-flops! But has any of that brought me some gravity defying, big busted stunner? Has it buggery! However, I digress.

"And do you know what?" she asked, looking at me as she cradled the cup of tea in her hands.

"What?" I replied.

"He's not a bad man. He looks after me. And I stand by him, too. He's had a lot go wrong in his life, and whenever it does, I'm guaranteed to be always there." She smiled and took a sip from her cup.

On second thoughts, I may just give the trophy girlfriend idea a miss. She sounds like a bloody jinx.

CHAPTER SEVEN:

Forensics

There seems to be some type of waving protocol within the Force. There is nothing officially in the Ladybird Book of Police, but as far as I can make out, it goes something like this:

We always wave to other police cars and always wave to the ambulance staff who, in return, always give a friendly full hand wave back. I wave to the firemen, however, they don't appear as friendly. Whilst we see a lot of the happy band of paramedics at assaults and deaths, we don't get to see the fire fighters much. I guess they are too busy going to hen parties or posing for calendars.

Waving school children are rewarded with a wave, as is the simpleton who potters around the town all day. Young mums who pretend that they are only waving at us to get a wave for their baby, also get a happy salutation back. Later on, when these same mums are with their boyfriends or husbands, they might give a discreet wave – offside arm facing straight down, wrist at ninety degrees, fingers spread, the only movement being a quick waggle of the hand from side to side. In return, I'll give them a discreet finger – hands still on the steering wheel with just the index finger of the right hand raised.

Sometimes, you might get a wave from a non-emergency ambulance. I'm not quite sure what to do in these instances. That, in essence, is just like getting a wave from a van driver.

There is something intrinsically wrong with that. I'm not a wave machine for God's sake! Waves are supposed to mean something. You don't just give them out willy nilly. That would devalue the whole special greeting, the mutual respect thing.

I wave back anyway, whilst secretly hoping no-one has seen me.

Occasionally, when I've been in an unmarked car, I've forgotten that I'm not in a liveried vehicle and I've waved to a police car/ambulance/young mum and have been met with a bemused look. Clearly, they don't recognise me and from the frown it gets in return, it seems I have now assumed the mantle of vile transgressor. Fortunately, I've yet to start waving at passing school kids as that would just be plain wrong.

It is with this in mind that I was, quite frankly, confused when driving down a quiet residential street the other day and a woman in her sixties ran out of her house and started to wave to me in much the same way as you would signal to a passing ship if you were stuck on a desert island.

I pulled over ready to remonstrate with her, when she told me that there was a body collapsed in her backyard. I got out and ran through to the rear of her house.

First aid is classified as an essential competency for police – when members of the public see an officer in uniform turn up to an incident, they expect them to know what they are doing and so at training school, my colleague Genevieve and I had been boning like pros. We practiced resuscitation skills on a life size model of a head and torso. She was called 'Annie' and rumour had it that Annie's face was based on the death mask of the daughter of the doctor who invented the CPR training apparatus. Her face was actually based on the features of an unknown girl who had drowned in the Seine and was discovered in a Paris morgue in the late 1880s. It is said that a worker at the morgue was so taken by her beauty that he made a plaster cast of her face. When, in the mid

1950s, Dr Peter Safar, a pioneer in emergency medicine, developed a method of mouth to mouth resuscitation combined with chest compressions, he approached a toy maker to make a life size dummy that could be used for training purposes. In turn, the toy maker decided to use the face of the beautiful, young, unknown Parisian girl for the figure, but I digress.

I vividly remember approaching the Resusci Annie doll in the final assessment and singing, 'Annie are you ok, so are you ok Annie, are you ok Annie, Annie are you ok'. It didn't raise a smile then either. By the end of it all though, I could resuscitate a plastic mannequin in my sleep, but a real person was a different kettle of fish.

I'm not the most confident person when it comes to administering first aid, but I am probably the most germ conscious. I hope you close the lid of the toilet when you flush. If you don't, the swirl of the water breaking up your poop sends millions of tiny poop molecules flying about the bathroom. And you know where they like landing best? On your toothbrush! And speaking of toothbrushes, what can be more horrible than going into the bathroom and seeing the bristles from your brush touching the bristles from your partner's brush! My God, you can almost see those germs running from theirs to yours!

And, if I feel like that about my toothbrush, you can imagine how much I was looking forward to doing some mouth to mouth with our collapsed person.

When we reached the rear yard, my waving lady pointed to the body and let out a hollow kind of sound before adding softly, "I think he's dead, officer."

"Thank God for that!"

She gave me a surprised look and I made a mental note not to speak my thoughts out loud again.

He was cold, cold as stone. He had obviously been there a while. I recognised him from the briefings. This was Tom Bowler, a notorious burglar and drug addict. Look, I know that as soon as somebody dies you are not allowed to say anything bad about them, but to me, it seems that this is often taken to extremes. If the story appears on regional TV news, it often makes you wonder if they are talking about the same person. The footage will show a relative of the recently bereaved person poignantly leafing through a photo album and then looking wistfully out of the patio window. The voiceover will describe someone who would give Mother Teresa a run for her money in the goodness stakes.

'*He was a devoted family man*' – Tom Bowler? I remember all the violent domestics I went to and how he left his pregnant missus to run off with the babysitter.

'*He had a bright future ahead of him*' – no he didn't, he was a smack-head, heroin addict. He had no future ahead of him.

(In fact, I've always been pretty confident that I won't pop off any time soon as I don't think that I've ever had a bright future ahead of me. No nice comments for me. I am *not* looking forward to my funeral.)

No, Tom Bowler was none of those things. He was a shit.

By all accounts, he'd been a shit for over seven years, too. I mention the seven year bit because all the cells in our body are continually renewed. Every single cell is replaced at some point: taste buds are renewed every ten days or so, you have fresh new blood flowing through your veins after 140 days, we have a new skin after five weeks, our livers are completely regenerated every month and a half and so on. After seven years, not one part of the old you remains – all the cells in your body have been replaced. Effectively, you are a new person. Yet, we all still seem to retain our prejudices, behaviours and old habits. As if to prove the point, seven years on and Bowler was still making people's lives a misery.

Maybe it's more a case of my grandfather's axe. He'd had it for well over four decades. Sure, he'd changed the head a few times, and replaced the shaft on a couple of occasions – but to him it was still the same old axe. And this was still the same old Tom Bowler.

Bowler's speciality was burgling the homes of pensioners and other vulnerable people, sometimes stealing not only their entire life savings, but also taking their precious memories in the form of treasured mementoes and trinkets. These were then pawned or sold on for a pittance just to fund his disgusting habit. He wasn't a modern day Robin Hood or some cheeky, nocturnal scamp. He was a horrible, vile man.

Someone once suggested to me that we should bring back the stocks. The olde worlde punishment oft seen in medieval villages and country fêtes. The victim, or to be more accurate, the offender, would be locked into a wooden frame, immobilising his head, arms and, occasionally, his feet. Then, as people meandered between the 'Splat the Rat' stall and face painting tent, they would throw wet sponges at the hapless incumbent for twenty pence a throw.

Well, actually, not quite. Back in medieval times, the stocks and its close cousin, the pillory, were devices used for torture, public humiliation and corporal punishment. Since the objective was to punish the offender, anyone could assault or aim filth at the victim. Rotten tomatoes and damp sponges were replaced by big, sharp, heavy stones. Just in case they tried to avoid the missiles, the victim's ears would sometimes be nailed to the structure. It wasn't unusual to find locals urinating on their troubled heads or punching them hard in the face. Exposed feet were often whipped and beaten – a particularly brutal and cruel form of torture due to the numerous nerve endings and small bones in the foot. It was known as 'bastinado' (named after, and I'm guessing here, what the poor bloke in the stocks would be calling the guy beating him). Most disturbingly of all though, whilst you were stuck in the stocks, you could also find your trousers pulled down and strange, dark experiments being carried out on your exposed rear end. It wasn't unusual after a stretch in the contraption for the criminal to end up blinded, permanently maimed, dead ...or at the very least, deeply traumatised and unable to sit down for a while.

I think, in comparison, Bowler had had it easy over the years, although I believe he had spent the odd stint in prison so maybe the last bit would apply to him, too.

No, Bowler was no loss to humanity. The last time I arrested him, he had spat in my face. It's disgusting. Goodness knows what ailments some of these druggies have. I dread seeing the doctor afterwards and imagine that he's going to tell me that he's got some good news and some bad news for me.

"The good news is that we've named a new disease after you ..."

I'd rather be punched in the face than spat at. Actually, I'd prefer it if they didn't even punch me either, but Sandford's criminals are slow learners ...just one lesson at a time to start with. Slowly, slowly, teachey miscreant.

To be honest with you, all in all, I was finding it hard to have much sorrow for Bowler's passing. Actually, substitute 'not much' with 'none'.

Anyway, I still cordoned off the area, informed Comms what I had found and they put in a call to the ambulance service.

Paramedics were soon on scene, along with CID. CSI arrived soon after along with the Force Medical Officer. To cut a long story short, it appears as if Bowler was climbing up the drain pipe to break in through an upstairs window when the pipe had broken off mid-climb, and down had come pipe, Bowler and all. He had cracked his head and died from the impact of the fall. Tom Bowler's luck had just run out.

As soon as everyone had done their bit and left, and I was stood awaiting the undertakers to take the unlucky burglar's body away, I got a private call from a detective in CID.

"What's he wearing on his feet?"

"Trainers."

"What about his soul?"

"It's probably going to hell."

"No, dummy, what are the soles of his trainers like?"

It might help if I explain: shoe prints are now being used to help stamp out crime.

The pioneer of Forensic Science was Dr Edmund Locard (1877-1966), who was regarded as the Sherlock Holmes of France. His principle was that 'every contact leaves a trace' ...and he famously said 'wherever he steps, wherever he touches, whatever he leaves, even without consciousness, will serve as a silent witness against him. Not only his fingerprints or his footprints, but his hair, the fibres from his clothes, the glass he breaks, the tool mark he leaves, the paint he scratches, the blood he deposits or collects. All of these and more bear mute witness against him. This is evidence that does not forget. It is not confused by the excitement of the moment. It is not absent because human witnesses are. It is factual evidence. Physical evidence cannot be wrong, it cannot perjure itself, it cannot be wholly absent. Only human failure to find it, study and understand it can diminish its value'.

Everyone already knows about DNA being used to identify offenders. As Locard asserted, fingerprints are also another age old, sure fire way of identifying those responsible for crime. Contrary to common belief, even identical twins have different fingerprints. The pattern on a fingertip – the arches, loops and whorls – are largely determined by genetics, but there are also other factors at play. Whilst a foetus is developing, the ridges along the patterns are altered by bone growth, pressures within the womb, and even contact with amniotic fluid. Whilst identical twins have similar patterns, and similar DNA profiles (they are indistinguishable to a standard DNA test), they never have the same minute print details. In fact, the study of fingerprints has been around for about two hundred years, and in all that time, no two people have ever been found who have the same prints. That's why baddies often wear gloves.

It's not just what the suspect leaves at the scene though; it can also be what the scene leaves on the suspect. For example, if a criminal breaks a window to gain access during a burglary, minute particles of glass may be found on their clothing. Following an assault, blood from the victim may have splattered onto the assailant. They may have brushed up against a particular surface that has left residue on them and so on. In these circumstances, it is just as important to seize the clothing of any suspect arrested for analysis, although this is sometimes easier said than done and not just because the offender may be forensically aware of what we could find. On a couple of occasions, I've discovered that some tough bully was reluctant to disrobe because he was wearing some delicate ladies lingerie under his attire. However, the ultimate discovery definitely belongs to Bob.

He explained to me that he had a male in custody and was confiscating his clothing piece by piece to bag up as evidence for CSI. Everything had gone smoothly, he relayed, until it was time for the trousers to come off. At that stage, our criminal had suddenly become rather coy and dug his heels in, refusing to take them off or cooperate any further. It was only after he was patiently informed of the two options available: that he could either remove them himself or that officers would remove them by force, that the suspect reluctantly gave in and stepped out of his jeans only to uncover something that instantly took Bob back to his good old days in Africa. Revealed, in all its glory, was the most realistic tattoo of an elephant that our Zimbabwean had ever seen. I'll let you guess what constituted the trunk.

"Although, after a week or so worth of growth down there, it looked more like a woolly mammoth," he added.

One can only speculate on what tattoo his girlfriend had on her privates. A watering hole, maybe?

Anyway, I digress.

Shoe prints from crime scenes are now rapidly becoming the third strand in linking criminals to an incident. The way that we walk wears down our footwear in a unique fashion. Different patterns, marks and scuffs contribute to the uniqueness of the tread mark. Angle of footfall and weight distribution also serve to make each mark distinctive. Marks can be left on floors, left on the surface when a door has been booted in, or even be taken from a person if he has been kicked or stamped on. These can be used to identify the offender concerned or even just give a lead as to who purchased the footwear. From a print or set of prints, a good forensic examiner can deduce other pertinent facts such as the approximate height of the wearer or the activity of the wearer. Or, for example, was he running or carrying a load?

The *Unabomber* (university and airline bomber), Theodore Kaczynski, knew how effective this strand of forensics was in identifying those responsible for crime and was known to keep shoes with smaller soles attached to the bottom of his regular footwear in order to confuse investigators as to the size of the suspect's feet. For seventeen years – from 1978 to 1995 – he terrorised America with his bombing campaign. It was one of the FBI's most costly manhunts, but in the end, he was simply caught when Kaczynski's brother recognised the bomber's style of writing and beliefs in one of his letters taunting police, as that of his brother.

Ear prints have also been used to detect crimes. In 1998, ear print evidence was used to convict a male of murder for suffocating an old woman to death. There was a print on the glass next to the window which had been forced to gain access to the property. Detectives believed the intruder had put his ear to the window to listen out for the presence of persons inside. Again, each person's ear, with its particular arrangement of cartilage and contours, is believed to be unique. In the case of rugby players, sometimes very unique. At the trial, our murderer, previously a small time burglar from Huddersfield in West Yorkshire, was sentenced to life imprisonment.

There was one criminologist years ago who was convinced that people with big ears were more likely to choose a life of crime over those with 'normal' ears. Nancy in Comms also shares this theory, but reckons the disruptive kids get their World Cup ears from being picked up by them by their angry parents when they were being told off as babies. On that basis, Prince Charles must have been one hell of a naughty kid!

Bite marks are another obviously unique way of identifying culprits – not just taken from the skin of their victims, but also from items left half eaten at the crime scene. Lip print identification is similar in principle to finger print comparison. Moving on, the particular firearm used in a crime can be identified from the rifling marks on the bullet. The microscopic striation marks left at a scene can be used to identify the tools used by a burglar to gain entry. Handwriting and voice recognition analysis can also be utilised as further methods of identifying a suspect. Even dog scent line-ups have also been mooted since everyone has their own distinctive and individual odour. Mine is 'High Karate'.

"So, what's the tread like?" the detective asked again.

"Well, sort of stripy."

"Get them off him before the undertaker comes. We can match them with the prints from the burglaries over on the Black Estate last month. If it's a fit, we can detect a whole stack of unsolved crimes."

I felt torn. This was a dead human being in front of us. A prolific burglar and career criminal who had brought misery and distress to his many victims, but he was still a dead human being nonetheless. I was facing a moral dilemma. It felt like the time when I stayed over at a friend's house one night. It was two in the morning and I wanted to use the toilet, but what then: do I flush and wake up the whole family, or do I not flush and people think I'm a dirty monkey in the morning (we're talking number ones here I hasten to add. I know the answer for solids)? OK, bad example.

OK, how about curtains? When you are going on holiday do you pull the lounge curtains or leave them open?

Actually, I get the feeling I'm not really getting the depth of my dilemma across here.

What I really mean is, do I let the victims of the crime down by not taking the trainers and, therefore, not let them have closure on their crime, or do I let Bowler have the dignity of going to the grave with his footwear intact? Sod it, it's not as if I was being asked to cut his ears off or knock his teeth out too. We had already ascertained that there were no suspicious circumstances here ...those Nike Airs would be heading into the property store.

These were all genuine burglaries that he was suspected of doing anyway – it wasn't as if we were trying to fit him up for anything. We weren't going to announce suddenly that we had evidence revealing the bloke who stole Shergar or anything like that.

"Lord Lucan found in back yard in Sandford. 'He's grown a few inches and is thirty years younger, but it's still him.' said a police spokesman."

And so it was that the woman who found a dead drug addict in the backyard and I developed a sort of bond – a tenuous link, born out of mutual experience. The death of Bowler had affected us both, albeit in different ways. She will never be able to look at her backyard the same way ever again, and I helped find the missing piece of evidence that cleared up a series of ten burglaries of frail and vulnerable people. We even managed to retrieve some of their property from Bowler's house.

So, when I see her now I wave ...and she waves back.

CHAPTER EIGHT:

Custody

What to wear? What to wear?

It's a beautiful May morning and the sun is already burning through the clouds in the mackerel sky.

I think I'll go for the white shirt today. Perhaps a pair of epaulettes with my warrant number on would be a nice decorative touch. I think that would go rather well with a black clip on tie. Trousers, trousers? Maybe that black pair would complement my outfit. Now, a pair of black boots would suit that. Accessories? Possibly a belt adorned with handcuffs, pepper spray and a hitting stick would set off the whole outfit. Stab vest? Why, of course! Headwear? Perhaps a Custodian helmet. It might be old-fashioned, but never out of style for the well dressed police officer. Or the peaked cap? I'd see, dependent on whether I was on foot patrol or in a car.

I do hope that nobody else at work has decided to wear the same outfit.

I arrived bright and early ready for the shift ahead. I was thinking how good it was to be an officer of the law, to be able to command my panda around the streets of Sandford, to be in a position to be able to help those in need in our community and to have the opportunity to right society's wrongs, only for the Sergeant to greet me with those four words that strike dread into the heart of any police officer.

"There's a cell watch."

"Shit." My heart sank.

"Daisy is off. She's got the builders in," added Barry. I do hope that wasn't some kind of crude euphemism. "Go and see Sergeant Ingarfield down the pokey."

By way of explanation, a cell watch involves slowly assimilating the pungent aroma of stale piss and over-ripe feet whilst sitting on a hard, plastic school chair that wobbles, in a dimly lit, draughty corridor outside a custody cell, whilst simultaneously listening to your police radio, hearing all the fun your colleagues are having outside. They are out there living the life, chasing down criminals, and there you are, feeling like a despondent veal calf slowly dying of loneliness.

This experience can last for between one and ten hours, dependent on how busy things are and whether the Sergeant remembers you or not. As a relatively new PC on the shift, you generally have more than your fair share of watches, too.

In the Sandford custody hotel, all the rooms have en-suite facilities and a room service buzzer. Well, the cells have a metal bog in the corner and a button to press. Frequently, this buzzer is used by the prisoners just to annoy you. They do this by leaning on the button for hours on end, or buzzing it every five minutes to ask "Has my brief arrived yet?"

"He'll be here at 2100 hours."

"Twenty one hundred hours? You're fecking joking, aren't you? That's weeks away, ain't it?"

"He'll be here by nine."

"Well, why didn't you just say that in the first place?"

I did have someone recently who, at my 6 am check, asked if the morning papers had arrived yet. Someone really does have to look at the way this establishment is marketed. In case you are wondering, the answer was 'No' ...nor do we have morning croissants and a cafetiere of freshly ground beans on the go, although a styrofoam cup of coffee flavoured drink and microwaveable beans and sausage are available to the discerning patron.

Inside the cell, a watch is usually required because the

occupant has been deemed 'vulnerable'. The definition of vulnerable can take many forms.

"That bloke in cell two – he sells farms."

I thought that this was an additional piece of information that the kindly custody Sergeant had told me in case I wanted to strike up a conversation with my charge. To be honest, having recently moved to the countryside myself, I must admit that I was quite interested in the rural market. Perhaps one day I could afford a small holding and settle down with a few pigs and a goat for company.

I know better than to try and stereotype people, but I must admit that I was expecting someone a bit older and maybe wearing a tweed jacket, rather than the pasty youth I was confronted with.

The first thing that struck me was the haircut. It was akin to something usually sported by a female Nazi collaborator in a newly liberated Holland.

He had what could only be described as a 'wanker's tan' – that is he had that extremely pale complexion you would expect someone to have who has spent long days sitting in their bedroom, curtains tightly closed, studiously avoiding any contact with natural light, bathing in the warming glow of their computer screen, whilst masturbating the day away – like poets do.

A ruddy cheeked glow from living some rural idyll this was not.

"So, what sort of farms do you sell, then?"

As I was greeted with a blank stare by our entrepreneur, the uncomfortable silence that had descended was broken by the roar of the custody Sergeant's voice as he boomed, "Donoghue you tit, he self-harms!"

It was so loud it sounded like the voice of God. If God was into telling someone that they were a tit, that is.

And so I discovered that even in this difficult real estate market, someone who sells farms is not necessarily deemed as vulnerable, but someone who self-harms is.

It's actually surprising to discover how many of our guests actually suffer from doubt and self-loathing, too. They may be full of bravado when we go to arrest them, but when they are tucked up in custody, it's another story. About two thirds admit to having tried to top themselves at some time or another.

There are also a number of prisoners who claim they are schizophrenic.

"You're not alone," I'd tell them.

Sometimes, the attitude of those banged up can be surprising. Occasionally, I've found the most aggressive and obnoxious criminal on the outside, to be the most polite, mild mannered gent when he is in the cells. When you are processing them – taking their fingerprints, photograph and DNA – you can usually get some good crack going with them. The career criminals seem to know the score. Sometimes, they will tell me how they got into crime in the first place, other times it will be their hard luck tale about how their mum left before they were born or more often than not, it's the football or weather. Bizarre as it sounds, they also seem to take pride in providing a good set of prints, too. Even 'Keith the Hat' does, despite his odd number of digits. Keith isn't actually some big London gangster as the name might imply, in case you were wondering, and in fact he just used to be called 'Keith the Thief'. All that changed though when he lost his little finger in a nasty accident whilst he was out burgling one day. The traditional LOVE and HATE knuckle tattoos suddenly became LOVE and HAT and a new nickname was instantly born.

Often, it's the white collar drink-drivers who can turn out to be the real arse, telling me how much they earn, and that they could buy me ten times over. What they would want with ten of me though, I can't begin to fathom.

Oh, and the violent drunk and disorderly youths never fail to disappoint with their mock macho posturing. The trouble is, we've seen proper hard men in here, and the youngsters just come over as pathetic wannabes.

Anyway, back to cell watch.

Inside the cell, our guest can be doing a variety of things, but in my experience, I have found that I either waste many valuable hours of my life that I will never get back, watching someone else sleep, or else I sit impassively listening to someone banging and banging and banging on the cell door like some demented laboratory rat, instinctively stomping their little foot on a lever waiting expectantly for another sugar cube to be delivered. Occasionally, to break up their routine, maybe out of fear of being labelled predictable, they stare through the little observation window screaming obscenities and slander at me. This is usually accompanied by a description, in minute detail, of how they know where I live and the quite imaginative ways they will employ to kill me.

As much as I don't really like either of these options, they are both preferable to the times when the occupant tries to engage you in conversation.

"Oi, copper! Knock, knock."

"Who's there?"

"Biggish."

"Biggish who?"

"Geddit? Big Issue, like those sad fuck tramps sell."

"Can you not go back to just threatening to disembowel me with a spoon?" I ask.

"What you doing out there?"

"I'm reading."

"Reading? A book? What are you, a poof or something?"

"Why don't you just go back to sleep in there?"

"A fucking book? That's just a slow version of TV. What's it about?"

"You won't be interested."

"I will. I promise. Tell me. Go on, what's it about?"

"OK. It's called Papillon – about a guy who is in the French penal system. He tries to escape time and time again."

"You what? You trying to take the piss? What's it really about?"

"OK. It's about a hungry caterpillar."

He seemed happy with that.

Occasionally – very occasionally – the shouted banter between the different cell occupants can be quite funny, especially if they sense that a 'newbie' has been banged up.

Occupant Cell 1: "I can't go to prison – you know what they do to people like me in there!?"

Cell 2: "Don't worry mate, by the smell of you when you came in, it doesn't look like you'd bend over to pick up the soap anyway."

Cell 1: "I don't want to go down!"

Cell 3: "It's ok mate, some nights it's just cuddling."

...but that's a rare phenomenon. Often, it's just the banging and banging against the cell door (actually, I should have reworded that after that last exchange), random shouts of the F, B or C word (or K word if you prefer) or it's just hour after hour of silence.

Normally, it's the boredom that gets to you first. Hour after hour of sitting and looking at your customer to make sure they don't hurt themselves.

After a while, you start looking around for anything to alleviate the boredom of the task in hand.

You've already smoothed out the creased A4 sheet of paper that asks the prisoners to *Please be patient for your meal – good food takes time to prepare*, and stuck it back on the corridor wall with the yellowing Sellotape (The food isn't really that good and takes one and a half minutes in the microwave, but still, perception is reality as they say. It's a measure of how bad the food is that I've never known a police officer take one of the ready-meals to eat himself, even if he has forgotten his sandwiches. Starvation is a much more preferable option. Believe me, I've been there).

The sign telling you only to give the cell occupier enough loo paper for the job in hand as otherwise they may try to block up the toilet to cause a flood, has also been read six or seven times. It's soft stuff, too – luxury – we only got hard greaseproof paper in the army – it was like wiping your arse with an empty crisp packet.

So, you update your pocket notebook and go back through the last few months, underlining everyone's name because it 'looks nice'.

You count up the number of arrests you've had and see what month was 'best'.

You check through your diary to see if you are working the next bank holiday. Working bank holidays are good – it means double time. I've got two out of the next three. Is that what Meatloaf was singing about? (I don't even want to contemplate what he was referring to when he sang *'I'd do anything for love but I won't do that'*, but I suspect he just might be alluding to what happens in the communal shower blocks in prison.)

But I digress.

You even start to look through the various conversion tables, lists of UK airports and other bumph at the beginning of the diary just for something to do. "Oh, Yom Kippur starts on the 28th this year. I really must let the shift know."

Then you spot a switch on the wall that doesn't look as if it turns off the lights in the cell or isolates the room service buzzer. You look at it for a while and then you flick it on and off to see what happens. Nothing happens. You flick it on and off some more. Still nothing happens. You sit back down and ponder. You get back up and flick it on and off really quickly for a few seconds – the way you would when you were small, before your dad would shout at you that you were going to fuse the whole house if you carried on doing that. Still nothing.

You sit back down. Then maybe, just maybe, you think ...somewhere at the other end of the County, the Chief Constable could be sitting at his desk, in his nice, big, warm office, trying to decide what he'll have for lunch today, and wondering why his computer screen keeps suddenly turning itself on and off.

When I get that thought, I like to get back up, flick the switch a few more times and then leave it in what I imagine to be the off position.

You sit back down on the hard, plastic, wobbly school chair and stare at the wall ahead. Then, after ten minutes or so of staring at nothing in particular, you notice that outside the cell is a pipe. You have no idea what the pipe is for, but it runs along the top of the corridor wall ending just before the cell door. And it has a capped off end.

I spent about four hours looking at the pipe during one cell watch. It didn't move at all. It just stayed there, much as it probably had done over the last twenty years. Eventually, the curiosity became too much for me. When I could hear that the custody Sergeant was busy elsewhere, I pulled my chair under the pipe so if I stood on it, I could just about reach the object of my desire.

As the Sergeant emerged from his office I quickly sat back down and pretended that the back of the empty sweet packet I had was *really* interesting. Hang about, what the hell is 'bovine gelatine' supposed to be? Shit, as well as wasting my life away, I'm doing it whilst snacking on a concoction of melted cows' hooves and E numbers! No wonder I feel like I'm going mental.

As soon as he'd popped back into his room, I was on the chair again. I could just about turn the cap at the end of the pipe. It was tight, but with a little help from the pliers on my Leatherman, I got it loose. A noise at the far end of the corridor and I was back on the seat. I tried a whistle this time; it was the cleaner. She popped in to see the Sergeant. This was it – this was my opportunity. They'd both be in there for a few minutes chatting. On the chair again, a few more turns ...YES! The end was off and a finger was poked tentatively inside the tube. There was something in there. It felt like ...paper ...a folded piece of paper. I could just about hook the edge of it with my pinkie. I slowly worked it to the end of the pipe. Damn! I almost lost it. I hooked about again with the blood slowly draining away from my arm as I defied gravity, but I continued to poke away in an attempt to retrieve my booty. I got it again, the corner ...I worked away and then success ...it was out!

I held the folded scrap of paper tightly in my hand as I screwed the cap back on, removing all evidence of my sordid little adventure.

I sat back on my chair, and after checking to see that no-one was about to spoil my savouring the fruits of my labour, I slowly opened out the note in front of me. This is what it said:

Are you bored too?

How very childish.

I got my pen out, and drew a picture of a monkey on the back and wrote *This is you*, and then stuck it back into the hole.

I sat back down on my chair and stared blankly at the wall. If I was a budgie, I'd have started plucking my own feathers out by now.

It's during times like this that you become grateful for any reading material – *anything* at all.

Of course, the Holy Grail would be today's newspaper, but if there is one, the Sergeant would be sitting in his office, feet up, drinking tea, laughing at the funnies.

Instead, we are left to see what we can scavenge. The Doctor's room is usually okay for something, or sometimes the top shelf on the blanket store. It doesn't matter how old the papers are, it's just something to read (wasn't it terrible about that Titanic!). More often than not, you will find burly police officers sitting reading 'Heat' magazine or engrossed in 'Woman's Realm'.

In addition to Cell Watch, I've also found myself on Baby Watch when, for example, a bad mother is found out in public, drunk in charge of a small child or indeed, when a shoplifting, pushchair-pushing papa has been apprehended. Whilst mum or dad is in custody, I've had to entertain the baby in an office somewhere until Social Services arrive.

I've even found myself on Puppy Watch, looking after ...well, a puppy, obviously. The clue is in the title, really. This was the result of some other criminal being arrested for drunkenness and cruelty, and whilst his callow and callous owner languished in the cells, I looked after our rescued four-legged friend until the RSPCA turned up.

Still, it's all still preferable to Poop Watch.

This happens when one of our guests has a surprise for us. Often, our drug using customers hide their drugs inside the little yellow capsule that comes in a Kinder Egg – where the little toy is. Toy discarded and replaced by their drug of choice, they then insert the capsule where the sun don't shine. I'm sure Mr Kinder would be most upset/turning in his grave (delete as applicable) if he knew how his invention, designed in all innocence to make kids happy, was being so horribly abused. Anyway, when we arrest a druggie, we have to carry out a strip search and see if our junkie has his/her own Kinder surprise for us.

Mind you, hats off to the criminals – they must have a higher than average pain threshold. I certainly wouldn't want anything the size of a Kinder Egg up my behind. A doctor once put her finger up my bottom and that hurt enough. Well, she said she was a doctor, but what she was doing in the swimming pool in the first place, I don't know (it's a joke!). I must say though, that however exceedingly unpleasant I found this digital penetration experience to be, I have since been reliably informed that it is still preferable to the old analogue version.

In this case, however, Kinder Egg was off the menu. Instead, as his door was kicked in during an early morning raid, instead of plugging the drugs ...sometimes I guess it's just too damn early for it ...our junkie swallowed a condom full of cocaine, prior to officers getting their hands on it.

However, no matter what entrance it goes in, it all comes out the same way. There was nothing else to do except to let nature take its course in order to get our hands on the evidence.

The drug pusher was arrested and taken into custody where a young officer was positioned outside the cell with strict instructions to act swiftly once nature's business had been done. He was to retrieve the condom full of drugs from amongst the faeces before the prisoner had a chance to tamper with the bag or flush it away.

So, he waited, and waited ...and waited.

Eventually bingo! The prisoner couldn't hold out much longer. After a meal in custody, *no-one* can hold out that long! Assisted by microwaveable chilli con carne, our culprit made a dash for the cell's en-suite facilities and, in an instant, the dirty deed was done. As quick as lightning, the officer snapped his gloves on and raced through the cell door only to be greeted by an even quicker worker. Snatching the condom from his own excrement, the prisoner resorted to swallowing the whole condom down again. The prisoner stood there beaming, looking like a messy baby who had just eaten a whole bar of chocolate. He was obviously delighted with himself that he had foiled the bumbling constabulary and he now would be free to go home. Except it doesn't work like that.

It was only as the officer sat back outside the cell in a resigned manner that our man realised that all he had succeeded in doing was delaying the inevitable by a few hours – and eating his own filth in the process. As the sound of someone retching was heard from within the cell, the officer outside comforted himself, secure in the knowledge that we were not dealing with a criminal mastermind here.

In fact, I think you'll find that the words 'excrement' and 'criminal mastermind' are very rarely found together in the same sentence.

As if to prove the very point, I'd like to produce Exhibit

A – a relatively successful businessman in the town.

Our entrepreneur was brought in on a drink-driving charge, and for some unknown reason, decided to stage his own alcohol-induced 'dirty protest' in his cell, smearing both the cell and himself liberally in his own produce (the report actually said 'dark matter' but that just makes it sound like he used depleted uranium to do the dirty deed).

Eventually, after sufficiently stinking out the whole cell area, he evidently thought that he had made his point, or maybe just sobered up, and demanded to be transferred to another cell and to shower. Unfortunately, being a busy Friday night, there were no other cells available, and being an antiquated station, the showers were on the blink again. It was, however, quite amusing to hear mahogany man make his phone call to his, I must say, rather classy girlfriend, to try and explain why he needed a new set of clothes and a box of wet-wipes.

"Quick ...before I set!"

Why they do it, I do not know. Whichever way you look at it, the filthy buggers are revolting.

Our dirty protester was eventually allowed to wash his hands and face in the basin in the doctor's room.

"Mind the hot tap, the water comes out almost boiling," I explained to the dirty businessman, who didn't really seem to be paying much attention to me, a mere PC.

"What are you saying to me, Constable?"

He spat out the words, purposely pronouncing my rank to make it sound like an unshaved front bottom.

"I was just saying make sure you use plenty of water."

"Ahhhhhhhhhhhhhhhhh!"

Dear me, it was very hot by the sound of it.

However, the final tale of poop debauchery belongs to Barry, who explained how 'the poop is mightier than the sword'.

A young prisoner had been brought in for being drunk and disorderly and had been placed in a cell. Everything had been fine and dandy all night until about six in the morning. Following a call on the cell buzzer, the custody assistant had gone down and opened up the cell's inspection hatch, used for passing meals and drinks through. Before he could do anything, an arm was thrust out of the hatch into the corridor. Not just any arm, though. This arm was clutching a pair of soiled underpants. Soiled with the sort of foul concoction only a curry and several pints can produce. Some voice in the prisoner's head must have then uttered those magic words, "If you have poo, fling it now!" In obedient response, the arm then started to windmill around and around, slowly at first and then gaining momentum, finally allowing the pants full access to the self-produced air stream and, in turn, allowing the evil contents to fly off in every direction, liberally pebble-dashing the corridor walls. The assistant instinctively dashed back into the safety of the office but not before his back looked like he had just finished a rather muddy stage of the Tour de France. On hearing the commotion, the custody Sergeant poked his head into the corridor, only to find he now had freckles where there were none before. An officer, casually pottering in to have a chat with the sarge, found himself dotted. As he darted into the sanctuary of the office, the officer following behind was plastered. The Inspector came to see what the fuss was about and he in turn got a share of the paste.

And, so it was that The Siege of Cell Three passed into history. A violent prisoner may have been charged down and contained, but no-one dared venture into the path of the poop maniac. It was only when the supply of filth had run its course and everything had sufficiently hardened that it was deemed safe to conduct a re-entry ...armed with a chisel, no doubt.

Yes ...a cell watch wouldn't be the best start to the shift, but at least I could catch up with what's on in last Christmas' TV Times.

CHAPTER NINE:

Who Lives in a Neighbourhood Like This?

The call came through to attend a house on the Yellow Estate. It was a night shift and I was on duty with Lloyd. We knocked on the door and waited. Eventually, a clearly very inebriated young woman answered. She looked like a fat Olive Oyl; to be more precise, a drunk, fat, buxom Olive Oyl. In fact, if we are going to be pedantic about this, a drunk, fat, buxom Olive Oyl with one of her ample charms hanging out of her top. Lloyd and I exchanged smirks as we were shown into the living room. She flopped drunkenly onto the sofa and started to tell us about her woes. I, however, could avert my coquettish gaze no longer. Besides, it was distracting me from the story in hand.

"Do you mind putting your tit away?" I asked.

"Shit!" came the reply. "Where's my baby?"

And that's why I quite like it when decent, law-abiding citizens are the victims of crime.

Don't get me wrong, I'm not wishing the worst on all you splendid things who have bothered to purchase this tome. Before you start to use this book as a coaster or to prop up that wobbly table, let me explain: it's just that I quite like going somewhere nice now and again. Is that too much to ask?

The trouble with this job is that wherever you work, you

just tend to see the worst of society. As much as I'd like to patrol the lovely areas of town, the beautiful parks or posh housing estates, there really wouldn't be much point as, generally, lawlessness doesn't occur there. I realise that I signed up to fight crime and that, by default, I find myself amongst the criminal fraternity and in the rougher estates most of the time.

Like us, criminals are happy in their own comfort zone. They tend to stay in the areas that they are familiar with, which generally means the area where they live. They generally commit their crime within that same area and, hence, as I am employed to prevent and detect crime, this dictates where I spend the majority of my shift. Consequently, most of my time is dealing with these miscreants, too, rather than with the more pleasant members of society. And, it's generally the same people who we keep coming into contact with. One week they will be the victim, the next week they are the offender. In fact, over a million crimes a year in this country are committed by re-offenders. One local drug dealer even had the temerity to call into the station once to complain that he wanted to report a theft. He explained that he had been conducting a drug deal when the buyer ran off with the drugs without paying him. In some circles these are known as 'SOS Crimes' – Shit On Shit.

It's as if they have Sandford Police loyalty cards ...and some of them would be able to obtain some fantastic prizes with the amount of points they'd get from the number of times they revisit the cells. It's the same old faces who constantly keep appearing in custody – our frequent flyers.

I was actually contemplating getting a brass band, a couple of dancing girls and the local newspaper reporter to accompany me when I made my hundredth arrest, but I don't think this crowd would appreciate it. Unfortunately, one of the side effects of this job is that it does make you quite cynical about society in general.

It makes a pleasant change to go somewhere and get offered a cup of tea without suspecting that the owner may have wiped their privates around the rim first. It somehow reassures you that civilisation hasn't totally broken down. In a sense, as the police, we are the thin line keeping the two factions of society apart – keeping the criminal element in check in order to allow the decent people in this country to get on with their lives, hopefully, as unhindered as possible from those wishing to spoil it.

In case you are in any doubt yourself as to what sort of area you live in, graffiti can be an early indicator of good or bad residential potential.

If you enter the Yellow Estate in Sandford, along with other general obscenities, you are greeted by the charming sight of an enormous phallus plus associated accoutrements painted on the gable end of a house. I locked up the kid responsible for it.

"I'll have the shaft but not the bollocks," were the memorable words used in interview by the street artist, aka vandal. Whilst taking responsibility for the penis, he swore that some other vandal had added the balls afterwards. I wasn't entirely sure what order they had been drawn in, but as his surname was Adcock, I suspected that it may have been the other way around. Who in their right mind would just draw a giant cock on its own anyway? Where's the artistic merit in that? Or was this some post-ironic statement about one of Hitler's closest associates – one of his most devout and indeed most evil followers? He, who as the Reich's Minister for Propaganda, perpetrated the 'Big Lie' principle, based on the theory that a lie, if audacious enough, and repeated enough times, will be believed by the masses.

'Hitler has only got one ball, the other is in the Albert Hall, Himmler has something similar, but ...' Yes, Mr Goebbels, we all know how the song goes. Hoist by your own petard.

Case proven methinks.

Well, I say we all know how the song goes, but in the interview, Adcock didn't know what the hell I was on about. Ultimately, I ended up charging him for the full set of genitalia anyway.

Don't get me wrong, not every house is a bad house just because someone has drawn an almighty shlong on the wall – even if the appendage does appear to be crying. In some homes I've received a very warm welcome. I'm not criticising the people on the estates – you can't help where you live – but if you live there, you'll know who the local bad apples are: the ones who cause the majority of the trouble and bring the area down. It's these houses that your immune system dreads you entering and often the warning signs are there when you approach the house.

At the front of the house, you'll often find dirty nappies thrown into the mud patch that used to be a garden. These are often accompanied by the revolving washing line that looks like it's had an accident, the old, damp sofa, broken bicycle and a dozen empty tinnies. Alan Titchmarsh would be turning in his grave – if he was dead that is, but he isn't, so he's not (information correct at time of going to press).

Some paths can be like a dog poop minefield. One house even had the poops arranged in the centre of the path like a plate of Ferrero Rocher at some bizarre ambassador's reception. You spoil us ... The only consolation is that if you do accidentally step in one of the dog's offerings, at least you're treading it *into* their house. Not that you would be able to notice it if you did.

I've even seen homes with human excrement inside the house, although dog or cat seems to be the waste product of choice for any discerning scuzzer; solids for the floor, pee for the walls. In these houses, carpets always seem to be thick with animal hair even if they don't seem to actually have an animal. I'm not quite sure how that works – there must be a pet hair share scheme that I don't know about. Recently, a colleague went to a house where there were over sixty cats climbing over every available surface. Maybe they were selling the fur on to other local residents? He went on to tell me that one of the rooms was just used as a giant litter tray.

Piles and piles of soiled clothes seem to be commonplace

and a pile of empty, greasy, takeaway pizza boxes seems de rigueur for any worldly wise slob. Naked walls may occasionally have a lopsided bare frame containing an old style family portrait, the glass having been punched out long ago during some alcohol fuelled domestic. Bathrooms are usually covered with black mould and contain the obligatory un-flushed dump. Elsewhere, light switches seem to have some yellowy earwax effect on them. I tend to rack my baton and use that to push the switches if I'm ever searching one of these places instead of touching the switch myself. Their knobs are just as bad! Cookers are caked in a layer of grease and filth, whilst over-filled rubbish bins look like the residents have been playing some form of garbage Jenga. There is often something growing in the sink which is barely recognisable under the mounds and mounds of dirty dishes. I can't do justice to the disgusting state of some of the houses, seeing is believing, but worse than the seeing is the smelling. It's a 3D experience – the sights, the smells and the feeling as your boots stick to the floor.

The worst thing is that the people who live in these states don't seem to realise that they have slowly descended into this quagmire. Shelves, that ten years ago might have had a gymnastics award and a statue of a small horse, now strain under a thick layer of dust, a three litre bottle of cider and a dildo. Drugs and Special Brew seem to have a lot to do with it, I do recall. I don't think I've ever seen a book in any of these homes, not even to steady a wobbly table.

But I digress.

You half expect a big sign to be hanging over the front door proclaiming: *Abandon soap all ye who enter here.*

However, one of the bright, shiny things standing proud in each of these hellish domestic wastelands, is the requisite massive TV. I stand to be corrected here, but it appears from the houses I've visited that a big, flat screen telly is given free after six months on the dole. After a year, it's the massive trampoline that covers what used to be the front garden.

I attended one such house about some damage to a fence. The bloke looked like someone had sewn a head onto a beanbag and then propped him up on the sofa. He didn't stir from his seat during my entire visit. As I was about to leave, I noticed a breeze block in the middle of the lounge.

"Where's that from?" I enquired, pointing at the block.

"It was thrown through the window," came the response.

I checked the printout with the crime tasking on it. There were the fence damage details, but nothing about a broken window.

"Let's see the window," I requested.

The occupier pointed at the front window and I drew back the curtain. I was expecting to see some 'Sandford double glazing' which is a sheet of chipboard over a shattered pane, but no, the glass was perfectly intact. Clear glass and not a scratch on it.

"I thought you said it was thrown through the window?"

"It was, but that was months ago. The council has been out and mended it. Just haven't got round to getting rid of the block yet." Brilliant.

No matter what they do to the estate, the big cock gives it away. The Government can spend millions tarting it all up, but it will always be the same shithole. You just can't polish a turd ...although I guess you can lacquer one ...but you get my drift anyway.

In comparison, the posh estate in the town is the sort of place where, my old Nana would say, 'they have fruit on the table, even when nobody is ill'.

Mind you, the posh houses aren't totally immune from the street art that blights the council estate either, although the only graffiti I saw just consisted of the single word *Poo!*, written in chalk on the side of a bus shelter, which, in the overall scheme of things, doesn't seem that offensive. Although the residents of these estates are the people who actually pay most for the police service, they actually get to see very little of us.

I guess it's like health insurance. If you pay for it and don't ever need it, it must be a good thing. There are doctors in China who have taken that principle to the extreme. They believe that it is their job to keep you healthy. When you are healthy, you pay them and when you are sick, you don't pay them. The wealthiest healthcare practitioners are the ones who keep you in tiptop condition and fighting fit. They have a vested interest to keep you that way. Everyone's a winner.

So, if you don't see police patrolling the streets where you live, hopefully, it's because you live in a decent, relatively crime-free neighbourhood, although it could just as easily be a result of continued Government cuts in police numbers (did I just say that out loud?). If numbers are reduced too much, the felons will start to party and crime flies when criminals are enjoying themselves. So, whilst crime is considerably less prevalent on these estates it still does exist.

When I've called at one of these homes on the posh estates to discuss an incident, the welcome has been altogether more pleasant.

"If I knew you were coming I would have taken my knickers down!" was the friendly greeting from one rather attractive householder.

"That's very kind of you, but I'm on duty. A cup of tea will do nicely though," I replied.

She then blushed from her head to her toes as she took her smalls off the radiator.

I also got a Kit-Kat.

Offers of partial nudity are nothing though to Lloyd. He had turned up to a job where the whole family were naturists. As he sat there with mum, dad and eighteen year old daughter all sitting in the buff, happily chatting away to him and sipping tea, he told me that he felt a little overdressed.

"I felt like lobbing my knob out just to get a little bit of empathy going with them," he reported.

His empathy, however, quickly turned to nausea when

the eighty year old granny came in and bent over in front of him to pick some lint off the carpet. It did help him remember where he had parked his bike, though.

I, myself, attended a call at a play area in the nicer end of town where there was a report of a 'lout' shouting obscenities. The adventure area was set out in the form of a pirate ship. I saw the so-called lout as I walked in. This so-called lout was in the crow's nest, calling out to the other children below. Actually, the rather prudish woman who called us might say lout but I'd say he was just a ten year old boy playing pirates. I had to explain to her what he was really shouting, and that it wasn't actually offensive at all. Eventually, she agreed with what I was saying and admitted that maybe she had over-reacted. I can, however, understand where she was coming from. 'Weigh Anchor!' does sound a little like 'Wanker!' if you say it fast enough.

Even when the kids are actually naughty in the posh estates, a certain amount of thought and deliberation goes into their pranks. To be honest, I have a quiet sense of admiration for the children who perpetrated the disappearing rope trick. Basically, two groups of youths stand on either side of the road and make out as if they are playing tug-o-war with an invisible rope stretched across the road, causing the oncoming vehicle to take, what they perceive, as evasive action or at the least, ring up to demand what we are going to do about this reckless behaviour in their green and pleasant estate. I said 'quiet' admiration. I still tell them off.

But when the crime figures start to escalate, drastic action is called for. Well, in the case of some burglars spraying quick setting, expanding solution into alarm housings to prevent them operating, the drastic action was a couple of detectives going around and offering advice.

Arriving at a big detached mansion, the detective running the operation rang the front door bell. The echoes of the chimes could be heard reverberating down the long hallway. Eventually, the lady of the house came to answer the door, fresh from a bath, with a towel clutched around her. To all intents and purposes, she saw two men in suits. They could be Jehovah's Witnesses, kitchen salesmen or conducting some sort of survey as far as she was aware. Eager to get on with the task in hand, our colleague stepped forward, and without even introducing himself, uttered those words that have since gone down in Constabulary history.

"Excuse me, Madam, did you know you could have foam around your box?"

As the woman stared open-mouthed at her visitor, the detective's colleague had to turn away and bite down on the back of his hand to control his giggling. It was only when the woman glared at him that he suddenly realised what he had said.

"I didn't mean your fun zone ..." he stammered by way of explanation, but it was too little too late, as the door was slammed in his face.

Occasionally, it's in these really big houses that it seems we, as police, are sometimes viewed as a necessary evil to keep the underclasses in order, but we are also regarded as not much better ourselves. Whenever I've been required to attend such a property, I've generally found myself kept on the doorstep whether it be rain or hail, whilst the warm occupant relays their version of events, and then quickly shuts the door as we go, to keep the horrors of the world away from their haven of peace and serenity. Or maybe it's just that word of the detective's charm offensive had spread.

Mind you, despite this, there is always something exciting about going to see a woman with a double-barrelled surname. You can just imagine them with plums in their mouth, eyeing you up as a piece of rough peasantry. It's the same mildly erotic feeling you get when you see a grown woman on a push-bike. Sure, you overlook the fact that she is probably cycling down to the station to give you an ear bashing because someone has just stolen her car ...and that she'll be a sweaty, angry mess when she gets there. Still, hey, it's a grown woman on a bike! Maybe even with a ponytail!

Yep, just the mention of a female with a double-barrelled name conjures up those inexplicably erotic, poor quality VHS images in your mind. But, like hearing a supermodel speak, the reality is often disappointing. Those images are best kept on VHS rather than being transferred to DVD. In the cold light of day, very little is as good as you imagined.

In fact, the last female I came across who had a double-barrelled name almost killed off the whole name thing for me altogether.

In this particular case, I was on the incident response van on a Saturday night in June. Essentially, six or seven officers patrol in the van providing back up and responding to the more violent situations that develop on a busy Saturday night when people start to use the word 'glass' as a verb rather than a noun. It was three in the morning; most of the revellers had gone home and even the kebab shop was shutting up. It had been a relatively trouble free night, which normally could be translated as the calm before the storm. Saturday was never totally trouble free in my experience.

Then we saw it. As we turned the corner to enter the High Street, our attention was brought to a semi-naked female lying on the grass near the pub. She appeared to be unconscious, her skirt ruffled up around her waist, her knickers around her ankles.

Rape!

That was the first thought that came into our heads. We hurried from the vehicle and surrounded our victim.

"She's breathing," confirmed Gwen.

"She's snoring!" said Chad.

"Try and rouse her," suggested George.

I called for an ambulance whilst Gwen tried to wake our victim.

Thoughts were racing through my head. I'd not long come back from my rape training. How to help the victims rather than commit a rape, I hasten to add. Rape – actions to be taken: preserve the scene, identify any CCTV or witnesses, get a sexual offences liaison officer out, seize clothing for evidence, DNA samples, suspects etc?

...and that's the moment when my name theory took a nose dive.

Wendy Sainsgow-Marchenin was not your foxy, sultry, mysterious Pussy Galore, as the double-barrelled nom de plume might initially suggest. She was, instead, your foul-mouthed resident of the Yellow Estate, with the body of a potato (a baking one) and the head of a potato (King Edward) ...that had gone to seed.

In case you start being appalled and disgusted at my lack of compassion for the sufferer of the most heinous of acts, let me assure you that for a victim of any crime, I'll wrap them up in a cloak of caring, don a cap of sympathy, and I am the epitome of concern.

No, I feel justified in my description based on Wendy's own admission of how she came to be in the state she was in. In brief, with the expletives deleted (which also served to make the story considerably shorter), it involved various quantities of cider, alcho-pops and shots, going to the kebab shop, getting said kebab, walking home, stopping to answer the call of nature on the grass and falling asleep mid-pee. Her badly packed kebab had been on view for all to see. We should have known.

When we asked her why she got herself in that state, she spat, "I'm miserable and depressed! How does that (expletive deleted) sound?"

"Like the title of a Morrissey song," I answered.

It seems double-barrelled names have ceased to be the preserve of the gentry. I think they are now rapidly becoming the preserve of the indecisive. Whose surname shall we have? Let's keep the names of *all* the potential dads. Which my of my recent X's could be the father (and I'm using X as the Latin for ten in this particular case). I'm surprised some of the kids on the estate aren't walking around with surnames as long as a football squad. If you're going to lie back and think of England, at least make sure you know who's in the team.

CHAPTER TEN:

The Bomber

"Hello there. My name is Abdullah. I have planted bombs in Catholic facilities in Sandford that will go off in thirty minutes. Goodbye."

The 999 call was made to the police control room at ten on the dot. It had been quickly traced to a public pay phone outside the shops at Nelson Parade. At one minute past, I had a call from Comms telling me to get straight down to the phone box, see if anyone was there and preserve the scene. I left the incident I was dealing with and put on the blues, getting to the Parade within five minutes. There was no time to lose. It could be a hoax, but this was the fourth of July, three days before the anniversary of the London bombings. We could take no chances.

I'd like to say that all the resources were quickly mobilised, and I guess in some ways they were: I *was* the only resource. I think there is sometimes a public perception that there are about ten times as many officers on patrol than there really are. In reality, a combination of annual leave, sickness, covering sections elsewhere and secondments onto specialist teams, had left a shift of nine plus a Sergeant, depleted to the Sergeant plus Geezer and me. Geezer was already dealing with prisoners in the cells, so I was the only mobile for all the Kilos, or to put it in other terms, a population of about fifty thousand. It was a busy Saturday morning and the general public were milling about doing their weekend shopping, oblivious to the incident unfolding around them.

On arrival at the Parade, I secured the potential crime scene, making sure that no-one entered the phone box, pending the arrival of CSI. They would come and take swabs from the phone and look for any fingerprints.

The tasks were now two-fold.

The first and paramount priority was the safety of the public. Check all the Catholic facilities in the town for any improvised explosive devices (IED) and evacuate if necessary.

Secondly, ascertain who the caller was, and build up evidence enabling us to trace and arrest them.

More resources were required, and soon the Sergeant and the Inspector joined me. Between us we checked the bins in the Parade for any IEDs just in case it was a ruse to get officers down to the scene before detonating a bomb there. Next, we quickly checked the shops to see if anybody had seen anyone making a call from the phone box earlier. No-one had.

CSI arrived in record time and started their procedures. There was no time to lose; we now needed to check out the potential targets. There just wasn't enough time to wait for the Army bomb disposal experts to come out. Their base was an hour's drive away and lives could be in danger at this very moment. We needed to act fast.

Mind you, I wasn't planning on diffusing the thing if we did find it ...was it the red wire or the green wire anyway? All I know from watching all those films is that whichever one you choose, you need to change your mind at the very last second, ideally whilst also having a deep conversation with some girl at the other end of a telephone about how things between you could have been different. There is also a lot of perspiration and mopping of furrowed brows involved.

I think the best advice is don't go near the ticking thing in the first place. Still, that wasn't an option at the moment. We had no idea if there were innocent members of the public in the potential blast areas and that would never do – it would involve a *lot* of paperwork if half the town was blown up, and I wanted to be off by five.

There are two Catholic schools in Sandford: Our Lady Queen of the Universe Primary School is next to the Catholic Church, while Christ the King Primary, which has a small chapel attached to it, is over at the other end of the town. Luckily, as it was a Saturday, the schools should be empty unless there were some extracurricular activities going on. They still needed checking out, though.

Barry and I headed to the church and the school next to it, which seemed the most obvious target, whilst the Inspector headed to Christ the King. Ben was also starting to make his way over from the neighbouring sections having been notified of our plight.

Fourteen minutes after the call had come in we arrived at the church and the OLQU Primary School. A quick check revealed that the school was locked and unattended. We hadn't been notified of any alarm activation from the school during the night so we made the decision to devote what little time we had to the church. It had only just been opened up at ten, but there were already a few parishioners milling about inside. Barry started a quick search whilst I briefly spoke to the lady arranging the altar flowers. She reported that she hadn't seen anything that appeared out of place, but we were better off talking to the priest. We would have to wait until he returned later though as he was over at the chapel at Christ the King, preparing for a christening there at half ten.

I gave a quick shout to Barry which echoed in the vast emptiness and seemed most undignified in the house of God, but there was no time for adhering to religious protocol. If anything, the chapel at Christ the King Primary School, with its impending christening, was the most likely target. We raced out and back into the car, screeching out of the car park, the siren being the only thing disturbing the otherwise peaceful morning.

Barry radioed the Inspector as we raced across town. He was already at the chapel and had begun shepherding the congregation onto the school playing fields, ably assisted by Ben who had just arrived. As we sped through the town and carved a path through the traffic jam at the roadworks, Barry confided in me that he had felt a little uncomfortable inside a Catholic place of worship, not being of that faith himself. "There were these doors along the side of the main seating area," he told me. "I had to ask someone praying nearby if anyone was in there before I went and had a look. He said they were the confessional boxes."

"As long as you didn't say '*I'd give it five minutes if I were you*' to the guy when you came out of one, you'll be alright," I reassured him.

Ten twenty eight. We pulled up with a screech of brakes, only to see the priest letting himself in the side door with a key. Shit!

We ran into the chapel after him. I arrived first and looked around but couldn't see him anywhere. Barry was seconds after me. I looked up at the clock, ten twenty nine. The second hand was on its final ascent to the twelve position. I looked through the various doors that were open and then I saw the clergyman again. He was in the vestry picking up a brown paper parcel. It looked about the size of a book, but about four times as thick. Things started to move in slow motion as I saw him grab the edge and start to tear the top off. NOOOOO!

Then all I heard was a loud BANG!

Then silence.

I patted myself up and down. Yep, I was still alive. I looked over at Barry, and Barry was looking back at me. Yep, definitely alive, but this certainly wasn't how I imagined heaven to be. Nope, heaven didn't just consist of me and Barry unless I had been the victim of some dubious mis-selling of this whole religion concept when I was a boy. I couldn't imagine anyone looking less like a seraphim than my Sergeant. Maybe a slight touch of cherubim there, but he was most definitely no seraphim. I want my money back, you bastards.

I know that Vestal Virgins are hard to come by nowadays, but I must admit, I was hoping heaven would cater for my desires with something a little better than a bemused Baz. Where was the hot historian, Bettany Hughes, dressed in a PVC cat-suit? Where was the witty Liza Tarbuck? The sophisticated Victoria Cohen (actually, probably wrong religion)? Well, how about that girl from the band *St Etienne*? Or that angelic looking Carla MacNeil from *Too Many Sisters*?

"Sorry," whispered Ben. He had seen the priest enter too and had raced back in and let the door slam behind him just as the padre had been opening up the package. Heaven can wait it seems. It appears we weren't in the hereafter after all. It wasn't a letter bomb either.

God, in case you really are omnipresent and looking over my shoulder as I type, forget what you just read. I apologise. It's all a little embarrassing now. And cancel all that bastard calling stuff, too. Except me, calling Ben one now.

"You bastard, Ben."

The slamming door might not have stirred him, but the swearing did. The startled padre now looked up at us, open-mouthed. Barry explained why we were there, and why we shouldn't be, and we all exited again quickly, joining the christening party on the playing fields.

Questioning the caretaker outside, he told us that he had only opened up the school chapel just before we had arrived, and that as far as he was concerned, all was in order. The alarm had still been set the previous night and nothing appeared out of place. Still, this was our most likely target for the bomber. Allowing for the fact that terrorists are not exactly known for their punctuality, we gave the bomber a fifteen minute window of error before we re-entered. We then carried out a thorough search and in the process I discovered that someone would be going to hell, maybe not today, but one day for sure. In the box where you put a contribution before lighting a prayer candle, some cheapskate had put in an extra strong mint instead of a coin. It looked like they had been sucking it first, too. No nubile minx from St Etienne for you, my friend.

Satisfied that the chapel wasn't suddenly going to become a chapel of rest, we let the christening party back in.

A decent amount of time had passed by since the bombs were supposed to have exploded. No explosion had been heard from the far side of town, so we were now pretty satisfied that the call had been a hoax. Now, I had to start the other part of the investigation: find out who the hoaxer was ...and catch them before they did it again.

A few hours later, I was sitting in the review suite of the council's CCTV control room. There is a CCTV camera looking along the Parade from the end of the road. When the footage was played back, I could see a mass of people milling around just before ten, but at one minute to, a figure came out from the shadows in the area of the fruit and veg shop and entered the phone box. Less than a minute later, they left and walked back down the Parade in the direction of Goodhead Way.

I could just make out the fact that we had a white male in the frame. The figure was just too far away to ascertain an age or any other characteristics, except that he appeared to be wearing three-quarter length shorts and white footwear. Sadly, despite the CSI programmes showing images enlarged and enhanced, enlarged and enhanced, enlarged and enhanced again until they had a suspect upon which they could run a face recognition programme, that sort of technology doesn't exist yet ...at least not in Sandford. All we had was a very pixelated square of a person.

What I did have though, was the fact that our suspect

should pass the front of the Co-op store at one minute past ten and thirty one seconds. I knew that the other shops on the Parade didn't have any cameras, but the Co-op did. Several inside and one looking straight at the till area. This camera would also take in the main doorway beyond the tills. Hopefully, I might catch a glimpse of the suspect in the fraction of a second that it took him to walk past the door.

As I headed down to the shops, I mentally prepared myself; I'd now have to endure an hour of sexual harassment from the girls there. It wasn't particularly directed towards me, it could be any man in uniform with a pair of handcuffs. I hope they were proud of themselves. No, seriously, well done – I quite enjoy it. I got a piece of cake and a cup of tea to go with the abuse, too.

Patiently, we reviewed and reviewed the camera footage at the relevant time, waiting for the most fleeting of images, but nothing. Damn. I was confident that he had passed this way. I did a quick check with the council cameras and discovered that the shop's cameras were running six minutes and nine seconds fast. We did a quick re-calculation and did another review.

Bingo! There he was, walking past. Perhaps just a third of a second of footage, but freeze the frame and we had our man. It wasn't a fantastic image, but it added a bit more to the jigsaw puzzle: white, male, shaven head, tattoo on his left arm, green singlet, green three-quarter length shorts and white trainers. It was still difficult to put an age to him – anything between twenties and late forties.

If he headed *back* that way, there was a good chance he had headed *up* that way in the first place. Frame by frame, we diligently checked through the rest of the footage. After half an hour, another piece of cake, more tea and more bawdy comments from the girls, I was rewarded with an even more fleeting image of our suspect making his way past the front door on his way up to the phone kiosk. It was blurry, but I could see he had a tattoo on his right arm as well. Nobody recognised him, though. I trawled around the other shops repeating the description, but again drew a blank.

The next day I was back, and at every break between jobs I patrolled around the area hoping to catch sight of anyone matching the description. In the council footage he had appeared to walk confidently up to the phone box so I hazarded a guess that he must know the area to some extent. I checked the intelligence systems and scoured through the old incident logs to see if there had been any other bomb calls matching the same MO. Nothing.

Monday, and I was back at the Co-op again. They hadn't been able to burn off the CCTV onto a DVD for me as the manageress wasn't there at the weekend, but now she was back. We reviewed the footage again, and during lunch we sat and reviewed Sunday's footage in case our man had come into the store for anything over the weekend. After a couple of hours I was going stir crazy when suddenly YES! There he was ...in the shop ...wearing exactly the same outfit. The dirty bugger!

I now had a good face shot. I could age him now, too. More importantly, I had a better view of those tattoos. The one on his right arm looked like a Phoenix rising from the ashes. At least it did from this distance. I asked the staff if they could check the till receipts out in order that I could establish what he had bought, in case that might give us a lead. A ten pack of Pall Mall cigarettes, paid in cash. So, he's a smoker, too. He's only buying a ten pack so maybe money's a little tight?

I did another sweep of the shops with the updated description, but it still drew a blank.

Close, but no cigar. I went back to the station and rang Comms, asking them to check their systems for anyone who had a distinctive Phoenix tattoo on their right arm.

When anyone is arrested, as well as fingerprints, photograph and a DNA sample being taken, other information is also recorded such as whether the offender is right or left handed, their shoe size, but more importantly for me on this occasion – if they have any scars or tattoos, descriptions of those tattoos and where they are on the body, etc. Comms started to trawl through their records.

I was still troubled by the fact that no-one recognised him, yet I still believed he must have known the area to some degree. Then it dawned on me: there is a B&B a couple of streets away – the type where the DSS put up people on a short to medium term basis. That could explain why staff didn't know the suspect as a local. Anyone who lives there would take the route past the Co-op to get to the phone box, too.

I went around to the owner of the B&B and gave a description of our suspect. In return, I got the name of someone who had moved in a few weeks ago who had a number of tattoos, and who could, potentially, be our man. I went back to the station and checked the intelligence systems. The male used to live down South and had a domestic with his ex-wife when he was there. If the police are ever called to such an incident, details of both parties are recorded as well as the circumstances of the domestic. The ex-wife's phone number was on the report, so I gave her a ring.

Yes, her ex had moved up to the Sandford area a few years ago, and yes, he did have a distinctive tattoo on his right arm. No, it wasn't a phoenix, but she conceded that it looked similar. It was actually the image from the cover of a book by James Herbert – the cover of *Creed* to be precise, and she kindly arranged to email me a copy of the image. I updated Comms with the revised information on the suspect, and asked them to specifically check his description. They came back informing me that he was recorded as having multiple tattoos, with a distinctive one on his right arm. Bingo! We had our man: Peter Black.

His ex-wife believed he was now living with a girl in the Sandford area. She didn't know a telephone number or address, but knew her first name – Annabel. She also believed that she lived in a street beginning with an E.

By sheer coincidence, I had attended an attempted burglary at Endean Road a few weeks earlier. The owner had been an Annabel Evans.

I called around to see her.

"Are you going out with Peter Black?"

She told me she wasn't with the suspect anymore, that they had split up rather acrimoniously about a month ago and wasn't sure where he was living now.

"Were you at a christening at Christ the King chapel on Saturday?" I queried. It was a long shot, but worth a try.

"Yes I was. How did you know that?" she questioned in return.

"And was Black not invited?"

"Well, he was initially, but he was uninvited when we split up."

House! A motive, too – revenge. Discontented ex wants to disrupt christening his former partner is attending. That probably explained the wording of the call, too. Anyone else calling in a hoax would have just said there was a bomb in a catholic church. The term 'catholic facility' was unusual and was probably specifically mentioned to make sure we checked the catholic schools, too, and in the process, ensure the chapel was searched and the service disrupted.

"And have you heard from him recently?"

"Well, yes. He texts me on a constant basis. I'm sick of it."

"Anything in particular on Saturday?"

"Well, yes, there was a particularly nasty one he sent in the afternoon."

"Can I see it?" I pressed.

She read out the message. *'Fuck you, you evil bitch. See what you made me do. You big, fat trollop.'*

"Fantastic!" I said beaming. "That's excellent. Just what I wanted to see."

"I beg your pardon?" replied Annabel indignantly.

That's the trouble with this job at times. My mind is sometimes working on a different set of criteria when I'm talking to a member of the public, or indeed a victim of crime. In my head, I was delighted that I had a text from the suspect, indicating that he had done something earlier, which I believed, probably alluded to him disrupting the christening. It was another fragment of evidence in my arsenal, whilst poor old Annabel obviously thought I was having a laugh at her expense.

I often make the same mistake when I'm sat taking a statement from an assault victim, following some horrific unprovoked attack where someone has obviously mistaken them for a party pinata.

I can be sitting in a front room with some young bloke, and I'll be half listening to the details of their horrific injuries, and half working out how I'll nail the bastard responsible.

Victim: "I've got a black eye and the bruising is really starting to come up..."

Me: "Good."

Victim: "I needed stitches to a three inch cut on my scalp..."

Me: "Marvellous."

Victim: "My two front teeth have been kicked out..."

Me: "Brilliant."

Victim: "I've got a broken nose..."

Me: "Quality!"

Victim: "And a bite mark on my left buttock."

Me: "JACKPOT!" whilst simultaneously jumping up and punching the air.

Victim thinks: *'What an insensitive jerk that police officer is.'*

I think: *'Those injuries will come over fantastically in the photos and the doctor's report will convince any magistrate/jury beyond any doubt that the offender is guilty.'*

Whilst the physical marks from a violent attack are bad enough, it's nothing compared to the scars on the victim's soul. It's my duty and responsibility to bring the person responsible to justice, but I just can't seem to balance in-betweens. My overwhelming eagerness to catch the bad guy can sometimes mask the empathy I have for the victim. And I really need to do something about my habit of thinking out loud. I explained myself to Annabel and got her back on side.

I was too excited about the development in the case to linger with her too long – a case that only a couple of days ago could have been filed as an unsolved crime, our only suspect being a blurry, pixelated man that no-one had seen before.

But now I had an offence: Communicating False Information – a bomb hoax.

I had a suspect: Peter Black.

I had a motive: Revenge.

I even had an admission (of sorts): The abusive text.

Things were shaping up quite nicely.

Next task: arrest the man.

CHAPTER ELEVEN:

Court

"I am arresting you on suspicion of communicating false information, namely making a bomb hoax call from the BT phone kiosk at Nelson Parade on the fourth of July. You do not have to say anything but it may harm your defence if you do not mention, when questioned, something which you later rely on in court. Anything you do say may be given in evidence. Do you understand?"

I turned up early and cuffed Black as he arrived for work. In the background the radio was playing a tribute for the victims of the seventh of July bombings. How ironic. He asked my colleague if he could fetch his cigarettes from his locker for him. Chad came back with them – Pall Mall.

As we drove to Custody, I sat in the back with Black, making general chitchat. I find it's always easier in interview if you have built up some kind of rapport first, however unpalatable I may find it. As the saying goes, it's easier to catch flies with honey rather than vinegar. Small talk with some of these offenders may be an unpleasant task, but when they get a custodial sentence due to the admission in interview, it's all worth it.

My plan was almost blown out of the water, however, when we arrived at Custody. Black asked if he could have a smoke before he went into his cell.

Bunny, the detention officer told him that he couldn't as there was a strict no smoking policy on police premises.

"Can't or won't?" demanded Black.

"You choose," came the reply. "Either way, it's the same result."

Black swore at the detention officer and crossed his arms. It's the age old barrier instinct. He was in shutdown mode. Tests have shown that students who crossed their arms during lectures learned and retained 38% less than their colleagues who kept their arms unfolded. Not only is the student more negative in his thoughts to the speaker, but pays less attention to what is said, too.

I snapped on the rubber gloves to carry out a body search. It was only an external pat down, still, it's always best to protect yourself – you just never know people's personal habits.

"No, no, no, no, no!" Black cried out, walking backwards and pressing himself to the wall. "I know my rights – you've got to use lube!"

"No, it's not like that," I reassured him, "I think you've got the wrong end of the stick."

"You're going to use a stick?" he shrieked.

I reassured him that no stick would be used during the searching procedure, so neither the right end nor the wrong end would thus be employed. All we wanted to do was just make sure that he didn't take anything into the cell with which he could harm himself or, indeed, me, Chad, Daisy or Bunny.

When I was happy that he had nothing on him that he shouldn't have and Daisy had given him his rights, I gave him a tea-flavoured drink and slammed the cell door shut, leaving him with last Wednesday's copy of The Sun.

I then gave Special Branch a call to let them know I had arrested a bomb hoaxer, just to keep them in the loop, and then sought out the Inspector to get authorisation for a Section 18 search. This gives us the right to search the home address of the arrested person – in this case, Black's flat.

Inside, we seized the clothing he had worn the day the

call was made, and looked for anything else that would link him to the incident.

Arriving back in the office, I then started to prepare my interview. I enjoy these taped exchanges. It's a battle of wits and I'm always determined not to lose – to find out the truth – not just for my own sake, but more importantly for the sake of the victim. I always like to prepare for all eventualities, but my favourite is the 'no comment' interview. Villains think they are clever if they don't reply or give the 'no comment' answer to each question, but I just love those scenarios. In those circumstances, you ask all your questions regardless, backed up with your statements and facts. It just means that when the transcript is read out at court, a magistrate hears all your evidence in a logical fashion with no defence being offered up by the suspect. Even if he does decide to come up with a tale when he finally arrives at court, the powers that be take a dim view, assuming that he has just used the intervening time between arrest and trial to come up with a trumped up story. If that was the truth, why didn't he tell it when he was given the opportunity? They are even warned about this in the wording of the caution, but most villains don't seem to listen as I go through the spiel when they are arrested.

Some take it too far though and give a 'no comment' when asked to give their name at the start of the interview. To me, that ranks the same as asking to 'phone a friend' when asked the same question on '*Who Wants To Be A Millionaire?*'

You have to be as prepared as possible when you get hold of your suspect as the law seems to be stacked in the criminals' favour. Sometimes, it feels like getting a suspect convicted is about as easy as knocking in a nail with an inflatable hammer as the rulebooks give them a good few bites of the cherry when it comes to getting off with their misdemeanours.

First bite: the police have to establish reasonable

suspicion or build up enough evidence to identify who actually committed the act, then find out where they are and finally arrest them. If we don't find them, this is their first chance to get away with the crime.

Second bite: before we interview the suspect they are provided with the option of having a solicitor, free of charge, to defend them. Then, I have to tell this solicitor what evidence I've got on the suspect before I actually interview the offender. This is called 'disclosure'. The solicitor and suspect can then spend as much time as they want discussing the evidence or indeed, some cynical people might say, concocting a cover story, before we all meet together for a chat on tape. All I know is that there can be an amazing transformation in a suspect after his consultation with his brief.

Anyway, that is their second chance to get off.

Third bite: if I am still convinced that our suspect is guilty of the crime, I then need to persuade our own legal department – the Crown Prosecution Service (CPS) that we've got enough of a case. Like all government bodies, the CPS has strict performance standards to achieve and if they don't think we have a good chance of winning at court, the investigation ends there. It's not what we know, but what we can prove in court.

Fourth bite: finally the magistrate or judge and jury hear the case in Court. Obviously, the suspect can also get off at this stage too. Home run!

The Victorians seemed to have the right idea in exporting our criminals to Australia. If I could select twenty of the most prolific offenders in Sandford and deport them to some far flung island, I'm sure that crime would reduce by at least eighty percent ...until some other criminals eventually filled the void left by their departure. Mind you, Australia seems too good for them. I wouldn't mind going on holiday down under some time and I wouldn't want to be bumping into Sandford's worst while I'm firing up the barbie (and that's not some sordid sexual innuendo, I'll have you know).

Actually, even the Victorian's plan had its pitfalls, with some minor felons committing crimes just to get deported to the land of sun, surf and 'Fosters'.

Of course, before you start putting the book down in disgust at my draconian thoughts regarding sending our criminals away to keep them from the decent law-abiding folks, it's only a joke of course (although by sheer coincidence, it also happens to be what I believe).

You might actually think that prisons do the same job – removing the criminals from our streets and sending them to pastures new for a while, and I'd have to agree with you except for one thing: the magistrates and judges seem loath to actually send offenders down, preferring to give them a suspended sentence and 'just one more chance' to add to the numerous other suspended sentences and 'one more chances' that they've already had. I guess the decision to be lenient and let the baddies continue to roam the streets is made a lot easier if you live in a big, posh house miles away from the areas where these criminals are committing their crime – unlike most of us.

When Black's solicitor eventually turned up, I discovered that he was a former detective who had previously been with a neighbouring Force before realising he could make more money by defending criminals instead of bringing them to justice – a 'gamekeeper turned poacher'. I gave him written disclosure covering the text of the initial bomb threat, the fact we had CCTV footage of our suspect, that CSI had attended the scene, that I had ordered a transcript of the 999 tape and, finally, that I had seized phones and clothing from his flat. I didn't want there to be any ambiguity about what I had told him at a later stage.

A basic police interview is normally in two parts. In essence, following the legal jargon to start with, the suspect has their opportunity to tell their side of the story. Next, dependent on what is said, the police then ask their questions.

In interview, Black told me that he had walked to the newsagents at Nelson Parade on the Saturday at about ten, and then had gone into the BT phone kiosk to ring up a catalogue company. He said it was cheaper to ring from a landline rather than his mobile. He had pressed a few buttons but realised he had forgotten the number, and had then gone back to the B&B.

Damn, I suspected that he'd had a little prompting from somewhere – my CCTV footage and any forensics were now superfluous. He had admitted to being in the kiosk at the appropriate time, and given a reasonable account of why he was there.

But how could he explain the fact that a 999 call was made to police from that phone, at exactly the same time he was in the kiosk?

"I can't. It must be a mistake. I didn't make that call."

The last time I saw someone lying as blatantly as that, they were appearing on a blurry video and saying how well they'd been looked after by their captors. However, Black clearly thought he had got away with it. Even his conscience hadn't caught him leaving the scene.

Who was Annabel Evans? He looked taken aback that I knew who she was. He admitted that she was his ex-partner.

I asked him about the abusive text he had sent her. He stammered like Porky Pig before replying that he had got frustrated that she wouldn't go out with him again, and said the text referred to an earlier e-mail that he had sent her, calling her the 'c-word'. Well, I'm no relationship expert, I'll be the first to admit, but calling an ex-girlfriend *'an evil bitch'* and *'a big fat trollop'*, or indeed even the 'c-word' doesn't seem the best way of getting her back on side. I know, I've tried.

How about the christening he wasn't invited to? He became very indignant at this stage. He insisted he *was* invited but that the invitation was later rescinded when he had split with Annabel. Yes, he admitted, he was very angry, he was emphatic that he should have been allowed to attend but still denied making the hoax call.

I had no option but to bail Black until I got the 999 recording back, along with a statement from BT confirming beyond any doubt, that if a call was recorded as coming from that pay phone at that time, there was no other place it could have come from.

As we left the interview room, the defence solicitor patted his client on the back and gave me a smirk. He reminded me of a smug, self-satisfied cat about to ask a riddle.

Maybe you, like me, wonder why anyone would want to defend someone who they clearly believe is guilty? I've no problem with defence solicitors per se ...but how can they still try and get someone off who they know perfectly well has committed an offence? Maybe when we work that out, we'll also find the real definition of playing devil's advocate?

Some solicitors almost without fail, however overwhelming the case is, however guilty they know the prisoner in the cells to be, will try and get their client off. I recall a particularly belligerent legal representative dismissing my evidence with the immortal words, "Facts? Well, you can prove anything with facts, can't you?"

But I digress.

The next week, between the usual domestics, assaults and thefts, my time was spent closing the loopholes in Black's account before re-interviewing him.

The BT records showed that the call made from the BT kiosk on Nelson Parade, at ten in the morning, on Saturday the fourth of July, *was* made to the emergency services. It could not have come from any other phone box.

I played the copy of his 999 call back to him, but he still vehemently denied making the call.

He had put on a fake Middle Eastern accent for the message so, unfortunately, there wasn't much scope for forensic voice analysis. Maybe I could include a charge for attempting to incite racial hatred or was that pushing it a bit?

In his first interview, Black had said he had forgotten the number of the catalogue company he had tried to ring that morning on Nelson Parade. I asked him if he had rung them subsequently when he had remembered the number. He said he might have done. I pressed the point further and his solicitor interrupted, criticising my line of questioning. I explained to him that his client's alibi was based on him trying to contact the catalogue company. If the call was important enough to warrant a trip to the shops, surely it was important enough to try again when he knew the correct number to ring.

"Yes. I remember now. I did call the company a week or so later," Black volunteered, much to the dismay of his brief.

"What day? What time?"

Porky Pig returned with a vengeance. Black was stammering his way through some more feeble excuses. He was on the ropes. He had been too cocky and now it was coming back to bite him on the arse.

"Sometime last week, probably, maybe. Something like that, I guess."

"It's not a difficult question. You say you called the catalogue company from a landline as opposed to your mobile because of the cost of the calls. It's not everyday that you use a public payphone. Surely you can remember what day you rang?"

"Last week?"

"Is that a question or are you telling me it was last week when you rang?"

"Tuesday. It was Tuesday."

"You think?"

"I don't think. I know."

"You don't think you know?"

"You're twisting things, PC Donoghue. Yes. I rang from a kiosk in town on Tuesday."

"I just don't want there to be any ambiguity when the magistrate's read the tape transcript. Well, at least we've got that sorted. And what did you say to them?"

"Something about cancelling my order. That's all."

"And what did they say to you?"

"They looked at my account and cancelled it."

I thought it was about the right time to reveal to Black that I had a statement from the catalogue company confirming that they had received no communication from Black, whether it be in writing or by telephone during that whole month.

Porky Pig was bacon.

Black's solicitor asked for a recess.

Ten minutes later, we reconvened. Black appeared calmer now following the latest chat with his solicitor. He still denied making the call. The evidence was overwhelming – he was our man. Yet he was still holding out. I reluctantly bailed him again.

In the intervening time between interviews, I checked the CCTV in the town centre to see if Black had used the phone box on the Tuesday. He hadn't. The forensic report also came back from the attempted burglary at Evans' house, the previous month. The burglar had tried to remove the beading from around a double glazed window to remove the panes and access the house. And guess what? Black's prints were found on the inside of the beading.

I visited Annabel again and updated her. In return, she confided in me how things had been altered and moved around her house in the days prior to the burglary attempt. Bookmarks changed, photographs moved, contents of drawers re-arranged. She said she hadn't mentioned anything before as she thought she might have been imagining it all or going mad. She had suspected Black was the culprit and he still had a key to her house after they had split. Subsequently, she had got the locks changed. It was the next day that she had discovered the attempted break-in.

The trouble is, evidence rarely presents itself in a logical fashion. Clues and pieces of information just pop up randomly, and even the victims sometimes inadvertently don't always reveal the full story until late in the day.

My theory was that Black probably still did have a key to Evans' house when the relationship ended. He went back on a regular basis and moved items around in a bid to spook her, to make her think that she needed him back to look after her, and when the locks were changed, he tried to break in to carry on his weird antics. The bomb hoax and disrupting the christening were just an escalation of his harassment of her.

It's all a bit alien to me. Why do people pester their ex-partners? If they don't want to be with you, why badger them into trying to go out with you again? What makes a person think that they own someone? Nobody owns anyone else. Well, except for Barney the dog. I paid good money for him. He's mine!

I arrested Black again for the attempted burglary.

Unfortunately, for any burglary, you need your burglar to commit an offence when they were in the house, or else be able to prove that they intended to commit one when they were in there. And proving that intent is difficult, because it's not a tangible thing. Intent is a mental attitude, it's what is going on inside the offender's head, and therefore it can't normally be directly proven. It's something that needs to be inferred from surrounding facts and circumstances.

To make the charge stick, I needed to prove that Black had the intention to steal, inflict GBH on anyone within or commit criminal damage. However, it seemed Black's intention was just to mess with Evans' head.

I interviewed him again. However, our love struck bomber stuck to his guns and continued to deny the offences, despite the overwhelming evidence. I reluctantly dropped the burglary charge and charged him with harassment instead, and at the same time, charged him with making the bomb hoax.

So, at great expense to the taxpayer, it was off to Crown Court.

Now, I don't know if you have ever been to Crown Court, but it's a different world entirely. There is a strict protocol and a whole different legal language to master. I thought that we came across some bizarre phrases in the police:

Bilking: to defraud. *"He ran off from the taxi. He did a bilking."*

Uttering: offering a forged document. *"That is not a valid £5 note. You are uttering. I'm going to call the cops on you, you damned foreigner."* (This often happens when trying to spend a perfectly good Scottish note in any English holiday resort south of Blackpool.)

Actually, to be nerdy about it, contrary to what our friends north of the border might insist, or indeed, our uneducated shopkeeper might believe, whilst Scottish notes *are* legal currency, Scottish notes are *not* actually legal tender in England and Wales. They aren't even legal tender in Scotland.

It's a complex concept, but in short, legal currency means that the notes are approved by Parliament to be used as currency (as opposed to say, Monopoly money, which obviously isn't), and legal tender means that if someone owes you money, if they pay you in 'legal tender', you are obliged to accept the money and extinguish the debt. Scottish notes aren't legal tender but are actually 'promissory notes', much like cheques.

So is the shop legally obliged to accept banknotes from Scotland? Actually, no. But then again, they're not obliged to accept English notes either. It's the shop's right to sell to whomever they want. But more fool the shopkeeper who refuses, I say. Still, it doesn't stop me sweating like Anne Frank opening a bag of crisps whenever I try to buy an ice-cream using a Scottish fiver down in Hastings.

Legal currency and legal tender are the sort of detail that these highly paid barristers argue about in court, ad nauseum, using intricate case law and complex legal jargon.

How about this? Was the Twin Towers tragedy one event or two? Surely it was one single attack planned by Osama Bin Laden. There were various parts to the attack, but it was all part of one plan.

Or was it two events? There were two planes that hit different towers. That makes it two events, doesn't it?

Why does it matter? Should we really be dissecting such an abhorrent crime? Isn't it bad enough that it happened in the first place?

Well, teams of lawyers are arguing over the minutiae because the difference between one event and two events is the difference in billions of dollars in insurance pay outs to the owners of the Towers. One event means one payout, two events means double that amount paid out. At the last count, that was a difference of three and a half billion dollars.

So, continuing with the pedantic semantics, who do you think owns a letter – the sender or the receiver? I'll give you a minute to ponder, should you ever need to know – which you probably won't.

Finished? Well, the physical letter – paper, envelope etc – belong to the receiver, whilst according to copyright law, the sender owns the words in the letter. Did you get it right?

But I digress.

It just goes to prove the point that court and lawyers have a use of language and a formality all of their very own, and in a court room, that is exacerbated by its old fashioned conservatism and inherent stuffiness. It can turn normally confident people into nervous wrecks.

There is the tale of the callow youth standing in the dock, chewing gum.

"Is that man masticating in my courtroom?" boomed the judge.

"For God's sake boy, get your hands out of your pockets," chided the defence solicitor.

I once witnessed a similarly gifted hooligan give a frankly bizarre answer to the court. It was as if he was trying to admit to some strange kind of sexual crime instead of defending himself against a simple assault charge.

There had been a mass brawl in the town and yob X was alleged to have punched female Y in this melee.

He was clearly overawed with the verbosity of all parties concerned when he entered the court building, and was eager to portray himself as an educated man caught up in an unfortunate situation, as opposed to the dimwit he was, fighting as usual.

The defence solicitor had been reading an article in the Financial Times, no doubt checking on his ill-gotten stocks and shares, when our yob pointed to a headline on the front of the paper.

"What does 'frugal' mean?"

"Well, in this context it's implying we need to be less extravagant with our money and 'to save' lad," answered the perplexed solicitor.

He only fully understood why the accused was wanting to know this, when he heard him make his impassioned plea to the judge.

"It weren't me. When all the fighting and stuff was going on, I didn't hit her. No, it weren't me. I took her down the back alley and frugalled her!"

Anyway, not to worry, even if he does get sent down for a charge of assault, or even some 'frugalling', he can always appeal.

So, when I hear that someone has been found not guilty at Crown Court, and is stating they are totally innocent of all accusations, being the cynical person that I am rapidly becoming, I just remember all the hoops that have had to be jumped through first to just get to court, and that if they have only got off now, perhaps there is a little more to the tale than meets the eye. Some technical point methinks as opposed to any degree of innocence?

But I digress. Again.

At Crown Court, even more highly paid devils' advocates

are wheeled out to fight it out with the CPS prosecutor in front of the judge and jury, with the goodies wearing the white wigs and the baddies wearing ...well, white wigs, too. Well, I did warn you it was all a little old-fashioned and confusing in there.

For three days, arguments and counterclaims were bandied back and forth. I was called, questioned, and then the things I said were called into question. By the end I was feeling as though I was the guilty one. Even the response time to the initial incident was queried.

"You got to the scene of the incident within five minutes you say, Officer?" asked the old crow defending Black.

"Yes I did."

"I really didn't think you'd come so quickly."

I was tempted to say that I certainly wouldn't if I was with her, but kept it professional instead.

At one stage, in an attempt to belittle me in front of the jury, she felt compelled to inform me that she had probably forgotten more than I'd ever know. I take it by this that she was referring to her sense of humility.

However, in the end she turned out to be a sheep in wolf's clothing. As much as she tried to muddy the waters, the fact remained that she couldn't refute the evidence that her client had made the 999 call to police, saying there was a bomb about to go off, three days before the anniversary of the horrendous London bombing atrocity.

He was sentenced to three years in prison. That was a good result. No, that was a great result. I was as happy as one of those self-loving monkeys down at the zoo. Now don't let me ever hear anyone say a bad word about our fantastic judicial system!

A round of radio interviews followed. I told them how pleased I was with the sentence and that the courts had taken the crime so seriously. I was tempted to ask for a dedication – The Clash, with their version of 'I Fought The Law', but I thought this was perhaps pushing things a bit. I gave my daughter a call to tell her that I was going to be on the wireless.

"What's a wireless?" she asked.

But I digress.

Three years! I dropped a note to Special Branch to let them know the outcome of the case and then danced all the way home.

Not literally, of course. That would have looked stupid.

CHAPTER TWELVE:

Burglary

Three police cars were blue lighting across the town, converging on one location. A call had come in that the brothers Peacock – Drew and Chris, were burgling a house on the Red Estate.

They were career criminals. Chris had done more meters than Jesse Owens, whilst Drew would steal anything that wasn't nailed down. If you cut off his hands as punishment, you could guarantee that the next day there would be a spate of ring doughnut thefts around the town.

Chris had recently got a tattoo across his back reading: 'CRIMINAL'. He told us he got it done because that was what we were always calling him, saying, "I want to be unique, just like everyone else." He should have listened a bit closer to find out what we actually called him, and then he would have ended up getting 'TOSSPOT' tattooed instead and saved himself the cost of a letter. Chris could be described as an angry sea, full of torment and despair. Or indeed, the aforementioned 'tosspot'.

Drew on the other hand, relied on the simplicities of bigotry for his belief system. I am neither Romanian nor black, not that there is anything wrong with being Romanian or black, I hasten to add. They are just two things that I am not. However, these are just two of the things that Drew has vehemently accused me of in a wave of hate filled vitriol when I have previously arrested him, only for me to further arrest him for racially aggravated public order in the light of these both spurious and unfounded accusations. I was present when Chris informed his dimwit brother that some racist/fascist political party was having a march in a nearby town and that the Orangemen were coming over to join them.

"What the (expletive deleted) has it got to do with mobile phones?" was Drew's response.

Ah, Drew Peacock, there really is no start to his talents. Sorry, maybe I'm being little unfair there. If truth be told, he can actually do basic maths sums by stomping out the answer on the floor with his hoof.

Drew also has ACAB tattooed across his knuckles. Whilst readers of the Urban Dictionary, and almost everyone else in the business knows that it stands for 'All Coppers Are Bastards', whilst he is in custody at least, Drew maintains it actually stands for 'Always Carry A Bible'. Whereas I admit I haven't seen the Pope's knuckles recently, I hardly think that the Pontiff would have such an inking on his person. He'd probably have something like *'Jesus is coming ...look busy!'* or a bikini-clad Mother Teresa.

Drew looks like he's never seen a bible in his life. Mind you, the last time he was up before the custody Sergeant, I explained to Daisy that she would probably be seeing a lot more of him as he was a recidivist. Peacock was then suddenly at pains to point out to her that, "I'm (expletive deleted) C of E!"

Not only is Drew an illiterate, but he also has yet to understand the principle of a woman scorned.

When people like Peacock are in custody, we, unfortunately, tend to get used to a certain amount of verbal abuse. A few weeks ago, whilst locked up for another offence, Drew shared with us his dislike for the police by liberally showering us with the B and C word, which, after a while, was just like water off a duck's back to us all. Custody is not the best place to be if you bruise too easily. However, there are some comments that are just beyond the pale.

After one such outburst, a traumatised Gwen turned to me, her eyes betraying the shock at his latest remark. "Did he mean me? Did he just call me ginger? Do I look ginger to you, John?"

Not satisfied with upsetting Gwen, he then moved his attention to the custody Sergeant.

"Anyway, tart, what's up with you? Why the (expletive deleted) grumps? You look as if you think your shit don't stank. Shouldn't you be home making your hubby his tea? Is it your funny week or something?"

Daisy began with what sounded like an apology. "Look, Drew, I'm really sorry. I really don't mean to come over as an uptight arsehole with no sense of humour," but then really got into her stride, "but when it comes to people like you with your potty mouth, I am ...STRIP SEARCH!"

Whilst neither brother was a criminal mastermind, they were grafters to say the least. They may be bad lads without a shred of decency about them, but if there was a set of criminal top trumps, Chris and Drew would be good to have in your hand – and now, on this balmy summer's evening, they were almost within our grasp.

I was heading from the town centre, Ben was coming from Kilo 3 and Chad was travelling from the industrial estate. As we got closer, we knocked off the sirens – we didn't want to alert our quarry and have them hot foot it through the alleyways. A silent approach was called for.

Everyone loves a burglary in progress. An opportunity to catch the thieves red-handed. Burglary is a particularly unpleasant sort of crime. First, there is the mental element to the act – the fact that someone has invaded your privacy, broken into your Camelot – and secondly, there is the material aspect to this misdemeanour – the actual theft.

I attended one such felony at a council house on the Black Estate some time back to find out that not only had the intruders managed to gain access to the property without forcing any of the doors and windows, but in addition to stealing the occupant's dole money and fags, they had also stolen a Rolex watch and several expensive paintings. Actually, I forgot to add at the beginning that not all burglaries are as initially reported.

Fat Gemma had reported the burglary. As well as being the 'victim', Fat Gemma also happened to be a regular shoplifter. Fat Gemma, by the way, was the name given to her by her fellow criminals – I wouldn't dare to be so rude about our customers from the thieving fraternity. Well, not in print, anyway.

Other crooks, whom I have had the pleasure to arrest, that have been re-named by their fellow law-breakers, have included:

Tits – a girl who happens to be gifted with a size J bust.

Sheffield Ben – he's called Ben and he's from Sheffield.

Pig-nose – a young fellow with a nose like a ...hang on, I think you're getting the hang of this already!

The bad boys and girls of Sandford don't seem to be into the whole 'ironic nickname' thing. Maybe this is the other definition of 'thick as thieves'? At least they would do well on 'Catchphrase' – just say what you see.

But I digress.

Sometimes, our unemployed brethren complain that they have had their hard earned dole money stolen on the very day they got it. How unlucky is that? Under Government guidelines, the claimant would get a crime report, and then they could claim more dole money to replace that which was 'stolen'. Perfect.

Sometimes, you need to be a little more robust to stop the radgies perpetrating their grubby little scams.

Back to Fat Gemma and her alleged burglary.

"What were the stolen paintings of?" I asked Fat Gemma.

"Just the usual sort of thing, trees and shit," she replied.

"How many were of trees, and how many were of shit?" I queried.

"Look, PC Donoghue, can't I just get a crime number? There has been a teabag in my house. He's been teabagging me while I've been sleeping."

"Sorry, Gemma, it doesn't work like that anymore. And it's a tea leaf anyway. Teabagging is something totally different, but I can take a report of that whilst I'm here if you want?"

She declined. Back to our burglary in progress.

The Peacocks had reportedly broken into a house on Canute Way, so named after the infamous tide turning king. In fact, Canute didn't try and turn back the tide at all, but rather, sick of all his subjects flattering and fawning over him, he went down to the sea to show that, in reality, he wasn't that powerful and couldn't command the obedience of the briny. He was actually a very good king, bringing a much needed peace to this war ravaged land, but sadly is now only remembered as some turnip who thought he was better than the ocean. He died in 1035, probably out of exasperation.

All the streets on the Red Estate were named after old kings and queens. However, some politically correct clever dick in the council had decided to use their 'real' historical names for the street signs, don't you know? Boadicea, it transpires, is too Iceni-ist apparently, so the street is now Boudicca Road, much to the confusion of the locals. Luckily, someone in the council ivory towers saw sense and left Canute with its modern spelling. Cnut Way would have just been playing into the hands of the local kids.

I arrived at the back of the house and quietly radioed to Chad, who had now arrived at the front. It looked like the brothers had gained access through an open kitchen window. Hopefully, they were still in there. Then I saw it, a face peering out of the kitchen window and then just as quickly disappear.

Got you, you little fucker!

Front and back of the house were now contained. Ben arrived and set about calling on the immediate neighbours either side to check that there wasn't access through the adjoining loft spaces. Sometimes a gang has completed a crime spree along a whole terrace by removing a few bricks from the partition wall in the attic, climbing through, dropping down into the house, then climbing back up and doing the same at the next house. And that's why I've got bolts on the entrance into my loft!

A couple of caged vehicles arrived – no-one wants to miss out on the fun. A dog van then pulled up and a snarling, bitey thing got out and went around to the back and released the dog. A word of advice here: if you are ever chased by a police dog, or furry shark as they are sometimes known, don't sprint away, then crawl through a canvas tunnel, run over a see-saw and finally jump through a ring of fire – they're trained for that. The same thing goes for making off down the street with your right arm held out at ninety degrees wrapped up in a baby's mattress; you're just asking for trouble.

I went up to the window and shouted through.

"Come on out, you're surrounded. If you don't, we'll send the dog in."

No response.

"I'll count to ten. If you don't come out, we'll send the dog in."

Still nothing.

"One ...two ... three ..."

"Fourfivesixseveneightnineten." The dog handler took over the count. Clearly, he was eager to try out his new toy. Giving the dog a helping hand, he lifted him up and pushed him through the open window.

I could hear some snarling and screaming and a red faced Chris Peacock shot back through the open window and into our welcoming arms. He seemed genuinely pleased to see us. We closed in on him, handcuffed him and then quickly and simultaneously, we all backed away squealing "Ewwww". I think he might have pissed his pants. They don't call him the 'Sandford Slasher' for nothing.

With Chris safely locked up, only Drew remained – no doubt with his bible. Nothing had popped out of the window for several minutes now so we had to go in. The dog man went first. Whilst the dogs are pretty effective tools, they don't always recognise the good guys from the bad. When they are wound up, everyone is a potential target. As for me, if ever I'm out on a job and a police dog gets released, I just stand still with my hands over my privates. Both hands. Nudge, nudge, wink, wink, ladies.

The handler was through and as I clambered in, I could see him pulling the dog's head out of a box of Coco Pops. Chad then climbed through and we all started searching the rest of the house. We eventually found Drew behind a sofa. He sprang up like a jack in the box and launched himself at us. I felt a hard kick in the stomach, knocking the wind out of me before we all ended up on the lounge room floor. There was a flurry of activity before police dog, Elvis, brought order to the proceedings. It wasn't much of a fight. To be honest, I almost expected some of my colleagues watching through the lounge room window to ask for their money back.

We found a key to the front door and escorted Drew to the awaiting van. We then stood about outside, chatting with each other for a while whilst Drew and Chris sat in their separate caged vehicles. I could hear the steady thump as they both banged their heads against the cage wall, followed by shouts expressing their particular doubts on our parentage. Despite the fact they were brothers, they also then started to shout at each other, again casting aspersions on the authenticity of their brother's parentage, which by default, would also render some uncertainty over their own personal circumstances. When I informed them of this, they responded by mistaking me for King Canute.

Daisy was naturally delighted to see the return of the brothers. I waited outside with Drew whilst she booked Chris in.

When it was Drew's turn, he had to be escorted by two of us, holding his head down to stop him spitting at us.

In custody, Drew was as charming as ever, swearing and threatening one moment and then asking, rather impolitely, for a solicitor the next, without even saying please. He also demanded his phone call to his common-law wife. I'd met his wife, and never has the term 'common' been more aptly used. I certainly wouldn't want to meet her in a dark alley, although it would probably be preferable to a well lit one.

Out of the blue, Drew then started to accuse me of beating him up. He lifted his shirt to show his pasty torso covered in bruises. "That's police brutality! I want him done!"

That is one of the problems of being a copper. Anyone can make allegations, and because we are the police, those allegations need to be properly investigated. Whilst that is ongoing, the finger of doubt is hanging over us and could, ultimately, mean us losing our job.

As unpleasant as it sounds, warnings came out about illegal immigrants from the old Eastern Bloc who, seeking some hard currency, were now working as prostitutes in this country. When they are arrested and en route to custody in the rear of a police vehicle, some take to discreetly touching themselves in their most intimate places and then suddenly wiping their hands on the arms or face of the unsuspecting police officer who is sitting next to them. When they get to custody, they complain that they have been indecently assaulted by their police escort. Swabs are be taken from the officer, and with her DNA found on him, the worst would be initially assumed and the shit would hit the fan. This happened quite a few times before everyone got wise to their little game.

Luckily, the previous exchange between Chris and Drew had been an indication of some brewing disagreement between them. Chris was in his cell, evidently straining to listen to the proceedings outside. Actually, you didn't have to strain too much with all the shouting Drew was doing.

I was still standing in the custody area with a resigned look on my face when a shout broke the silence.

"You skanky liar, Drew!" yelled Chris from his cell. "You did that when we had a fight together last week, you sad fuck!"

Chris Peacock, the thieving, violent, incontinent, vicious bully – my heart went out to him.

"Looks like your pants are on fire, mate," Daisy said to Drew.

Hot pants were something that obviously our friend didn't like, and several of us now wrestled to control him as he flayed about, indiscriminately kicking and punching in all directions. In the middle of all this, Bunny came over and asked Drew if he wanted a nice cup of hot chocolate and did he want it sweet?

I, and my other colleagues, interpreted this as "Would you like a nice cup of boiling hot liquid to throw over these police officers here? And whilst you're at it, I can always add some sugar so it might stick to their faces a bit better?"

As far as I was concerned, there was a short answer and a long answer to this.

I opted for the short answer by shouting, "NO!"

Several of my colleagues opted for the longer response, yelling, "NOOOOOOOOO!"

"Maybe later then," she replied and went back to reading her book.

He was obviously a fan of cocoa based beverages because this seemed to tip him over the edge.

The final thing the custody camera then shows is us all disappearing from view in a flurry of arms and legs.

CHAPTER THIRTEEN:

Injury

"Well, Mr Donoghue," began the radiographer, "This is one of the healthiest X-rays I've ever seen ...now, if we just compare it to yours ..."

I hadn't been feeling too good after my little altercation with Drew and had gone to the Doctor, who in turn, had referred me to the hospital. I was diagnosed with internal injuries caused by Peacock and operated on immediately.

And so it was that I got high on my painkilling medication, had a lovely dream about Megan Fox, and finally found myself spending two weeks in August in the police convalescent home.

Before any of you get on your high horse about taxpayers' money, not that I think you would, you splendid things, it's all paid for out of contributions from our salary. I paid into another fund so I even got some pocket money when I got there.

Some officers can spend their entire career contributing and never getting to use the excellent facilities. I was one of the lucky ones, getting badly assaulted so soon in my career. Oh, wait a minute ...

For those of you into statistics, a police officer is attacked somewhere in this land every twenty minutes. So, if you are a police officer reading this, and haven't been able to enjoy the superb amenities at the convalescent home, don't give up hope just yet!

I'd come close to becoming a convalescent home inmate on a number of occasions, but until now it was a case of close, but no cigar.

Earlier in the year I had responded to a domestic in a small village in the Kilo 2 area. On arrival, the female informed me that her boyfriend, who had assaulted her, was also currently on the run from the police in Scotland where he was wanted on warrant for attacking her with a hammer and also for attempted murder. He had left the scene prior to my arrival but she provided me with a good description. Six foot tall, stocky build, short ginger hair, scar on his face and a swallow tattoo on his neck.

"Is he likely to fight when I arrest him?" I enquired.

"Oh aye. He's a maniac. A mentalist. A reet nutter. He's a professional cage fighter. In Scotland, they normally come in a couple of vans for him."

It was a busy day. We didn't have a couple of van loads of coppers waiting on standby. In fact, we *never* have a couple of vans of coppers on stand-by. I think there was only Chad available – all the rest of the shift were already committed with prisoners elsewhere. That's the problem with these small villages: normally nothing much happens, but when it does kick off, you invariably find that you're on your own.

I could hear him on the radio, racing over from Kilo 1. Never let it be said that I'm not a generous sort of guy. Why go and seek out this angry man mountain alone when the two of us could potentially spend a couple of weeks recuperating from our injuries at the rest home? A lot more social, I'm sure you will agree.

When Chad arrived we got into his panda car and started to scour the streets. Apparently, they had only moved to the village a few days ago so our assailant probably wouldn't know anyone who would hide him. My guess is that he would be prowling the streets nearby.

Then, there he was, like a ginger Desperate Dan, sporting an oversized gold coloured dog chain around his neck and stomping his way purposefully back towards his house. He looked like he was carrying two invisible carpets under his arms, his fists clenched tight, obviously ready for round two with his missus. My God, he was huge! I bet he even walks on all fours when no-one is looking.

Neither Chad nor myself are the biggest people you can imagine. We're both about average height, average build and I'd guess we both have an average pain threshold.

Redheads and gingers on the other hand, have been biologically proven to have a higher pain threshold than non-redheads. Scientists have found that the mutant gene that causes red hair – melanocortin-1 – also affects how redheads react to pain. Allegedly, they can withstand up to twenty five per cent more electric shock than non-redheads. I'll remember that when we eventually get issued with Tazers, but until then it is just pub quiz fodder.

I wasn't about to tell this fact to our Goliath, and I particularly made a mental note not to mention that the egghead who had spouted this theory had used the word 'mutant' in relation to ginger-haired people. You're not helping things, professor!

I felt for my weapons. Sure, we have the pepper spray and baton, but you need to hit someone directly in the eye with the spray for it to take effect, and you need to be at close quarters to wield the baton – about close enough for this gorilla to punch me hard in the skull.

Chad obviously had the same thoughts. "At least we'll go out in a blaze of glory," he intoned.

I thought less 'blaze of glory' and more 'hideous beating' personally, but I appreciated the poetic sentiment.

Still, we were police officers and had a job to do. I got out of the car and shouted the gargantuan's name to get his attention. I think a little tact and diplomacy was called for here. Our suspect looked like he was the sort of person who carried a massive chip on his shoulder at being held back in life by a cruel world that didn't sufficiently reward a bad temper, violence and shouting. At this stage, we were standing in the middle of the road and the cars had stopped in both directions, providing a natural amphitheatre for us. I asked him if he was Hugh from the corner house. He said he wasn't. I could see the scar. It ran all the way down his cheek, like he had a zip on face. I asked him to show me his neck ...he tilted his head to one side. There was the swallow. Six foot tall, stocky build, shaved ginger hair, swallow tattoo ...this was good enough for me ...despite his denial, I was confident that this was our man – Hugh Janus.

"I've had a complaint of an assault and the assailant matches your description. I'm going to have to arrest you on suspicion of that assault."

He just glared at me. I could see Chad out of the corner of my eye but I didn't want to lose eye contact with our suspect. No-one said a word. In the background, I swear I could hear people placing bets ...and I don't think Chad and I were odds-on favourite. Two average sized coppers against a giant who looked like he was someone Popeye would fight on shore leave.

I remember looking at the big bloke's t-shirt. It was blue and white striped and had a little emblem on the chest – a little man on a tiny horse. The man looked like he was about to bash the horse's head in with a mallet. I hoped it wasn't some sort of omen.

Janus gave out what I'd call a 'Hitler laugh' – when you laugh at the wrong time and for all the wrong reasons.

Then, to our surprise, he just shoved his fists out in front of him in the age old stance of someone who was showing he wanted to be handcuffed.

I looked quizzically over at Chad. This is not what we expected ...but it was an opportunity not to be missed.

I cuffed him, cautioned and arrested him, all the time expecting him to lunge forward or put the nut on me. Nothing. He was totally compliant. Was this the calm before the storm? Surely getting cuffed wasn't a good move on his part if he was planning to kick off.

Maybe our Glasgow hard case had thought we were too much of a match for him?

Hmmmm, if it takes two van loads of tough Scottish coppers to capture our offender, I doubt that Chad and I would have scared him too much.

Mind you, maybe he thought that if it takes two van loads up north to get me under control, and they are just sending these two mild mannered looking coppers to bring me in, these guys must be super ninjas? Maybe not.

Maybe he had reflected on his previous bad deeds and suddenly decided it was time to seek redemption? Most unlikely.

"I'm going to search you now, Hugh."

We have to search everyone we arrest before putting them in a police vehicle just in case they have a concealed weapon with them. Even if they appear calm and compliant, you just never know what people will do. Unless we have a caged vehicle to put the prisoner in, the arrested person sits in the back of the car along with an officer, the criminal always sitting behind the passenger seat in case they kick off mid-journey. At least they can't head butt the driver so easily from that position, but God loves a trier, and I've seen some triers in my time. Several times I've had to stop the car mid-journey and go and join in the fracas that is developing in the back seat. It's more dangerous if you are transporting a prisoner alone. Barry told me how he was once driving one prisoner to custody when he felt a double footed boot to his head, delivered by the unhappy passenger in the back.

Not everyone is so violent, though. I had arrested a regular shoplifter and was transporting her, single-crewed, back to custody. I'd cuffed her, but being a heroin addict, she was painfully thin, and had managed to slip her wrists out of the steel bracelets. A set of cuffs can be a fearsome weapon if smashed into the back of your head. I was navigating the big roundabout on the edge of town when I glanced at her antics in the rear-view mirror, so I couldn't stop the car to re-cuff her. Instead, I resorted to plan B.

"Listen, Patricia, you couldn't just slip your hands back in to your cuffs for me? The Sergeant will give me a right telling off if you turn up without them on."

"No problem, PC Donoghue. Sorry about that," and promptly slipped her bony wrists into their constraints.

Old and frail doesn't mean there isn't any danger either. A female officer was riding in the back of a car on the way to custody with an old lady who had been arrested for shoplifting. As she was a sweet old girl, they didn't bother with the search or even use the cuffs. Midway through the journey, the woman reached into her shopping bag, took out her knitting, and then plunged the knitting needle deep into the thigh of the female officer. So ...that's why I always search. Our Scottish friend didn't look like he had any balls of wool on him, so that was one less thing to worry about at least.

As I started to pat Hugh down, he started to make a series of funny noises. Chimp noises.

"Oooh ooh aah."

I stopped. The noises stopped.

I started again, the noises started again.

"Oooh ahh ahh."

As I continued patting down our charge, it started to sound like some sort of full on monkey gangbang.

"Are you OK?" Chad enquired.

"It's my sunburn – go easy on the search lads, please," he implored.

Aha, so that was it. He wasn't defeated by the thought of battling with us, he was defeated by a sunny day! His strength was also his weakness. His gingery-ness, whilst being the source of super pain resilience, was also his Achilles heel ...making him more susceptible to sunburn. Sunlight was his kryptonite.

Again, when we arrived in custody, the girl who reads the books asked the big fella if he wanted a cup of boiling hot liquid to throw over the two officers who had just taken away his liberty. I said I thought he might like it better when he was sitting comfortably in his own private room.

After all that was sorted, I rang the police station in Scotland.

"We've got your Hugh Janus arrested."

"Splendid. How many of you did it take to get him then?"

"Just the two of us."

"You what? I take my hat off to you guys!"

Well, let him take his hat off if he wants to. Let him think we had super hero powers if it makes him happy. Let me have at least a few minutes to bask in the glory. I wasn't about to spoil the moment and tell him that a flea with asthma could have arrested him in that state. Like I said, you just never know how someone will react.

But I digress.

In the past I had been punched in the face, wrestled to the ground, spat at, kicked down the concrete stairwell in a block of flats and kneed in The Cock Inn ...none of which have been particularly rewarding experiences, but this time, it was. Following my trip to the hospital, and as a result of the injuries sustained during my tussle with Mr Peacock, I was rewarded with a stay at the police convalescent home.

Officers were there from all Forces spread across the land, all different ranks. The only thing we shared in common was that we were all officers who were injured in some form or other. It was all first name terms at the home. The usual rivalries between different departments was pleasantly absent. CID always think they are better than their colleagues in uniform – as if they are The Beatles and we are just The Monkees. However, at the home, we were all just The Police (before Sting went off and became all tantric with his seven hour masturbation marathons). Constables were sitting next to Superintendents, chatting with detectives who were swapping tales with traffic officers. All had tales to tell, and all were better than mine!

Tales of bravery, tales of violence, and tales you won't believe. One officer was there having crashed his police vehicle whilst blue lighting to a report of a female being assaulted. He had to swerve violently to avoid a car that somehow, oblivious to the blue lights and sirens, had pulled out of a side street directly in his path. His police car had then crashed through a barrier at the side of the road, and as he sat there unconscious, some local thugs had opened the car door and climbed through the smashed windscreen to steal his pepper spray, baton and police radio. They were only stopped from taking more when they were chased off by some of the other local residents.

Another officer was there because of a 'misunderstanding'. To me, a misunderstanding is normally something that is probably embarrassing at the time, but can be sorted out to everyone's satisfaction at a later date.

It's Nancy from Comms furiously complaining to the manager of Boots because one of the staff accused her of being a smack addict.

"What I actually said," explained the exasperated pharmacist, "was *are you asthmatic?*"

Or, it's Charlotte texting one of her friends when she heard that her six week old cat had just passed away.

'I hear yr kitten died. LOL'

As I explained to her, she probably got the negative response from her (former) friend because, whilst I'll concede that technically LOL could indeed stand for 'Lots Of Love', in text speak, it was generally universally taken to mean 'Laugh Out Loud'.

A 'misunderstanding' is my friend, Sharon, teaching a class of children about the life of young soldiers during the First World War.

"I'd have run away, Miss," said one of the kids after hearing about the hardships, the rats in the trenches, the terrible injuries and the bloody battles.

"Well, what did they call men who deserted or refused to fight?" she asked the class, only to be met with silence and blank stares.

"I'll give you a clue," she continued. "It begins with the letter C."

"Miss, Miss," a hand shot up at the back and in all innocence, a voice asked, "is it a cunt?"

No, usually a 'misunderstanding' does not land one in a police convalescent home.

Oh, it was a misunderstanding between a police motorcycle and a four ton truck. I can see how that might end up with someone spending time here. It seems you can't always trust some of these foreign truckers to understand the road signs in this country.

Personally, I don't trust fish – it's all those tiny bones. As a police officer, it's also advisable not to trust someone who says that their dog doesn't bite. Hearing the words, 'Well, he's never done that before,' uttered in a surprised tone of voice isn't really much comfort when forty two teeth are biting hard into your behind.

One injured Superintendent mused about how he missed the action on the front line, now that he was so office-bound these days, bogged down with Government crime targets and department budgets. He told us the tale of his first riot as a newly qualified PC in his early twenties. He explained that as the petrol bombs and bricks started flying, as the flames and smoke filled the air, and how the sound of the explosions and shouting filled his senses, it all became too much for him. He just took fright, threw down his shield and ran. He ran through the lines of reinforcements, ran past the support vehicles and just kept on running and running until he eventually collapsed with exhaustion in a shop doorway. After about twenty minutes, he told us, he sensed a figure standing over him. The person then knelt down beside him and put a comforting hand on his shoulder before gently speaking.

"You know, son, there is nothing to be ashamed of in being scared. We all feel those emotions but what makes you different as a police officer is how you handle your emotions. The public look to you to protect them. They say 'evil prospers when good men do nothing'. You son, are one of those good men. Go back, pick up your shield, and walk back proudly to the front line. I have confidence in you to do the right thing."

"You're right," said our young PC as he stood up and dusted himself down. "I'll go back now. But before I go, can I ask who you are?"

"I," came the reply, "am your Superintendent, in charge of this incident."

"Bloody hell!" our PC exclaimed, "I didn't realise I'd run *that* far!"

Whilst I was there, I also had a chance to speak to others who had had similar injuries to me in the past. In essence, it seems that when discussing injuries, people can then be divided up into two distinct camps.

There are those who tell you how much agony they were in for months, and they are still not the same years later ...or...

There are those who inform you that they were out and about the same afternoon and scaling Mount Everest the day after.

Fundamentally, it appears to me that if I listen to either camp, I'm a loser either way. Either I am in for a life of agony hereafter, or else I am a wimp for not being back at work within twenty-four hours. Very helpful and not really what I wanted to hear. What I really wanted to hear was a more effective way of getting dressed in the morning rather than having to sit on the end of my bed, trying fruitlessly for half an hour or so to lasso my sock to the end of my toe.

At least no one tried to show me their bandaged wounds or scabby scars. This usually only happens when I visit some felon at their home and happen to casually ask if they are working at the moment. In a bid to justify why they haven't been in gainful employment for the past decade, they will show me all manner of disgusting body parts, even though I try to tell them that it's ok, and I'm not a spy from the government trying to establish if they are 'DSS disabled' or actually disabled.

Altogether, I spent two happy weeks at the convalescent home recovering, allowing my bones and scars to heal, having physio, doing pilates, gym training, sleeping a lot and drinking ...a lot. And to anyone who says that women don't pass wind loudly ...I sat in on the yoga class ...so I have evidence to the contrary.

I even got my own personal training plan from the instructor for when I got back home. Our programme included new techniques for stretching prior to our exercise. We were told that every morning the first thing that her dog did when he got up was to stretch, adding that we can all learn a lot from our animals' behaviour. She's probably right but, personally, I draw the line at trying to lick my own balls.

I was also told that I had to change my exercise schedule every four weeks though, otherwise my body would get used to the same routine, and I wouldn't get the best from my workout. Essentially, if I understood correctly, she was saying that I had to try and fool my body into thinking I was doing different sorts of exercise, otherwise my lazy carcass would just rest on its laurels. Fool my own body? Who was boss here? I had known for a while that some parts of my body had a mind of their own ...but my *whole* body? That seemed a bit of a tall order. Then I remembered the time when my body had actually fooled me ...the time when I was out drinking in Catalonia ...the time it told me I was *only* going to fart. My body must really hate me.

CHAPTER FOURTEEN:

Roaring Days

"Smoke 'em if you've got 'em." Barry was addressing us at the shift briefing. It was going to be a busy ten hours ahead of us, by all accounts. The late shift was still out, responding to immediates all over town, and it didn't look like letting up.

I was on night shift, starting at nine at night, going through until seven the following morning. All the indications were there earlier in the day that something was brewing. It was one of those long, hot, late summer days. Barney hadn't wanted to go on his morning walk, preferring to lay limply half in and half out of his kennel. The hound up the road had stopped his barking and even the flies had quit their buzzing. Even as the evening stole the afternoon, a still mugginess cloaked the town.

There are over sixty thousand people arrested for being drunk and disorderly in the UK every year; that's about one person arrested every five minutes, and with sixty percent of these crimes being committed after dark, it can all add up to a busy night. It seems a day full of drinking in the baking heat had served to charge the tempers of the residents of Sandford's estates. It never ceases to amaze me how a little sun can drive some folks crazy. It's the prodigal sun. What I wouldn't give for a mackerel sky right now.

Combined with that, it was a full moon night. Incidents of violence and disorder always seem to peak at this time of the month. We'd be working like Trojans tonight.

This was my first full shift back after a month or so off following my operation which had included those two glorious weeks down at the convalescent home. I had come back on light duties for a while but had started going stir crazy, so despite the mayhem that was unfolding in the town, I was still glad to be back at the sharp end again.

In case you aren't aware, light duties are roles that a police officer can undertake that are non-confrontational in nature and have no danger attached to them. Well, that's the theory. In reality, they are tasks so mundane and boring that you either vow never to get injured again or want to volunteer for the riot squad just to get some sanity back in your life.

My first light duty tasking was to attend a computer course to introduce me to some new systems that had come in whilst I had been off recovering. At the door, I was asked to sign in and put down my next of kin details. Hang on a second, how dangerous can a computer course be? I wasn't even asked for NOK details when I had been smashing people's doors in during drug raids or been policing some violent football stadium clash. Were we going to be sitting typing with our feet in a bowl of water or something?

In the end, it turned out to be not even that exciting. No footwear removal was required at all. The course turned out to be five hours of instruction, shoehorned into two eight hour days. I've never drunk so much tea in my life (except when I was on my CID attachment) and the highlight of the whole course was getting a furry tongue on day two after one of the girls bought me a hot, milky beverage and I thought it was a cold, milky beverage.

On light duties, you are also asked/shafted by your colleagues to do all the statements that they didn't have time/couldn't be bothered to do now that they had a light duty lackey on shift (me).

Things didn't get much more exciting when I was told to help out on the front counter. This is where members of the public drop in to report a crime, or if you are a resident of one of Sandford's estates, drop in to ask some bizarre pub quiz question. Let me assure you, this is one role that has the capacity to drive any sane person around the bend.

At the time, following an increase in the country's 'state of alert' status due to possible terrorist activity, there were severe restrictions in place at all of the airports. There were limitations on what you could and couldn't take on-board the aircraft, and even baby milk was being tested before it could be taken through security. One woman had come in and told me she had recently had a baby and was still breast feeding ...and how would the testing procedure affect her?

One portly girl came in to complain that her ex-best friend at school had called her a fat elephant. A rude kid isn't really a police matter, but I did what I could. I tried to put it into perspective for her, to try to get her to rise above it. Sticks and stones, and all that stuff.

"A fat elephant? Come on, you're bigger than that!" I told her, but that just seemed to make things worse. There is just no pleasing some people. In the end, I just stopped trying.

I recognised the next guy who came in. He owned the quarry that I passed on my way to work each day. His wagons would just pull out into the country lane without taking any notice of the traffic on the basis of *I'm bigger than you and you'll come off worse if we hit, so I'll do what I want, and you take the evasive action*. Often, I would be forced to brake so violently to avoid being crushed under the wheels of some enormous lorry, that I was sure I'd end up giving myself whiplash. His fleet would thunder past, irrespective of the road conditions, be it summer, winter, rain, sleet or snow. I had already started building myself up into a simmering rage before he had even had a chance to speak to me.

It seems he was worried about the security of his site, and wanted to know what actions he could take to minimise the risk of being broken into. Despite my personal feelings, I am a professional. I spent the best part of half an hour talking to him about lighting, fencing, security patrols and the like. It was only when he was leaving that I felt justified in adding an item from my own personal agenda into the mix.

"And if you are worried about someone stealing any of your wagons, I suggest a simple sticker on the back might help."

"Really, PC Donoghue, and what would you recommend it says?"

"How about *'If this vehicle is being driven well, call the police. It must be stolen'* "

The next day I was greeted by a very angry man who burst in and demanded to speak to the Superintendent. After I explained that the Superintendent wasn't based at the station, he insisted on seeing what he obviously thought was the next best thing.

"I want to see the (expletive deleted) Intendent then, you (expletive, meaning 'monkey spanker' deleted)!"

"It doesn't exactly work like that, Sir. The Superintendent isn't here. There is no Intendent and before you ask, there isn't even a Mediocreintendent."

Before I could find out what was so urgent, he told me to, "(Expletive deleted) just forget it then, you (expletive, meaning the monkey thing again – he obviously doesn't have access to a Thesaurus – deleted)!" and he stormed out from whence he came. Ah, what a charming man.

Another came in to report that she'd seen a male look through her kitchen window, which had spooked her. I asked what he looked like. Now, normally, when describing someone, we go through a ten point plan. This breaks the description down into little identifiable segments, ranging from their colour, gender, age, hair, body type, right through to what they were wearing or carrying. Now, I don't expect people to remember all the finer details, but I think they should at least have a stab at it. However, in response to my question, our complainant had just replied that the bloke who had looked through her window was ugly, "like the elephant man." To me that is just a lazy description. For goodness sake, even the 'elephant man' didn't look like an elephant. More like fresh ginger.

I sometimes tried to liven things up by throwing in some humour to the procedures now and again, but even that was wasted on some of our clientele.

"I want to report three men who came and stole some decorative fencing from my garden."

"Did one of them walk with a distinctive gait?" I queried.

"You what?"

"Forget it."

I'd also have to check an endless stream of vehicle documents from people who have been given producers (requirements to show their insurance, driving licence etc at a police station) by the traffic boys and girls.

"Can I see your photo card for your licence, please?" I asked one woman who had come in with her papers.

"Well, it's a terrible picture. It really doesn't do me justice," she replied coyly, before handing it over.

I did a comedy recoil when I saw it. "It's not justice you want, it's mercy by the look of that."

"I beg your pardon!" she barked indignantly.

Oh dear. Another joke falls flat on its arse.

After a week of this, I was like a pressure cooker slowly rattling away on the stove. It was eventually decided to move me away from front counter duties after a particularly exasperating encounter with an elderly lady who had come in to report a minor traffic bump.

"And what was the registration of the other vehicle?" I asked.

Why, oh why, do people try and use the phonetic alphabet when they haven't got a clue?

"Ooh, let's see. It was N for ... mmmm, oh, I can't think. What starts with an N? N for... oh yes! N for....oh dear, it's gone ...N for ..."

"N. I've got the idea. It starts with an N," I interrupted tersely.

"N for pneumatic, dear, then it was an F for phlegm..."

"NF, what else?" I said tapping my pen on the table.

"Then four for ...for ..."

"Four, four, four?" I queried.

"No, dear. I'm just running through the twelve days of Christmas in my head. Four for four calling birds, that's it! And then Five for Hawaii Five O." She looked pleased with herself. As for me, I had just snapped my pen.

"You really don't need to go through all of that, you know. Just tell me what the registration was as you saw it."

"Oh no, dear. I've seen 'The Bill', I know what you do. Now where was I? Then we had a K for cagoule, C for ...C for ...oh no, I can't use *that* word. It's on the telly all the time now. 'You C'. 'You filthy C'. Oh it really appals me the language nowadays."

If there is one thing that irritates me, it's people who won't stick to the point, who digress off the subject at every opportunity. Actually, whilst I'm on the subject, the politically correct brigade have even tried to PC the phonetic alphabet. India and Zulu are apparently too xenophobic for their version, and there have been moves afoot to attempt to change I and Z to Indigo and Zebra instead. I for idiot more like. Those politically correct zealots are taking over everywhere and bullying you if you try to resist in any way. Don't like Fair Trade coffee? Then you must be racist! Anyway, where was I ...oh yes, the annoyingly digressing woman.

"C for cantaloupe."

"You what?"

"It's a type of melon, dear. And finally B for ... B for ...B for..."

I was starting to tear my hair out at this stage, but she continued on regardless.

"B for ...B for ...B for ...I've got it! B for Butternut squash!"

"BRAVO! BRAVO!" I shouted in exasperation.

"Oh thank you, dear."

At this stage, I was quietly being led away to sit down in a darkened room by one of the girls from the front office as I just kept on muttering, "It's B for bloody Bravo. It's Bravo...I'll give you butternut bloody squash."

No, the town may be ready to implode, but it was still better being back on full duties than being slowly driven mad on light duties.

The first immediate came from the Black Estate. A domestic at Avery Walk.

Gwen and I raced over with blues and twos. We knocked and knocked and hammered and banged on the door and were eventually let in by a person of restricted growth – a little person or, indeed, vertically challenged personage. Apparently, the word 'dwarf' is no longer acceptable in modern, politically correct parlance. If India and Zulu are merely minor irritations, dwarf is full blown Chlamydia. I had found this out to my cost only a few weeks earlier.

I was on that computer course at Headquarters – the dangerous one – when, during one of the many tea breaks, the instructor casually mentioned that she wasn't looking forward to doing some much needed DIY over the weekend. I quipped that she should get a little man in. Instantly, I recognised the error of my ways. Headquarters may be many things to many people, but to all, it is the bastion of political correctness. I staggered back under a volley of withering glances. I started to back peddle ...badly.

"When I said *little man*, I mean it could just as easily be a little woman. I didn't actually mean a dwarf or anything. Or a midget. Actually, they're not the same. A dwarf has a bigger head. Anyway, it could be a big person for that matter ...not too big mind you ...not obese or anything ..."

I didn't go on to say they could be transgendered, didn't have to have all their limbs or could even be special needs or anything of the like (although that could be a bit dodgy if they were using a nail gun or super glue). Instead, I just sort of faded out and looked at my boots, sipped my milky beverage and got a furry tongue. God must have it in for me. She must have got up on the wrong side of the cloud this morning.

But I digress. Where was I? Oh yes, we were back in the flat of our person of restricted growth.

"Hello, Stumpy," I said when I saw him. "What's been going on here, then?"

Gwen almost choked, and looked at me as if something had short-circuited in my brain. I had to explain as we left that I knew Stumpy from old. He had done some gardening work at a friend's house and had informed me that was his name. I had told him that I couldn't possibly call him that, it was ...well just plain wrong, but he was adamant. That was what everyone called him, and that was all he answered to. Even his wife called him Stumpy.

I later found out that he was also a petty criminal with previous for theft and had never held down a regular job, except an annual stint across the country at Christmas pantos in Snow White. However, at the moment, Gwen was blissfully unaware of all of this and her diversity credentials were being severely tested.

"What's been going on? Nothing. What makes you think that, PC Donoghue?" Stumpy replied innocently.

"Because we got a call from your wife, who was very distraught on the phone."

"Oh that," he began. "Well, if I'm honest..."

"...Which of course you're not," I corrected.

"Which of course I am not, you're right, I forgot that you knew my previous..."

As Gwen went to speak with Stumpy's wife, I then got the full story from Stumpy himself.

As many of you may know, a marriage is something that needs to be worked at. Unfortunately, Mrs Stumpy had been getting a man in to do that work whilst Stumpy was away at panto each year. And not a little man. Stumpy had found this out, and after a few drinks, things had got a bit out of hand. The end result was that Stumpy was coming with us for common assault on his wife. The first lock up of the shift.

Elsewhere about the town, other crews were responding to an endless stream of emergencies and fights. A report of a glassing came in from a pub across town. There are 87,000 glassing incidents reported each year in the UK. I remember thinking that we hadn't had one of those in Sandford for a while. A few minutes later another glassing was phoned in, as if to justify the statistics. Officers arrived and soon found out they were connected. Both males were coming in for affray. Two more lock ups and another crew out of the picture, escorting the worst of the injured to the local hospital.

A criminal damage in progress. A female pouring paint over a love rival's car. A crew raced over, but she had gone before they arrived. The lucky male, who was the object of two females' attention, fingered his ex-girlfriend as the culprit. Chad and Geezer went round to her house and found her car bonnet was still warm. After several knocks on the door, a female answered, yawning. "Oh officers, you woke me up. I decided to have an early night. No, I don't know what you are on about. I haven't thrown paint on anyone's car. What? What's that paint doing on my nose? Oh shit." Another one en route to the cells.

In the dead centre of town, a funeral wake had got out of hand. I soon realised after joining the police that it was one of those occupations where, to outsiders, you are forever known by your job as opposed to your name. Whilst I long to be introduced to new acquaintances when I'm off duty, with a simple, 'This is John, he's a nice/ friendly/ handsome/ well endowed guy' (select most appropriate for particular circumstance), I usually find it's a case of 'This is John, he's a police officer', and often, I have to say, it seems to be said as if it's some kind of warning. It's as if we are not regarded as individuals – we are regarded as a breed apart. Chad told me he once popped into a corner shop when he was on duty to buy some cigarettes.

"Are police allowed to smoke?" the shopkeeper asked.

"We're actually allowed to do most things that humans do," he responded.

Anyway, the other great preserve of titles is the traditional Working Men's Club. We have the Chairman, Vice-Chairman, Secretary, Treasurer and finally, last but by no means least, Committee members. The residents of Working Men's Clubs though, seem to glory, nay, relish, in introducing themselves solely by their position of office. Never shall their real names be revealed.

Anyway, on this fair evening, and at this funeral party at this Working Men's Club, too much alcohol had been imbibed and a fight had broken out. When I arrived, the transgressors had already slipped out of the side entrance, and the staff were busy stacking up chairs and mopping up the spilt beer. The hierarchy of the establishment didn't seem to be bothered about the scores of mourners injured as a result of what appeared to be a good old Wild West saloon bar fight, but they were thoroughly outraged over one transgression.

"You do NOT hit a committee man!" the Secretary informed me in no uncertain terms. This, it appears, is a cardinal sin in this form of institution. Beat anyone else half to death by all means, but do not *dare* to strike a man of appellation. I'm pretty confident that flicking the V's at the Treasurer would warrant a flogging. I took some brief details of the fight and reluctantly, names were eventually revealed. I needed to know where I could get hold of people during working hours next week in case I needed to get a full statement. All bar one, it transpired, were unemployed. "But I thought this was a working man's club?" I queried. I was informed I'd have to speak to the Secretary about that.

A concern for safety call followed soon after. A frightened householder was reporting an unknown male in her garden, apparently pulling out his own teeth with a pair of pliers. We often get drunks banging on the wrong door demanding to be let in, but an amateur, self-operating dentist was a new one for me. I actually knew the guy concerned. I had been called to a domestic a month earlier. He had been going through a nasty separation from his wife at the time and had the usual barrage of heartless solicitor's letters adding insult to his misery. The last letter must have been the one that broke the camel's back and something in him must have snapped that day. When I arrived, I found him busy cutting all the furniture in half with a chainsaw – chairs, sofas, beds, tables. Luckily, the cat had already ran outside. He had shown me the letter informing him that his wife wanted half of everything. I couldn't really argue with that. Anyway, back to our hectic night and George and Ben duly arrested him under the Section 136 of the Mental Health Act and he was taken to the mental hospital for his own safety.

About the same time as that was happening, Barry, in company with Charlotte from the previous shift, was called to a public order incident outside the town's nightclub. Normally, things quieten down when police arrive on scene. And mostly it did on this occasion, except for one male who wanted to mouth off still. Barry had tried in vain to get the guy to calm down and go home, but the drunk still wanted to create. It finally got too much for Sarge when the male threatened to ejaculate over him. This was just a step too far. He was cuffed and ended up in the bin along with all the other offenders of the evening.

All in all, a sad end to a night out, but it's Charlotte that I really felt sorry for in all this. She is a lovely girl and I'm sure she must have been slightly crestfallen that the man wanted to do the dirty over the Sergeant and not her. Her self confidence must have taken a bit of a knock. I tried to cheer her up later and told her that if I had been in that position, I would have definitely chosen her. She seemed pleased.

Still, Charlotte can be a tease, too. She is a pretty girl and

I know of at least one guy who has asked for her number when she has attended an incident. "Of course you can," she replied sweetly, before writing her number down, folding up the piece of paper and popping it into his top pocket whilst giving him a wink.

It's only when she left that he eagerly opened up the note and found it just read '999'.

As Gwen was still dealing with Stumpy back in the cells, I was teamed up with Ron when a call came in about a robbery in a local pub. A male had walked in, bold as brass, and imbedded an axe into the bartop. He had ordered two bottles of brown ale and then, after extricating the blade, had held it against the landlord's chest, telling him not to phone the police, "Or I'll carve you up. I'm fucking mad me. I'll kill you."

I think he had something there. You have to be pretty mad to rob a pub at axe point and just ask for two bottles of dog. As he left, the landlord followed at a discreet distance. We arrived just as the male had disappeared into the maze that is the Black Estate. I jumped out of the car and accompanied the landlord in the search for our robber, whilst Ron scanned the deserted streets nearby.

"There he is," whispered the publican, pointing to a male with a bottle of stolen beer to his lips, silhouetted against the brightly lit kitchen of a house.

I called Ron on the radio and stood at the rear gate, my pepper spray in hand. I was giving it an extra shake to make sure it worked when I needed it, when the male appeared, poking his head over the top. He was perhaps in his fifties, dishevelled, clearly drunk, with mad, staring eyes. The eyes always give it away.

"What have you been up to?" I asked.

No reply.

By now Ron had turned up.

"Show us your hands and open the gate," Ron instructed.

A grunt this time. No hand show, but I could hear the gate being unlocked.

I pushed the gate open cautiously with my foot and could see the male making his way back to his kitchen.

"Oi, come back here!" we called after him, but he was intent on getting into the house. We ran after him and caught him just as he was stepping through the back door.

"He's getting the bloody axe!" cried Ron, as he grabbed the man and tried to pull him backwards out of the house. I could see the shaft of the axe on the kitchen bench and our offender's hand hovering literally millimetres from it, but as long as Ron kept pulling him, it was *just* out of his grasp. His hand kept flexing, his fingers clutching for the handle. Our robber was bracing himself against the door frame. I joined in, trying to prise the axe man out of the house, away from the weapon. He was definitely a strong bloke, and neither Ron nor myself felt as if we could loosen our grip in order to effect some blows to encourage our would-be attacker to desist struggling. Let loose of the man by one iota and I'm sure our robber would spring into the kitchen, and if he got hold of that weapon, I'm confident that we'd be goners. We couldn't even afford to let go to reach our radios to call for assistance. He was making an unholy roar as we struggled to contain him. It seemed as if we had reached an impasse, us pulling him back, him bawling at the top of his voice, when suddenly the mad axe man's wife appeared from the living room.

"What the fuck is going on in my house? What do you think you are doing with my husband?"

"Stay back!" I shouted. This wasn't looking good. If she passed him the weapon, he could spin round in one swift move and it would be me who was the first human obstacle in the arc, closely followed by Ron ...that is, unless by some fluke, the axe head just embedded itself in my head, allowing Ron to walk away scot-free. I guess Ron could only hope.

The other option was to let loose now and try and extricate ourselves from the situation and at the moment, I believe that this option probably involved running fast ...in the opposite direction. A little undignified maybe, but perhaps preferable to getting a chopper embedded in my skull. But then again, we couldn't just have him marauding about, waving his weapon at all and sundry. If any members of the public got cleaved in half, there would be a lot of paperwork involved in explaining that to the powers that be. I'd take my chances hanging onto the crazed axe man for now.

I shouted at her again, telling her to stay back.

Despite my protestations, I could see her move closer, closer to the axe that loomed so ominously. I was too wired to be nervous, still firmly holding onto the mad loon whose hand was constantly grasping at the axe shaft. As he struggled, our grip loosened, and millimetre by millimetre he got closer to it. Then, he just started to touch the handle with his outstretched fingers. This wasn't good news. I glanced up at the wife.

"He's a fucking bastard!" she shrieked, before taking a three yard run up and launching a powerful kick into his nuts. He immediately let loose of the frame and all three of us shot back ending up in a heap in the back yard. Ron and I quickly wriggled from under him and turned him onto his front, twisting his arms behind his back as he continued to struggle violently. By the time we had actually got him cuffed, it didn't match anything from the Home Office approved manual, and I concede that one of his arms looked to be in an unnatural position, but when you are fighting for your life, you can't always do things perfectly.

"And don't bring him back here, neither!" the wife shouted after us before slamming the door. We called up for a caged vehicle and soon our robber was off to custody where he got into his cell and immediately fell into a drink-induced slumber. Well, I guess even bastards have to sleep.

Domestics, public order, mindless vandalism, and various assaults later and the cells in the county were all full. The emergency overflow cells were filling up too, and after that it would be a case of taking felons to the neighbouring county to house them for the night. It was only one in the morning, but the staffing numbers were already decimated with officers tied up either at hospitals or with prisoners. Barry shook up the vehicle crewings, and those of us who were left were then out – single crewed in pandas for the rest of the shift, responding to what came in.

Three in the morning and the balloon went up. A call for all available units to travel to the neighbouring area. A near riot in the town square. It was one of those places that by day was full of open air cafés, boutiques and bistros, but sadly this was not cosmopolitan Milan, and on a night time, the piazza was reclaimed by the binge-drinking idiots, fighting and carrying on. Units started to converge on the town from all corners of the county. Comms had caught it on camera and described it as New Year's Eve all over again. On the stroke of midnight last year, the gathered throng had either started kissing or scrapping. Apparently, it was hard to sort out who were grappling and who were snogging. Despite pleas to 'make awkward sexual advances, not war', the carnage continued. Kath, from the other shift, said that at one stage, she had one delinquent in cuffs when another jackass came over and punched her charge hard in the face. "That's not in the rule books," she told me.

You could tell who were the old hands amongst the officers on scene. Whilst we took hold of the offenders in Home Office approved escort grips and arm entanglements, the old sweats, usually the hardened traffic cops, simply grabbed the guilty party in some form of headlock and marched them to the paddy wagon that way. It seemed to be pretty effective anyway.

There was some sort of fancy dress party going on in one of the clubs, as there was a steady stream of beautiful, young girls dressed as bunnies and fire fighters entering the fray. Well, they looked beautiful until they opened their mouths and let loose a barrage of filth at one another. Whilst the males within the square were gradually getting the message that if they continued misbehaving, they'd get locked up, the girls seemed to think they were immune to any sort of punitive action, and continued with their cat fights. Even when they were cuffed and being led away, the little ball of anger in a dress would be screaming, "But I've done nothing wrong, you (expletive for 'front bottom' deleted ...several times)."

Whilst males seem to demonstrate a steady and predictable route before violence finally erupts: taking a fighting stance, clenching fists, glancing at potential target areas and the like, drunken women, however, don't seem to display any of these indicators. Whilst a male will weigh up the situation to ascertain the possibility of winning prior to any action, this doesn't seem to be a consideration worthy of their drunken female counterparts.

I concede that, occasionally, they may put their handbag down first, and maybe I should take more notice of that, but even that's not a certainty before they lash out. And that, dear reader, is why I've been assaulted more times by women than by men. I currently sport a scar above my left eye as a result of my inability to understand the female psyche. As a ten year old, I would have been delighted to have such a scar, to contribute to some imagined action man persona, but as a forty-something male, it's not so welcome, and just *another* reason why I'll probably never get to date Jacqueline. Jacqueline, by the way, is the sophisticated, cool, smart young woman from the CPS office upstairs, who takes out all the confusion from the red blood, yellow bruises, purple knuckles and blue language of the witness statements, suspect interview notes and police reports and then efficiently and effectively transforms them into one logical and straightforward black and white report for court purposes. Whilst most of the guys in the station just want to get into her Agent Provocateurs, and I can't say I blame them, they are missing the point with a girl like her.

Anyway, bit by bit, and arrest by arrest, our imitation New Year's Eve was once again restored to a balmy August night/morning, which was just as well as each arrest took another couple of officers from the scene.

We were down to less than a hundred stragglers left in the square, when I was greeted by the sight of a young woman sitting on the v-shaped tow bar of the burger wagon, her pretty, floral skirt hitched up around her waist, defecating in the street. I expressed my disgust in no uncertain terms and told her that she could have used the facilities in the club if she was so desperate. She was told to clean it up or I'd arrest her, although I had no idea where I'd house her, as even the overflow cell facilities were almost full. I'm not sure what I expected her to do, but I wasn't quite prepared for what happened next.

Standing up, not even bothering to clean herself, she first rolled her eyes at me, then picked up the offending turd with her bare hands, put it in her handbag and then got in the queue for the food. I decided at that stage it was time to return to the comparable sanity of my own section.

We had survived until half-six, only thirty minutes to go. Surely nothing should happen now.

"Any Kilo mobile, can you investigate a report of a car crashed on the border? All traffic cars are currently tied up."

As much as I make fun of the traffic officers (although I made a mental note to stop this after seeing their escort technique), I wouldn't like to be in their shoes. They have a difficult job and they do it well.

There are almost 400,000 cars stolen each year in the UK, over a million drivers are driving without insurance (costing millions to those of us who do pay for it) and over 300,000 men, women and children are injured on our roads annually; of those over 40,000 are either killed or seriously hurt. Hundreds upon hundreds of deaths are caused where someone has exceeded the speed limit, driven too fast for the conditions or driven carelessly or aggressively. A further 3,000 are killed or seriously injured in collisions where someone involved was over the drink drive limit. And sadly, if everyone wore their seatbelts, about 500 of those deaths could be avoided.

So, if you are ever stopped by one of my traffic colleagues for a driving offence, you can always indignantly point out to the officer that they could better spend their time arresting 'proper' criminals but, personally, I wouldn't recommend it.

As for me, I prefer crime and disorder myself as opposed to road policing, but every so often I have to get involved in traffic incidents, usually in the form of accidents and collisions.

"I'll attend from Kilo 1," I told Comms and set off for the border to search for the crashed car in company with Bob, who jumped in with me in case we needed to close a road off. Someone had rung in saying they thought a car had run into a tree, but couldn't be sure. Hopefully, this would be a quick check, find nothing, and then back to base ready to hand over the keys to the dayshift team.

There was a low fret covering the area as we made our way to the border, so we drove slowly, scanning the woods either side for any sign of a vehicle. Eventually, we saw something. It looked like old damage. Part of a car's bodywork against a tree, nothing more. Still, whoever had rung it in was well intentioned. We pulled up the panda, put the blues on and got out to put a 'police aware' sticker on it to avoid any more calls.

It was only as I got closer that I noticed a hand protruding out of the broken window. As I got closer still, I could see the back of a head. Shit, this wasn't old damage, this was a recent crash. But there was no front of the car – no bonnet or engine, and there was no back of the car – no rear seats or boot. There just seemed to be the driver's side, no passenger side either. This must have been one hell of a major impact. There was no sign of life in the car, the driver was clearly dead, and we couldn't have even got to him even if there were any.

Bob got on the radio and called for fire, ambulance and

traffic, as I started to search deeper into the woods. About twenty yards away I found the engine block. Ten yards on was the battery. I started to find bits of car bodywork scattered amongst the trees. I then started to feel something dripping on me from above.

"We'd better get the helicopter out," I told Bob. For all we knew, there could have been passengers thrown from the vehicle on impact, flung into the undergrowth or up into the foliage. The helicopter's infra-red cameras would pick up any body heat if there was any. On the other hand, it could just have been water droplets condensing from the morning fret dripping down on us, but I wasn't going to take any chances.

Soon I heard the reassuring sound of sirens in the distance. Meanwhile, cars sped past on their way to work, not bothering to slow, despite our presence at the side of the road.

"Can we get a couple of units down to close the road off?" I requested Comms.

Soon the road was quiet, and the site was illuminated by the blue strobes of all the emergency vehicles in attendance. The Traffic Accident unit was now on scene, taking measurements and photographing the wreckage. It later transpired that the driver must have been driving so fast, that when he left the road and hit the tree, the engine had just carried on travelling deep into the woods. The rest of the vehicle had just concertinaed. When the fire brigade recovered the car from the tree, it was evident that the impact had crushed the vehicle from almost six feet in width to just twelve inches.

As the fire brigade started cutting the vehicle away, a few bits of paperwork fluttered from the car door. I retrieved then and showed them to the traffic Sergeant. One was a speeding ticket issued the previous day. I just wonder if he had made a comment about doing some 'proper police work' when it had been issued.

Eventually, I was stood down as the accident unit took over the scene and continued its investigation. The drunken antics of the idiots in the town seemed a world away. A pointless death like this seemed to put things in perspective. As I slowly drove with Bob back to the station, I made a simple request.

"Can you not do that thing you do that really annoys me?" I asked him.

"What's that?" he replied.

"Talk," I answered.

The new shift was waiting in the office when I got back, and I fetched my uneaten sandwiches and my kit bag out of the panda and handed over the keys. It had been a full on shift, full of arrests, drunken idiots and domestics. However, I'm pretty confident that the new relief would happily swap the last shift with me a thousand times over to avoid having to go and inform the dead man's family.

When you attend an incident like that, sometimes the humour in the job just deserts you. I felt useless, yet there was nothing I could have done. Still, it didn't help me feel any better. My mind just kept on mulling over scenarios again and again. What if the driver had had an argument with his wife that morning and just ran out of the door before the 'sorrys' could be said? How would she be feeling now? Would some child be waking up this morning and wondering where her daddy was? Had he told her that he loved her recently? Would some dog be eagerly waiting for its owner to get back home ...and waiting...and waiting?

I booked off duty and made my way home, patted my own dog on the head, had a bottle of beer and got into bed.

'Dear sleep, I like you very much. Please can we be friends?'

Sleep wasn't answering me. I just lay there. What a loser. I can't even lie in bed and close my eyes properly. I just stared at the ceiling. Eventually, I turned over the pillow to see if the cold side would work any better.

'Dear sleep, I feel we got off to a bad start. Can we try again?'

CHAPTER FIFTEEN:

BOBO

There is a rare creature that police in the big city talk about in hushed tones. In the theatre, it is unlucky for the name 'Macbeth' to be uttered, supposedly bringing bad luck on the play and anyone acting in it. In police circles, it is also considered bad form to mention the name of this creature out loud in case this shy, retiring animal is scared off, never to return again. Many have waited and prayed for a fleeting glimpse of its majesty, for amongst the hustle, bustle and frenetic activity of the metropolis, it can be a thing of beauty to behold. Sadly, I've also been told that some metropolitan coppers have *never* sighted this rare beast in decades of service to the Crown.

However, like most creatures, they are more abundant in the countryside. Indeed, police in the rural provinces see far too many of them. They are a veritable nuisance. Their sheer profusion has led to many a good officer seeking a transfer to avoid their menace. The way that they pop up uninvited, day after day after day, can sap morale and de-motivate entire shifts.

They still exist in the towns, occasionally making an appearance on a Monday or Tuesday night before hibernating for the rest of the week. They are both revered and loathed with equal measure. Initially welcomed, but like a visiting relative, you quickly tire of them. Have you ever met my dad?

In essence, this delicate being cannot survive where the population is dense (insert your own punch line here).

This mythical creature is known by many different names. Sometimes good, other times bad, sometimes referred to fondly, other times in derogatory tones, sometimes spoken of adoringly, other times muttered in a disparaging manner. In Sandford, it is known by one name alone. In Sandford, it is known as the BOBO: Book On, Book Off – nothing happens. A quiet shift.

Usually, we tick over with a mix of domestics, nuisance youths, assaults, thefts and the ever popular 'missing persons', but every now and again the BOBO comes to visit.

A few weekends ago, I was sent to cover duties over at a country market town when they were short-staffed. It was a veritable BOBO fest. During our briefings back at Sandford, we normally talked about the active drug dealers, the intelligence on potential drink drivers, the known burglars we should be targeting, the violent domestics and the tension indicators pointing to areas where we could expect trouble come pub closing time. During the briefing here, we all had a nice cup of tea and a piece of homemade cake that one of the girls had brought in, whilst we heard about Farmer Jones who had a chicken stolen ...or it might just have been eaten by a fox. "Either way, keep an eye out. He's a Bantam, and answers to the name of Keith."

The rural police station covered a vast area – about six hundred square miles, but generally nothing happened there. The patch consisted mainly of farmland with the occasional well-to-do village dotted amongst it. The market town itself was an enclave of wealthy retirees and artistic sorts – not normally the types to go on a lager-fuelled rampage and ending up painting the town red. Maybe after one too many glasses of Shiraz or even a cheeky Pinot Grigio, a light wash with a delicate cerise or a gentle terracotta was more on the cards, but even that was a long shot. Even the village pubs were self-policed with the farmers preferring to keep their drinking holes trouble free, normally sorting out any rabble-rousers themselves.

As I drove down the pretty country lanes, the police radio would be silent, nothing disturbing the beautiful sounds of the birds singing in the trees. Occasionally, I'd change channels over to the Sandford frequency to hear the shenanigans and mayhem over there, and then change back. Still nothing. I'd even give a call to Comms just to make sure the set was still working. It was. It was just another quiet day in the shires.

One shift of driving around the spectacular countryside with nothing to do was wonderful. The second shift was less fun, and by the third shift I was really starting to miss the action over in the Kilo sections. This would probably be a good posting when you were coming up to retirement, but at this stage in my career, it wasn't really my cup of tea, even if it did come with some shortbread biscuits, courtesy of the Sergeant.

I did my bit for the community though, stopping traffic to allow all types of creatures across the road: from ducks with their ducklings in tow, through to various sleepy hedgehogs, and even a short-sighted Mr Mole. I did get one call though from a concerned townie who was out on a Saturday afternoon jaunt. He was worried about another sleepy country resident – a badger, who the caller believed 'seems to have fallen asleep on the side of the road'. He was anxious that our torpid carnivore might come to grief if he stayed there. I travelled over but had my suspicions that things had already gone a bit pear-shaped for our white striped chum ...and indeed I was correct. He wasn't going to wake up any time soon. My initial thoughts were confirmed. He had been run over. It hadn't been a good year for our badger, more likely a Michelin radial.

Back in Sandford a week later, it was seven thirty on a Tuesday morning in September and I was having my own Michelin moment, albeit of a different sort. Geezer and I were sitting in an unmarked vehicle on the edge of the green, in a village not far from Sandford. We were in full uniform, including our body armour, but had our civilian jackets over the top, so as to resemble two large Michelin men. I'm sure we didn't look conspicuous at all.

Today, we were on what Americans might call a 'stakeout', but without the coffee and doughnuts. In fact, we don't seem to have an awful lot in common with our US counterparts when it comes to the whole process of eating. In America, the public love to see their law enforcement officers in their local diner. It's a presence in the community. They know that if a police officer stops in for a coffee, there is less likely to be any criminal activity in the area while he's there. Over here, even popping to the 'drive-thru' attracts snide comments about not being out and about chasing down muggers. It seems that in Great Britain we like to get the maximum out of our public servants, and even if an office worker is out on his own lunch break, he doesn't seem to think that anyone in uniform has the right to eat during their shift, too.

I think the other big difference between us and the US police apart from the obvious of not carrying guns, is that only one of us chases criminals up to the county line and then, when they cross it, stop the police vehicle, get out and shake their fists.

"Darn it, Earl, he's crossed the county line. Next time! Just wait till next time!"

But I digress.

After arriving for work that morning, Geezer and I were told to take a plain, unmarked CID car down to the village green. A resident had seen some suspicious activity.

I love those sorts of calls. Suspicious can mean anything. To me, a clearing in the woods is suspicious ...and slightly sexy. What bizarre, depraved, carnal rituals went on here? And why wasn't I invited?

To me, anyone who has an oriental girlfriend is also slightly suspicious. Hmmm, I wonder how that pot-bellied, balding, old bloke managed to get such a stunner in tow? Nothing to do with e-bay was it?

How about the size of those chicken pieces in your curry? I, for one, have never seen a bird that big. Have they been cultivating some form of genetically mutated, oversized rooster in that outbuilding? Or maybe it's donkey?

Or, how about when your girlfriend becomes overly romantic? Something's definitely up. Nothing to do with that pair of Jimmy Choos you saw in town earlier is it perchance?

Anyway, down at the village green, suspicious meant something altogether different.

Apparently, several times a month, a car pulls up, a male gets out, sticks a small parcel under a bench on the village green and drives off. Several hours later, another car pulls up, someone picks up the package and leaves. Such a drop off had occurred at six forty five this morning. Following a call by a concerned member of the public, the Inspector had put a quick operation together. It was our job to monitor the drop-off point. More units were parked at other key strategic points around the village, ready to move in if anyone approached the target. What was in the packet? Drugs? Laundered money? A gun? It was anyone's guess. All I knew was that when an approach was made, the balloon would go up and all units would converge on the target ...but until then, we just had to wait.

After a poke around the vehicle, the first thing Geezer and I found out was that the civilian radio had been taken out of the car. I suspect it was just in case we tried to have any glimmer of fun for the next five hours.

You can find out a lot about someone when you are stuck in a car with them for hours on end, especially when nothing is going on. Most of it is rubbish.

Recent interesting snippets/useless trivia that I have found out from spending far too much time in close proximity with colleagues have been:

If you put your thumb over the face of Paul Simon on the *Bridge Over Troubled Water* record, it looks like Art Garfunkel has a big Cossack style moustache. Thanks Barry.

A horse owner has named his horse *My Face*, just so he could have a secret snigger at the posh ladies at Ascot as they cheered on the steed as it raced for the finish line. Thanks Geezer.

George's new girlfriend has an amazing body and huge boobs. Thanks George.

George's new girlfriend only has an amazing body in 'roll up, roll up' sense of amazing, and she's got huge boobs because it's part of an overall weight problem. Thanks Ben.

When he left Zimbabwe, inflation was hitting over eleven million per cent and a loaf of bread cost 1.6 trillion Zimbabwe dollars. You wouldn't want to spend too much time browsing at that rate. Thanks Bob.

Meanwhile, Ron added to my collection of trivia when he told me about the wedding of one of the traffic officers that he had recently been to. The traffic lad had lost his first wife in unfortunate circumstances a few years earlier – but even he had conceded that it had been one helluva game of cards. Apparently, the officer was determined to make sure that his second marriage would be a success – everything that his first marriage wasn't. In a bid to start it off on a truly romantic note, he had asked the DJ at the reception to play 'Something Stupid' for that very first dance with his new wife. However, as the bride and groom took to the floor, instead of the Nancy Sinatra classic, they were met by the unmistakable strains of 'The Birdie Song'.

Anyway, back to the interesting snippets and, according to Chad, Satan is dead. Actually, this one may need some further explanation.

Satan had been the name given to the monster that had been discovered in trap two of the gent's, back at the station.

"Had I seen it?" Chad asked. How could I not have seen it? It was the talk of the station for days. Someone had laid the biggest turd imaginable in one of the toilets. It was big enough to make its own pension contributions. As it lingered at the bottom of the pan for days, immune to flushings and bleach, it had become something of a tourist attraction. Women from the front office even made escorted viewings to marvel at its majesty. It was indeed a thing to behold as it lay there, slowly rusting away. It was even widely believed that in the case of a nuclear war, just cockroaches and this homage to bad eating might be the only thing left in a post-holocaust environment. They had named it Satan.

There had been numerous quests to find its original owner, but to no avail. My suggestion had been to look for someone who looked like they had been crying when they had left the scene. It certainly would have brought tears to my eyes. However, despite the best endeavours of our highly trained CID colleagues, the identity of Satan's owner remained a mystery.

Eventually, after four or five days, Satan disappeared as mysteriously as whence he had come. Some say it was beaten into submission by a specialist cleaner, brought in for the job from 'oop north'. Others say it was blown up by the Coastguard Service (you wouldn't want that thing getting out to sea in one piece!) Some say it was beamed back up to the mother ship. Others say it just lost the will to carry on after the adulation of the early days had subsided.

Whatever the truth of it, we shall never know. All that now remained was a note written in black biro on a piece of toilet roll, stuck onto the cistern.

RIP. Followed by the dates of his short, but joyous life.

However, perhaps the most shocking piece of trivia came from Gwen, albeit inadvertently.

We had all been in the parade room one quiet night, discussing the habits of certain drug addicts in the town.

Barry had mentioned the lengths some of the heroin users went to after years of abuse. "Due to the veins in their arms collapsing through over use, I hear some of the druggies are injecting straight into their scrotum."

Gwen had then chipped in the immortal line, "I don't like the sound of that! I wouldn't want to inject *my* testicles."

We all chorused a communal, 'Eeeeeeeeeewwwwwwww!' whilst simultaneously adopting a puzzled expression, looking agog at Gwen, putting our hands on our own jewels and scraping our chairs backwards away from the table. I had tried to blank out the mental image but to no avail. That was the stuff of nightmares.

She had tried to explain, but it was too late. It had started to develop into urban myth, to be passed down from shift to shift as soon as the words had left her mouth. That is the thing with the police. Make one mistake, or say the wrong thing, and it gets around the place faster than a fast thing that's been greased up good and proper to make it go even faster. Within hours, you'll no doubt find yourself sporting some new nickname based on your revelation/calamity/mistake.

Just talk to 'Shit-Crack' about it. Actually, on the other hand, don't talk to Shit-Crack. He got his particular name based on his lack of ability to have any decent banter.

In return, of course, the various shift members got to know my useless trivia.

How I was back on the market. How I had recently split up with my girlfriend. She was meant to be the last, but she turned out to be just the latest. She kept going on about how she wanted me to be like her ex, so in the end I made her wish come true and became exactly like her ex – by finishing with her.

What I didn't share with the shift though, was the fact that I was finding out that there is a fine line between being 'back on the market' and 'reduced to clear'.

They also heard about the time I turned up to the small fire on the nature reserve.

A call had come in from a slightly concerned member of the public. He had wanted to report a fire, "...but it's only a small one and I didn't want to bother the fire brigade."

I'm not sure if that type of call ever happens the other way round.

"Hello, Fire Control, can I help you?"

"I'd like to report a burglary. It's not a house or anything, just the shed. I didn't really want to bother the police with it."

I suggest not. I don't think Trumpton would be overly impressed with someone waking them for that.

However, Gwen and I had responded dutifully. We found the burning bush down by the pond. I stood about for a few minutes, listened intently, but it didn't speak to me. I decided that it was down to us to put this minor inferno out of its misery, despite the fact that we didn't have a working extinguisher.

"Can't you go and get your helmet and scoop some water out of the pond?" suggested Gwen.

Well, yes, technically I could have done. I would also have been lumbered with swampy smelling head attire for the rest of my service as a result. The solution appeared more obvious to me and instead I unzipped, told Gwen to stand well back, and I peed the thing to death. Gwen just opted for kicking the embers around a bit instead to make sure the blaze was totally extinguished. Spoilsport!

Occasionally, the talk during the quiet times would turn to royalty. What does the Queen do with all those half hours?

I only found this out after I joined up, but we don't get paid for the first thirty minutes of any overtime worked. It is 'for the Queen' I was told. I suggested to the Sgt one day that I'd like to come in an hour or so late on the next set of early shifts – have a bit of a lie in and cash in a couple of those half hours back that I'd kindly (and unwittingly) donated to Her Majesty over the last year. I soon found out that where the House of Windsor was concerned, it's a one way street ...and I suggest that you don't bother asking for time back yourself if you are easily offended by coarse language or gestures that look like someone is agitating a slack handful of coffee beans.

Occasionally, the talk would turn to space. It seems that astronomers are no longer content with discovering stars and giving them a rude name or calling them after a cartoon dog. No, now they like to dream up bizarre hypotheses about the universe that can never be proven, nor disproven.

Apparently, we are not alone. There is another, better us out there. And a worse us. One potty professor, no doubt wearing a white coat and sporting crazy hair (or maybe wearing a jacket with elbow patches, greasy barnet and glasses), has come up with the theory that there is a parallel world out there in which another one of us exists. But no, my friends, not just one parallel world, but many. Loads in fact.

It seems that each time we take a decision – do I turn left or right, should I take a pen or a pencil with me, have I got time for a pee before I go out or not – we split off into a different world. We live in the world where we made our decision, whilst another us potters off into the new world, with a pencil, no doubt. Until the next decision is made that is, and the next parallel world is created.

Somewhere, there is another me who didn't fail his French exam. Somewhere, there is another me who knew the difference between chapeau and chateau. Somewhere, there is another me who didn't make the examiners laugh their socks off by going into a long, involved story about living in a hat.

Who knows, in some other world I've made all the *right* decisions and I could be living with CPS Jacqueline. This is, of course, dependent on CPS Jacqueline making all the *wrong* decisions in her life.

We also talked a lot about the nice looking girl from the Sugababes.

Back at the stakeout, we spent another four hours in situ before we were relieved. In fact, just to show how un-American we are, we don't even call it a stakeout. It's just called 'waiting for something to happen', which doesn't sound half as exciting, probably because it isn't.

All the other incidents that day were covered by a skeleton staff as the Inspector insisted that the operation be kept going throughout the shift. Other jobs had to go by the by ...the potential prize here was too good to miss. When the trap was sprung, officers would close in from every direction and tackle the suspect to the floor. We would not only have the package, but the people behind it, too.

This was the Inspector's opportunity, his big chance to bag some major criminal players. If we took a weapon out of circulation amongst the criminal fraternity, the top brass would be singing his praises. If it was laundered money, the higher echelons of CID would be writing to congratulate him on his quick thinking. If we got a major drugs bust here, maybe even a commendation from the Chief.

At one in the afternoon, another unit had secreted themselves in situ, watching the collection point from a discreet distance, and no doubt more useless trifles and trivialities were swapped between them. At just before midnight, after eighteen hours of observation, the decision was finally taken to stand the operation down. Maybe we had been compromised, maybe we had a criminal informant in our midst, maybe the bad guys just sensed that something wasn't right.

Either way, the operation was terminated and the Inspector moved in to see what was in the package.

Have you ever been on a treasure hunt? The ones where people leave clues all over the county, so you have to drive all over the place working them out? If you ever find yourself in a village near Sandford, just watch out when you go to pick up your clue in case you find yourself being charged at by a handful of eager coppers who:

Manhandle you to the floor, twisting your arms into positions they shouldn't go.

Drag your wife through the passenger window whilst simultaneously shouting, 'STOP RESISTING!'

Smash every window of your car with their batons in case anyone tries to escape from the scene in the motor.

Sitting in a vehicle for several hours with nothing to do can make you go a bit manic when the balloon eventually does go up.

I guess I don't need to tell you what was in the package now. There was no gun, no drugs, no dirty money, no big criminal players involved ... just a handful of geeky treasure hunters.

Luckily, nobody came to collect the clue ...so no one was a winner. Neither the treasure hunters ...nor the Inspector.

Some felt a bit sorry for him ...but not me. I never really got on with the Inspector. He left recently and we got a new one who is great, but the old Inspector still had a pop at me even after he had departed.

It was a purely innocent remark; I had met a retired Chief Inspector at the gym and he had been asking if I knew so and so, as they do. If we discover a person we both know, I think we are expected to stand in contemplation for a little while, and then let out a little sigh that says 'we both know the same person'. I'm not sure what it achieves, but we all seem to like to play the game from time to time.

Unfortunately, we had drawn a blank, so the conversation turned to which of my senior officers he knew. Who was my Inspector he asked. I replied he used to be Inspector Soaper, but now he's Inspector Jeavons.

"Really? How interesting. I wonder what prompted that? Most bizarre, that Dick Soaper always was a strange one," came the reply.

I thought nothing of it until a few weeks' later when I got an angry call from Soaper, demanding to know why I had told old colleague of his that he had changed his name. I tried to explain that it wasn't like that, but the phone had been slammed down before I had a chance to say much at all.

I'd never really got on with Inspector Soaper. He seemed to take great delight in pouring cold piss on my enthusiasm.

It can be hard enough battling with the drunks and criminals outside without having to contend with Mr Ego Deflator inside the station.

I don't know from whence his initial dislike of me developed, but I think it may have started during my first week.

I was sat waiting in one of the interview rooms with a young teenager when Soaper looked through the small inspection window, opened the door and then strode purposefully into the room.

"What's he in for?" he asked me, nodding towards the young man. Clearly he didn't think that the guy was even worthy enough to be asked directly himself.

"Robbery at knife point, Sir," I replied.

I could see the rumblings of a volcanic eruption brewing up inside Soaper. As he got angrier and angrier I could see the veins on his forehead pulse. If this was a cartoon, there would be steam coming out of his ears. Eventually, he could hold it in no longer, and with a mighty roar, he turned his full attention to the adolescent.

"You disgust me!" he boomed. "Robbery! Knives! Have you got no inkling of decency, no shred of morality?"

The juvenile was clearly taken aback, looking both shocked and petrified, shaking visibly, his knuckles white as they gripped the seat. He was clearly terrified by this onslaught.

Soaper continued his righteous monologue, lambasting the lack of standards in the youth of today and I guess, delivering the sort of home truths that we would all like to dispense to the wasters who turn innocent people's lives upside down by their selfish and violent actions. By the time he had eventually vented all his anger and frustration, our teenager had almost turned white and was perspiring profusely, tears welling up in his eyes.

It was only then that I managed to finish what I was originally saying to the Inspector.

"As I said, Sir, this gentleman is in regarding a robbery at knife point. He's the victim."

Fair play to Soaper, he was a quick thinker. He stepped up to the lad, sat him back upright in his chair, ruffled his hair and said, "And that dear boy, is what I shall say to the miscreant who did this to you when we find him," before shooting me a withering glance and leaving the room.

I had felt decidedly ill at ease with the Inspector thereafter.

At one stage, I thought that he had let bygones be bygones when I approached him with a report that I needed signing.

I had been at home on a day off when I had received a call from Dave, the farmer up the lane. He had had three sheep killed by some unknown animal. I'd often heard tales of the beast of Sandford, possibly a wild cat that stalked the countryside, occasionally attacking livestock, and even more occasionally, being sighted ...just like Elvis (the occasional sighting that is, not attacking livestock).

The whole country abounds with tales of wild beasts that terrorise sheep and cattle, and I'm sure that these predators exist. There was a wide variety of exotic animals kept by private collectors in the days before stricter legislation came about. When it did, many of these animals were just released into the wild with no thought about how this would affect the local ecosystem.

Technically, the farm fell within the bounds of the next police division, but they were normally far too busy with the problems in the city to bother with the goings on in the smaller, outlying villages. To them, a few dead sheep would figure low on their priorities, but I could see that to the farmer, this was his livelihood. I pulled on my Wellingtons and made my way up to his farm.

When I arrived, and Dave showed me the killing zone, it was quickly apparent that things didn't quite stack up. I could see two puncture wounds on the sheep's throat, but that was it. Other than those wounds, the ewes were unmarked. A big cat kills to eat, not for the enjoyment of it. I would have expected the animal's stomach to have been torn out, blood to be everywhere, carnage, but the scene appeared forensically clean. The wound seemed almost surgical in its appearance.

A loose dog, on the other hand, could have attacked the animals, but generally they would have been messy kills. Cue the blood, guts and gore again.

There were a few large paw prints in the wet ground near where the bloated sheep were lying, but nothing other than that. No human footmarks to examine. The killing beast had come alone.

I phoned the station and requested CSI to attend. Meanwhile, Dave showed me photos of a couple of lambs that had been killed on his land a few years back. Here the sheep had virtually been skinned alive, probably by the rasping tongue of a big cat. Today's scene was nothing like that.

An hour later and I could hear the rumble of the forensic van trundling up the lane. Another visit to the killing zone and casts were taken of the paw marks.

"It can't be a big cat," explained our crime scene expert. "A cat retracts its claws when it is walking. These marks clearly show they weren't."

So, it must have been a dog. Strange.

The CSI once again examined the dead sheep which, by now, were so swollen and distended, they looked like they were going to explode any second, like some grass eating version of Mr Creosote.

"A single bite to the neck," was confirmed. No other marks, no other clues.

I gave Comms a ring to find out if any other incidents had been reported. Twenty minutes later and I received a call back from Nancy.

"No kills, John, but the farmer at the other end of the village has reported a stray dog. I don't know if they are linked at all?"

I wasn't sure either, but it was the best lead we had ...the only lead we had. So we made our way to Tom's farm to view our suspect.

"That's a Japanese Akita!" proclaimed the forensics expert, who, it was turning out, seemed to be the font of all knowledge. As much as they look like cuddly, fluffy Husky dogs, they can be vicious animals. I was trying to gain access to a house a few months back to secure the arrest of a suspect inside, when he threatened to set his Akita on me if I entered the property. They are also known as Japanese fighting dogs for good reason. He wound his dog up into such a frenzy in a bid to scare me (and Chad and Lloyd who had now arrived as back up) ...and was doing a pretty effective job of it, when the dog turned on his owner, and started to rip into him instead. Ain't life a terrible thing?

Our current suspect though, was happily pottering about in the barn where the farmer had contained him. He looked well cared for ...these aren't the sort of dogs that usually end up abandoned. They are pretty expensive pedigrees.

We tentatively made our way in and were greeted by sniffs and licks. I kept the dog's attention while our expert studied the paw size.

"It's a fit," he informed us.

There was no blood on the animal's face, but that could just as easily have been washed off in the nearby stream or as he made his way through the long grass in the fields.

Tom explained that he had just found the dog wandering in the yard at about seven that morning. Dave had found the sheep on his early morning rounds of the fields, so the times seemed to tie in. It looked like our suspect had just become the defendant.

The clean kill aspect of the incident still bothered me, though. I got onto the wildlife inspector in the north of the county to tell him my findings, and the final piece of the jigsaw slotted into place.

In Australia, Akitas have been trained to help on the massive sheep farms, and to make clean take-downs of sheep, killing with a single bite in order to keep the carcass in good order for sale. So our dog *was* capable of such a precise kill.

It finally all made sense. We could have taken swabs from the dog and the wounds on the sheep to try and match them up, but it was extra expense when we were pretty sure that we had solved our case.

It was cold comfort to Dave, losing his stock, but the positive thing is that we knew that there wasn't another beast of Sandford loose in the area. It was a relief to both him and Tom. It would be up to the Council now to collect the dog and decide what to do. Wait to see if anyone reported their charge missing, and then take whatever actions councils do in such circumstances.

All that was left for me to do now was something that I couldn't do normally if I had been on duty, that was to have a few well deserved beers at the farmhouse.

When Soaper heard about it, he sent me a note saying he wanted a report ASP which, I'm guessing, is an impatient version of ASAP. You've got to be a man in a hurry if you are in far too much of a rush to put in that extra 'A'.

"Good report, Donoghue. You've made a very slight mistake here, though, on the form to forensics," said Soaper studying my account.

"Oh sorry, Sir. I'll get it altered."

"No problem. It's all part of the learning process," he said as he smiled, wrote something on the front sheet and handed it back to me. Maybe he wasn't such a bad sort after all. It was only when I got back into the parade room that I saw the big red line across the page and in big capital letters the words: 'COMPLETED IN ERROR BY AN IDIOT.'

In hindsight, I guess his smile did look like the sort of grimace that people pull whilst they are peeing in a swimming pool. And this was straight from the high diving board.

The next day, Soaper came into the morning briefing. He explained that we couldn't win them all and then, rather unexpectedly, thanked me for my help at the treasure hunt yesterday. Well at least I thought he had, until I played it back in my head again.

"Thank you, Donoghue. Without your input, things would have worked out exactly the same."

Cheers.

Someone mentioned having a collection for Inspector Soaper when he left. I suggested that it would probably be a bit more beneficial to have one for the *incoming* incumbent.

No, seeing the Inspector was about as pleasant an experience for me as seeing a dog with its ear turned inside out. I didn't shed a tear at his surveillance operation gone wrong ...well not a tear of sadness anyway. I almost pissed myself laughing.

No. Some shifts are BOBO ones, but even BOBOs can have happy endings.

CHAPTER SIXTEEN:

School

The new Inspector was in the morning briefing. Something was not normal. I like normal. I don't like not normal. I like my routine. I don't like changes to my routine. I like the Status Quo – *Rockin' All Over The World* is probably my favourite. He coughed and then addressed us all.

"The Superintendent is coming to visit the station at lunchtime. If you've got any questions for him, make sure you come back into the station, or else drop your question in this box."

There were two reasons that I didn't really want to meet the Super. Firstly, I tend to think life is less complex if you strive to avoid those people in the higher echelons of power, and secondly, and perhaps more importantly, the Super also held the highly dubious title of 'Force Rape Champion'. Whilst I know fine well that this meant he was the oracle of all knowledge within the Constabulary where rape cases were concerned, the title just sounded like some form of bizarre and rather unsavoury accolade and, quite frankly, conjured up images of some sordid little contest that I certainly didn't want any involvement in whatsoever. Maybe they needed to go back to the drawing board with that particular moniker.

They are always inventing fancy titles for all sorts of positions, some of which, to be perfectly honest, can be downright misleading. Take the 'Airline Executive'. Sounds impressive, doesn't it? Well, it does until you find out this guy works at the local garage and is in charge of the hose used for pumping up your tyres.

Well, forewarned is forearmed. I'd take my sandwiches with me. I wasn't going to be coming back to meet the top brass. I'd pop a question in the box though.

I'd thought about suggesting that we start prosecuting drug dealers for using non-metric weights and measures, but eventually decided on a more immediate question that I needed answering.

Who do you think would win a fight between a badger and a baboon?

I posted it into the receptacle and got ready to make my way to Sugar-Rush Infants School.

Just before I left, the Sergeant called me into the office to ask if I wanted to re-check the spelling on my statement before submitting my file. Did I still want to crime it as a fight at the local comprehensive, or else did I wish to re-classify the incident as a sexual offence? By way of mitigation, firstly, I did type up the report at 4 o'clock in the morning, and secondly, 'K' and 'L' are very close on the keyboard. I re-read my transcript and corrected my mistake … there's a world of difference between getting a good kicking and a good licking.

I was ashamed at my lack of attention to detail …or the fact that it had been discovered, anyway. I thought back to training school where the emphasis had been on reporting the facts both clearly and without ambiguity. I also thought about my colleague, Genevieve, who was the master, or should that be the mistress, of factual reporting, and exceedingly proud of the quality of her statements. It had been drilled into us that we should always use plain English. The example given had been where the person providing the statement used a phrase like 'bonkers in the nut' – we would then clarify this in the statement, explaining that this meant 'mentally unstable'. If the person said they were smoking a 'tab', we would clarify that it meant a cigarette, and so on.

On one particular occasion, Genevieve was taking a report from a shy teacher who had been flashed at by a male near the boating lake. The school ma'am had explained that she couldn't really say what the flasher looked like as she wasn't really looking at his face, but agreed to provide a comprehensive statement to police. Our rather refined teacher commented that, *"the male stepped out onto the pathway in front of me, and pulled open his raincoat to expose his genitalia."* Genevieve, in her quest for clarity, had then helpfully added in brackets, *'cock and balls'.*

Anyway, it all provided a tenuous link for the Sergeant to tell me to go back to school ...or in this particular case, the school crossing at Sugar-Rush Infants School.

Today, I was the replacement lollipop person. The lollipop lady had gone off sick at short notice, and they wanted me to control the traffic. I was, however, not to be entrusted with the actual lollipop, which to be honest, I was quite pleased about. There must be special lolly-stick training for which I was not deemed suitable.

Whilst my colleagues all had a laugh at my expense, I was secretly pleased. School crossing patrol meant lots of grateful, young mums and possibly a coffee and biscuit in the school staffroom afterwards. Surely, on such a cold, damp October morning, it was the least they could do for someone who had kept their charges safe on such a dangerous stretch of road? Well, that's how I'd sell it anyway.

It turned out to be one of the nicest mornings I've had. People actually thanking me instead of swearing at me, and believe me, that doesn't happen that often in Sandford. The thanking that is ...lots of swearing, but very little thanks. A few young mums also asked if I'd be back that afternoon. Things were just getting better and better.

Then, coffee and a biscuit in the holiest of holies, that most mysterious of places, the school staffroom. Oh, how I had wondered what it was like inside the staffroom when I had been at school. What sort of depravity went on inside? What treasure lay within?

If you were wondering, it didn't really live up to expectations. Just a few easy chairs, a collection of chipped mugs, a couple of old coffee tables, and stacks of books for marking.

Still, I was in the warmth, with a cup of coffee, some shortbread fingers and Miss Jones – a warm looking, twenty-something, coffee making and shortbread-supplying teacher. She had recently moved to the area. She also had a dog it transpired. Maybe I could get the conversation around to Barney, and offer to show her a few local dog walks?

"Would I come into Year Four and answer a few questions from the children?" Of course I would, Miss Jones.

So it ended up that I was sat on a tiny, child's chair in front of thirty or so inquisitive children.

Introductions over, and a stern warning not to swear, Miss Jones invited questions from the floor.

The warning about cursing was needed, believe me. Only a week earlier, I had been chatting to a woman on the Yellow Estate who told me that she had recently taken her baby to be baptised ...and had been petrified that the baby would start swearing in church. The baby! In church!

They can be like little parrots at that age. The parents must have been ever so proud.

"Awwww Darren, the babe's just said his first words. Come and listen, he might say *fucker* again."

But I digress.

"So, who has any questions for Mr Policeman?"

"It's actually officer," I corrected.

"So, who has any questions for Mr Policeman officer?"

As an array of hands went up, Miss Jones pointed to a girl in the front row.

"Why do you wear a clip on tie?"

"It's so we don't get strangled if someone pulls on it."

A murmur went around the class. They seemed happy with that answer. Good start, John.

"What are those things on your belt?"

It's the same question that you get in every house with an inquisitive eight year old. This was easy. Let's hope they didn't stick one in about the recent changes to the Fraud Act later on.

"There's an 'asp', which is the extendable baton that we hit people with, then there is pepper spray which we can spray in a baddie's eyes if he is being naughty and I've got a small but powerful torch ..."

"Shine it on me! Shine it on me!" the class chorused. So I did.

"Miss, I can't see! I can't see!"

I looked over at Miss Jones and she glared back at me.

"I did say it was powerful," I explained by way of mitigation. "They'll be ok in a minute."

I don't know why I was even bothering to explain. The little buggers were hamming it up. You don't put on a pained expression like that even if you've stared into the might of the burning sun. I should have shone the 'turd melter' on them – the massive torch that is kept in the back of the pandas. That would give them something to moan about! Still, I wanted to keep Miss Jones on side, so best pretend to be concerned. A bit.

"...And I've also a pair of handcuffs."

"My mum's got a pair, too." Suddenly there were hands shooting up all over the place wanting to tell what their mums had at home.

"OK class!" Miss Jones was now shouting above the melee, trying to regain some order, "that's enough!"

Children seem to have a talent for embarrassing their parents. The same thing has happened in people's houses when the kids have spied the cuffs. When I tried to save one mum her blushes and turned the conversation onto the lovely weather we were having, her boy started telling me, in all innocence, how he had come down late last night and found his mum and Uncle David 'sunbathing in front of the fire'.

Miss Jones was able to top that though, and later had told me the tale of one of the mums who had been out shopping with her naughty son.

"I want sweets! I want sweets!" the boy had stomped and cried out in the middle of the supermarket.

"No sweets today. You've had enough this week," came the steely rebuke.

"I want sweets! If you don't give me sweets, I'll tell everyone a secret about you!"

"I will not be blackmailed by a nine year old boy. No sweets, and I mean it. Now behave!"

"I saw you with Daddy's willy in your mouth!"

The mother had told Miss Jones that as those words were shouted out, everything seemed to suddenly go into slow motion as she saw heads turn towards her from every direction. She could feel a hot flush start from her feet and spread upwards, burning her cheeks en route. Everything fell silent as those words echoed down the aisles.

Just as quickly, everything slipped into normal speed again, noises returned as the trolleys clashed into each other and chatter filled the store. She quickly put her head down and reached out to the nearest object she could find.

"Oooh, chocolate buttons, they're nice, let's get some of them."

Back to class Four...

"Have you ever been to a murder?" Children seem to love the gruesome questions.

Sadly, yes. I had been to a murder, or 'murrr-dah' to give it the official title. As is the way, uniform arrive on scene first. That uniform had been me. After an initial assessment, I concluded that foul play was involved, carefully retraced my steps, secured the scene and contacted CID.

"Where do you start?" I asked the DS when he arrived half an hour later.

"It's not rocket science," he responded, "just take things step by step."

He went on to tell me that he held a lot of credence in the old adage: 'find out how they lived and you'll find out how they died'. Stick to the facts – don't get taken in by the rumour mongers, "Otherwise, what was a fart on Monday will end up being a shite by Friday." Very eloquently put.

"And," he continued, "not everything requires complex detective work or some highly paid Chief Inspector driving round the countryside in a vintage car playing classical music. Sometimes, Donoghue, the answer is just staring you in the face. Don't ignore the elephant in the room."

I looked around and then gave him my best puzzled expression, turning the edges of my mouth downwards for added effect.

He put his hand on my shoulder before adding softly, "It's an idiom."

I guess that'll be the ones with the big ears, then.

I stood up to address the class. "Yes, I've been to a murder but don't worry boys and girls, we caught the animal who did it."

Nods of approval spread and even a few handclaps. You're winning them back, John.

"Can I try your hat on, Mister Policeman?"

"No."

Miss Jones looked at me quizzically.

"They've probably got nits," I whispered. "You can try it on if you want, but not them."

"Really," she sighed in exasperation.

"Why are you called 'the boys in blue'?" asked one girl.

A good question. When the police were originally formed, blue was the colour worn by the Royal Navy, who also happened to be very popular with the public. It was decided to adopt this colour to distinguish the new service from the army, who were unpopular at the time and wore red (the Army went around breaking up the protests of the day, and this never tends to endear you to anyone I find). The newly formed police officers had to wear their uniform on and off duty. In addition, they were equipped with a truncheon and a top hat that they could stand on to look over fences. It was a long answer, so I decided to summarise.

"We are called 'the boys in blue' because of the colour of our uniform," I answered.

"So why do they call you black bas..."

"I think that is enough about the uniform," interjected Miss Jones. "Now Ryan, what's your question?" she added, pointing to a familiar looking kid in the front row.

"Are you the policeman who beat up my dad?"

Miss Jones was getting quite practiced now in looking at me in a slightly disapproving, quizzical way. A sort of *what have I let myself in for* type of way.

"I didn't *'beat him up'* exactly," I whispered to her. "He was resisting arrest. I had to take him to the floor."

I remember the job well. In fact, I remember promising myself mid incident that if I actually made it to the end of the shift alive, that I would reward myself with copious amounts of alcohol.

The job had started out innocuous enough. A report had come in from ambulance requesting assistance in a barber's shop over in Kilo 3. It was the traditional type of establishment – not a hairdressers or unisex salon – just a good, old fashioned barber shop. Not 'British Hairways', 'Kropps & Bobbers' or 'Blojobs' – no, this was just 'The Barber Shop'. It had a red-and-white striped pole painted up one side of the door, a window display consisting of an oversized box of Wilkinson Sword razors nestled between a couple of sepia toned photos of models with hairstyles of yesteryear, whilst inside there was a wooden bench along one wall where blokes would sit, waiting to be called to the holiest of holies – the sumptuously padded red leather chair. I say blokes, because that is what they were. Not callow youths or trendy go-getters – just blokes. The whole place was only about the size of a front room. The unspoken rule of the barber shop also meant that those waiting had to sit in silence, or maybe glance through the old copies of Readers Digest magazine that adorned the place. Conversation was the sole preserve of whoever was sitting in the chair and the barber, who seemed to be an authority on whatever topic was being discussed at the time. What could possibly be so urgent as to warrant a blue light run to this place at half ten on a Tuesday morning? Had they run out of 'something for the weekend'?

I had been transporting Andy, a new starter to the shift who had yet to gain 'Panda Commander' status, to a job at an old people's home. Instead, I diverted to this incident, promising that I'd drop him off in a few minutes after we sorted out this little misunderstanding.

We casually walked in to find two young female paramedics struggling to keep hold of a male in his early thirties who appeared intent on climbing into the window display. He certainly didn't look like your usual customer of this sort of establishment. He had already stamped on the big cardboard razor box and knocked over a photo of a Warren Beatty lookalike before they had dragged him back into the main part of the shop. One of them managed to inform me that the guy had clearly taken something and needed attention, but they were having problems getting him to go to the hospital. My query asking the guy his name was met by a clenched fist that narrowly missed my left ear. My follow up attempt to inform him that we were just trying to help generated a similar response which Andy managed to deftly avoid by tilting his head to the right in the nick of time. Andy and I then grabbed hold of an arm each in a bid to control him, when, with an almighty roar, he sent us both crashing back into the door. The guy seemed to have super human strength. He then tried to push past us and get into the street. We were both taken aback by the ferocity of his attack but we quickly rallied. We clearly couldn't let him get out amongst the traffic in his state and I took the decision to take him to the ground so at least the medics could get a better look at him. I swept his legs away and the three of us tumbled onto the floor whilst the ambulance staff stepped back. All attempts to gain control of the maniac now failed miserably as he flayed about indiscriminately, punching and kicking in all directions. I remember wrestling amongst the hair cuttings, coins spilling out of my pocket as I did so, my notebook and pens falling to the floor and getting rolled on. This wasn't a nice, managed arrest – this was a grappling mess. Our un-named male was clawing, biting, punching, kicking and headbutting his way around the floor as we struggled to gain control, whilst at the same time, trying to avoid getting seriously injured in the process. I yelled that I was going to use my pepper spray if he didn't stop struggling. He didn't, so I managed to get it out and spray him at point blank range. I could feel the splash back burning as it rebounded onto my face and arms. I was expecting him to reel around in pain and I let my guard down, awaiting the cessation of hostilities. But nothing. Instead, the male's head suddenly appeared in front of me, his teeth bared as he tried to bite my face. Luckily, Andy managed to deflect his head as I felt for my radio and called for urgent assistance. Something was wrong here. I had clearly got him full in the eyes. He was supposed to have lost the will to fight – it should have caused him severe pain, temporary loss of vision, breathing difficulties – but there was nothing of the sort. We were told in training that it would even work on a grizzly bear! Instead, this guy seemed possessed with the incredible strength of an angry bear combined with the intensity of an irritated wasp that had just survived a failed swatting attempt. He seemed to be super human. After only a few minutes of this hard physical exertion, I was beginning to get exhausted. We had now subtlety changed from fighting to gain control, to fighting just to survive. As we continued to roll about the barber shop, I just kept on thinking that we couldn't let this madman get to his feet and grab any of the scissors or cut throat blades that were abundant in the shop. If he was armed, goodness knows what he would do. I genuinely now believed we were fighting for our lives. It was mayhem.

I quickly glanced up, only to see the barber snipping away, pleasantly chatting away with his customer, whilst the other patrons sat, stony faced, pretending to ignore what was unfolding around them. I couldn't see the paramedics as my face was now being grabbed and shoved back against the wall. An audience had started to gather outside now, looking in through the window at the live floor show. They saw me manage to get a cuff on him, but as the male jerked violently about, it started cutting into his wrist and blood was added to the mix of sweat, hair and kit that we were rolling around in. We seemed to have migrated around the floor of the shop as we scrapped on. I could hear Andy shouting at the male over my laboured breathing as we all fought and rolled around the room. Suddenly, the door burst open and all six foot six of George strode into the room. He grabbed the man's legs in an effort to control him, but he was easily kicked off. He shouted for leg restraints and I managed to pull out the Velcro strips from my side pouch and throw it towards George. He tried to get them around the man's legs, but they were getting twisted in his trousers as he struggled. I got my baton out, but wasn't able to rack it open due to the confined space. Instead I just jabbed it into his ribs to little or no effect. I was rewarded by a punch to the head.

I could hear more sirens in the distance as we fought on. Then, the door was kicked open and Jennifer burst through the door. I like Jennifer. I'm normally thrilled enough just to be in the same postcode as her, but now I was even more overjoyed with her womanly presence. She had come off her normal shifts and been on standby for Court when she had heard my shout on the radio. I owed her two quid for a sausage sandwich she had bought me the week before. I think she wanted to make sure I didn't die too early so she could get her money back.

She quickly surveyed the scene, pulled the window blind down, stopping the free show for the bystanders outside, before yelling 'GET HIS TROUSERS OFF' and kicking away a pair of scissors that our loony was grasping for. George then yanked down the guy's strides. They had been covered in hair and that was the reason the Velcro had been getting clogged. Jenny quickly wrapped them around his feet and then his thighs and at last we had his legs under control. We were now winning the battle. George and Andy held him down as I extracted myself from under the male and applied the other cuff. Job done.

And that, dear reader, is how I 'beat up' the child's father. I hope you can see that this could all have been avoided with just a little bit of friendly cooperation.

As a post script to the incident, I had to go to the admin clerk to request a new set of handcuffs as, following the incident, mine were covered in blood. I also asked for a new set of Velcro leg restraints as mine were in a pretty poor state following the tussle. On hearing about this, Jenny obviously thought that this was an excellent opportunity not to be missed to get some new leg restraints too. Five minutes later, she marched up to the bemused clerk and delivered the startling revelation – "Mine's covered in hair."

I also caught up with the two paramedics later in the shift, who informed me that they had to disappear midway during our struggle as they had an emergency call to assist an elderly gent who was having a stroke in a car (it's amazing what you can get on the NHS nowadays!).

Our struggling male, it turned out, was on a veritable concoction of illegal pills and was taken, rattling, to hospital and then custody, before going home it seems, and telling his son about how he was the innocent victim of police brutality.

Oh, and it appears that the barber's patrons weren't so disinterested either. Apparently, they had picked up my money as it had rolled on the floor ...and pocketed it.

However, I thought it best to skip the bits about the drugs, theft and Jenny's hairy apparatus and instead counter the scandalous accusation by our druggie's offspring.

"He was resisting arrest, children," I loudly explained to the class. "Now, you must never do that if a policeman asks you to do something."

"Because you'll hit him with the stick?" asked a girl.

"Well no, no ...not always, children."

"You'll spray his eyes?" volunteered another.

"Does it knack?" asked a third.

Another good question: does it knack? To be honest, I was having a crisis of confidence in my equipment after the incident at the barber's. The pepper spray was a key weapon in my arsenal and it had failed at the very moment I needed it. Had the cocktail of drugs the nutter had taken made him temporarily immune to the effects of the spray, or was it just poor kit I had been issued? I needed to find out and, as luck would have it, I had my opportunity the following weekend.

I was on patrol with Emma, a Special Constable, when a report came in of a domestic in one of the outlying villages in the Kilo 2 area. The occupants were well known to us – a pair of alcoholics who would battle furiously on a regular basis. On arrival, however, everything appeared in order. In fact, the husband didn't even know who had called us. I chatted amicably to him in the kitchen whilst Emma sought out his wife to check that everything was ok with her. The wife, though, had different ideas and suddenly announced her presence to us by bursting through the door, sending Emma sprawling back onto the floor. She then launched herself at her husband, punching and clawing at his face in the process. He seemed just as surprised as us at the attack of this killer banshee. I stepped in between to separate them, only for her to start yelling in my face and begin punching and clawing at me instead. From what I could make out, she was accusing her husband of stealing her benefit money and had bided her time, waiting for us to arrive before announcing this heinous crime to the world.

I tried to grab her arms, as did Emma, who had now got up following the wife's ungracious greeting. However, the little banshee was thrashing about so violently, kicking and punching in all directions, that it was difficult to control her. As Emma took a blow to her chest, I thought enough was enough. Now, not only did we need to regain control quickly before anyone got badly hurt, but I also realised that this was an excellent opportunity to test my new canister of pepper and answer my question – does the kit work? Pushing our battler back, I took the can from my belt, levelled it at her eyes, shouted for Emma to stand clear, and directed a steady stream of pepper spray into wifey's eyes.

It worked perfectly. She let loose a scream as she reeled back in agony, her hands instinctively shooting up to cover her face, before she curled herself up into a protective ball. I admit, in hindsight, that it was probably a little unprofessional of me, but I allowed myself a little cheer when I saw the incapacitant take effect. Unprofessional and also ill advised as, although disorientated and in severe pain, she then launched herself in my direction, intent on harming the person responsible for her current predicament. Luckily, I was easily able to harness her forward momentum and sent her onto the floor, where she wriggled maniacally until I restrained her.

Emma, who had used this intervening period to usher the husband through the back door out of harm's way, now glanced back in to check on me, only to see me holding the wife's face in the cat litter tray as I cuffed her. It wasn't intentional – it was just there. And it wasn't exactly the way I wanted to be remembered by my colleague either but, as she has informed me on several occasions, that's the image of me that is etched on her brain to the present day.

Well, it was a long explanation, but at least I had my answer for the class.

"Yes," I answered emphatically, "it does knack. It hurts a lot."

"I thought you were here to help us," protested one child.

"Yeah, not hurt us," joined in another in the front row.

A few of the kids were starting to 'boo' now. More joined in. What the feck! Maybe I shouldn't have been laughing when I said it, but that doesn't excuse their hostility.

Beam me up, Scotty!

This was rapidly becoming my worst nightmare. Even worse than the one where I'm wading through a big tub of guacamole with no trousers on and being chased by Hitler carrying a big black dildo.

"Look, who wants to try on my hat?" I said, passing it to a kid in the front whose head looked cleaner than most.

"My uncle says a monkey could do your job," said a fat kid with big ears.

Shit! What's the world coming to? Things were starting to get increasingly raucous now.

Don't get me wrong, it's not that I don't like children. I have a daughter whom I love to bits. But when I was at school when Tufty came to visit we didn't bombard him with insults and dubious allegations.

No, when Tufty graced us with his presence, we were just pleased that he showed us how to cross the road safely and in turn treated him with the due deference that his office dictated.

Instead, I come to Sugar-Rush, expecting some lively debate about policing, and some little kid has to bring it down to such a puerile level. A monkey doing my job? Charming.

Maybe I should counter with one about him looking like the FA cup?

What about a '*Where's Noddy?*' joke?

No, no ...control yourself John, you're better than this.

"... But then tea breaks could be a problem," I replied. Aha, touché, you little twat.

Miss Jones stifled a snigger. Maybe I was winning her back onside. The room quietened as the class tried to wonder what was funny about that, and then another hand shot up from the middle of the throng.

"Have you ever arrested anyone famous?"

The answer was 'Sort of'.

I had once arrested a girl called Candice whose pictures were plastered all over the West End of London. Sadly though, just in the phone boxes. She was a semi-professional porn star with an hour glass figure ...a rare thing indeed, coming from an area where the sand has run to the bottom for most of the other girls.

She had returned home to visit her family when her Dad had thrown a wobbly about her photos. Come on, think man – you named her! What sort of career do you think she'd end up in with a name like Candice?

I had been called to the domestic and witnessed the tail end of their argument. He was having a go at her for wasting her education by doing porn. She had countered that by saying that it was art. Ah, the great 'Art or Porn' debate. Historians, critics and artists have long voiced their opinions on this matter. Some say that art should be something that makes you think, something you'd want to look at and wonder about and admire for its own sake, something that you might hang on your wall. Porn, they argue, does not engender these emotions. Others say that the difference between porn and art is the shadows and is the metaphor of perspective, whatever the hell that means.

Personally, I think that the way to tell art from porn is simple: if you were looking at it and you feel the need to hide it under the bed when you hear your girlfriend coming up the stairs, it's probably porn. If it costs £3.99 and has a wipe clean cover, it's another good indication that it's probably porn we're dealing with.

I've seen some of Candice's photos. I was torn. Yes, they made me think and admire them for their own sake, but at the same time, I'd felt compelled to hide them.

The debate had descended into a free-for-all, and blows had been traded. Candice had to come in for assault.

She was a pleasant girl and had confided in me on our way to custody that she had been troubled by a stalker for the past year. I thought it best not to confide back that I was often troubled by one after seeing her photos. So, the answer to the question is 'yes', I have arrested a minor celebrity. A very hot, and very flexible, minor celebrity.

But I digress.

The class looked at me expectantly. Maybe I had been pondering on the issue for a bit too long.

"So have you ever arrested a celebrity then?" Miss Jones prompted.

"No. Never."

C'mon, give me a break. I was just getting the teacher back on side. I didn't want to spoil things now.

The buzzer rang for break-time.

A few hands still shot up from the kids, eager no doubt, to hear more tales of drunkenness and cruelty.

"No more questions children. I'm sure the nice policeman has other things to do."

Saved by the 'belle'.

I sat for a minute or so more before getting up – just to let those pleasant memories of Candice subside.

I felt drained after my interrogation from those unruly urchins. Some things in life always just end badly. I was hoping Miss Jones would have given me an easy ride. Well, I guess answering a few questions from a classroom full of small kids was the price I had to pay for it.

I ended up asking Miss Jones out but, as I said, some things in life always just end badly.

Take 'doing a comedy bounce' off the sofa each time the other person sits down. Not too big a bounce, just a little spring. It's just meant to be a little bit of fun that's all. A word of advice here – check first to see if your new girlfriend has any self-image problems, otherwise you will spend the rest of the night texting, 'No, I was not trying to say you look fat'. This will probably be in addition to the, 'No, I was not suggesting that your flat looks like a crack house', just because you dared make an amusing quip (well I thought it was), about how it was obviously the cleaner's day off.

Or, offering to cook Sunday dinner when you don't really know too much about the mechanics of defrosting ...or indeed the cooker. Ah, diarrhoea ...so hard to spell, so easy to contract. So *that* was the devil in Miss Jones.

Let's just say I didn't see much of her after all that. After a few weeks she phoned me and ended it, trying to let me down gently by telling me, "It's not you," before thinking for a moment and then adding, "no wait, it is actually you."

CHAPTER SEVENTEEN:

Bad Dog

I have a small, furry, financial black hole that wanders around my house. A farting, attention-seeking, financial black hole. As you will have probably guessed, that particular monetary drain is Barney the dog.

Barney has cost me a lot of money over the years. This started out with chewing everything he could get his paws on. Table legs, chair legs, the connection end of the telephone, the flex to my lamp, my welcome mat, shoelaces ...I could go on, so I will ...the garden fence, my notebook and fridge magnets to name but a few.

Then he started eating between meals. At night, Barney has a bed in the kitchen. He'll pretend to be asleep, but as soon as I pat his little head and go upstairs to bed, he'll open one eye, check I'm not around and then start his search. Up on the work surfaces, inside bags, up on top of the table to see if I've left *anything* out that he could possibly consume. Loaves of bread, my sandwiches for the next day, avocados, peanuts, apples ...anything that could possibly be regarded as edible ...and even a few things that couldn't. I'm sure he doesn't enjoy some of them. I think he must still be harbouring a grudge against me for that time I had him neutered, and wants to slowly bankrupt me in revenge by eating me out of house and home. *C'mon fella, that was ages ago ...let bygones be bygones.*

Yes, he can be naughty ...but not *that* naughty really. In fact, Barney's misdemeanours fade into insignificance when I was called to a *really* naughty dog one day.

The call came in as an immediate response. A dog on the other side of town had bitten his owner's thumb off.

What the ....! I had to check again to see if I'd got the message right. Chomping his owner's thumb off – talk about biting the hand that feeds you. Yep, I had got it straight, this was one wayward scamp we were talking about here.

To be honest, as I drove over with blues and twos, I wasn't exactly sure what I was going to do when I got there.

To date, my 'dog trying to eat person' antics had been limited to:

1. Being bitten by Matthew Quinn's dog when I was in junior school. I had gone over to Matthew's house for tea. I remember the day vividly. His mum had cut his hair the day before and he looked like a chimp. It was back in the days when Curly Wurlys and Wagon Wheels were huge. I had never seen a biscuit as big as my head before, and neither had I seen a bar that was so incredibly long. It never really occurred to me it was that size because it was mostly holes. Matthew had a toy rifle from the cowboy series 'Bonanza' and we were playing cowboys and Indians, taking it in turns to be the goody and the baddy. I don't think you're allowed to do that anymore. Out in the garden, his dog was busy playing wheelbarrows with another dog. Matthew's dad saw it and came out with a bucket of water. Apparently, the dogs were in a same sex relationship and he didn't approve. After the water was thrown, Matthew's dog ran in circles around the garden and when I went to shoot him with the toy rifle, he came over and bit me on my leg. I remember thinking that I was the cowboy, so why was he biting me?

2. Being bitten by a wild, rabid beast whilst on duty. OK, not exactly a wild, rabid beast ...but a beast nonetheless ...OK, a Westie. The West Highland Terrier had been running in and out of the traffic on the High Street, so I stopped the patrol

car, and tried to get him off the road before he caused an accident. The dog catching device, or to call it by its proper name, 'the stick with a hoop at the end' was back at the station, so I was left to go it alone ...just me pitted against the forces of nature ...or a small dog at least. After much Keystone Cops antics, I managed to get the dog off the road and to the safety of the pavement, at which time he then rewarded me with a bite to my hand. I called to update Comms, telling them, "I've been bitten by a dog." To the best of my recollection, I said this in a coherent and controlled manner. Nancy in the Comms room, however, has re-interpreted this as being said in some sort of over-emphasised Welsh accent, and likes to repeat the phrase to me each time I chat to her. I've often thought of telling her that she can be arrested for impersonating a police officer ...especially impersonating him badly ...but I guess this law is generally reserved for the type of people my brother arrested down in his Force area.

The felon in question would approach the working girls in the red light area and then pretend he was an undercover police officer, offering them the choice of 'sausage or summons'. Now *that's* the crime of impersonating a police officer.

3. The third of my 'dog eating person' antics (just in case you had forgotten what the hell we were on about originally) was listening to 'Marie Provost'. This is the Nick Lowe song about the true tale of an old black and white film star who faded into obscurity when 'talkies' came along. She became a recluse and lived alone with her small dog for company. Eventually, when no one had heard from her for a while, they became concerned about her welfare. Apparently, when the cops eventually kicked in the door to her cheap hotel room up in Hollywood West, she had been dead for several weeks. In desperation, her pet Dachshund had started to dispose of her. I sang along with Nick – '...*well even little doggies have got to eat! ...That hungry little Dachshund!*'

4. Finally, as a last minute stand-in, due to the officer in the case being sick, I attended a case conference on my first day at Sandford. I heard the desperately sad case of an unfit mother and her badly neglected two year old who was repeatedly found wandering the streets. In the latest incident, the police had found the baby crawling across a main road in the town. The social worker waxed lyrical about the dangers to the child, finishing off with, "Anything could have happened to the baby. She could have been eaten by a dog!" Eaten by a dog? What sort of place was I coming to? Baby-eating dogs roaming the streets of Sandford? Shit, was it too late to re-enlist in the Army? It seemed a bit safer there.

Psychologists say that obsessive compulsive list makers (and I guess that includes me) are trying to create an illusion of control in otherwise chaotic lives. I've never been that deep, but maybe that is what I was doing now. I always thought I had a pretty ordered life, although I know that sometimes when I've made my 'to do' list, I've added on things I've already done, just so I can tick them off straight away and feel that inflated sense of achievement. Actually, if anyone reading this has the time to analyse the motivation and reasoning behind people's compulsions to create checklists and inventories – get a life!

But I digress.

None of these previous dog-related experiences gave me any clue as to how I was to deal with this snacking dog. Maybe there *were* baby eating dogs on the prowl in Sandford. Maybe our hound just happened to be on a diet. Maybe tonight was doggy Weight Watchers night. '*Oh I couldn't eat a whole baby today. I'll just have a thumb, that's only forty sins. I'd just die of embarrassment, darling, if I didn't reach my target.*'

No, Mr Dog, if you ate a whole baby you'd die from a bullet in the head from the firearms unit. I'm sure one of the girls on the unit has a pair of .38 specials.

Anyway, this reminiscing and conjecture wasn't helping at all. What should I do when I got there? Arrest the hound? Stick the cuffs on his little paws? Beat the pooch till he regurgitated the offending digit?

If he did regurgitate it, what should I wrap it in? Chad once found an ear at the scene of a particularly nasty fight. It had obviously been bitten off by the offender, and then spat out. He took it back to the station, emptied the ice tray from the fridge into a Netto carrier bag, put the ear in with the ice and happily set off to the hospital where the owner of the ear was being treated for other injuries.

"Well, that's fucked that ear up," said the ungrateful doctor. Apparently, you need to keep the body part cold, but letting it come into direct contact with ice 'fucks up the ear' – it's a medical term. Chad didn't hear the last of it ....neither did the victim.

Biting ears seems to be in vogue at the moment ...all the best criminals are at it, don't you know. Actually, scrub out the word 'best'. Two Sandford brothers had a grudge against another villain in the neighbourhood who was breaking into houses and nicking all the best stuff before they got to it. They decided to teach this usurper a lesson. This lesson in question consisted of kicking his door in and then biting off his ears. A lesson, I'm sure you will agree, that if executed correctly, would certainly be a lesson that one wouldn't forget in a hurry. The trouble is, as all teachers will tell you (except maybe PE teachers), that you need to do some preparation and planning beforehand, or things have a tendency to go terribly wrong. Cue embarrassed brothers who didn't adhere to the '6 P principle': Prior Preparation Prevents Piss Poor Performance. Instead, they broke into the wrong house and, consequently, bit the ears off the wrong man. He may never wear glasses again.

Back to the Sandford digit devourer. Was he still an angry young dog? What's to say he wasn't going to bite my fingers off? From the information I'd been given, it didn't sound like our canine would be that respectful of the office of constable. They might call us out to incidents like this, but my digits can get bitten off just as easily as the next man's.

Was he loose? Would he need rounding up? The stick with a hoop on the end was back in the station somewhere. We had been hooking Bob with it last week, but goodness knows where the hell it was now.

Comms confirmed that ambulance and the Council's dog warden were en route, but they were still a good ten minutes away.

As I arrived on scene, Ron pulled up in his panda. We walked over to the house in question and peered over the fence to see a very pale looking man sitting on a stool with blood all over his hands, looking like he'd just been shaken awake. He was, to put it in local vernacular, 'shaking like a shitting dog'. Nearby, our actual shitting dog was pottering about, licking his doggy lips.

Dogs are essentially like small children. I'm sure that at this juncture some smug, softly spoken, liberal, holier-than-thou social worker type, possibly wearing sandals, will beg to differ, but just hear me out. Apart from the obvious fact that they both potter around on all fours and are stupid, they both live 'in the moment'. They don't know all about cause and effect. Causality is the relationship between an event (the *cause*) and a second event (the *effect*), where the second event is a consequence of the first. Even I had to read that twice and I can play chess. If I started to admonish the hound now, he'd wonder what the hell I was doing it for. They say that one dog year is equal to seven human years. On that basis, although the dastardly deed happened ten or so minutes earlier, to the dog it probably seemed like days ago. Anyway, we hadn't heard what he had to say in his defence yet.

Despite the universal assumption of innocent until proven guilty, I wasn't about to take any reckless chances with my own digits. I'm quite attached to them. Instead, I put my leather gloves on, leant over the fence and tried to shoo the dog back into the house. When that failed, I moved onto Plan B. This entailed retrieving my packed lunch from the car and chucking bits of my cheese sandwiches towards the back door, hoping to lure our hungry hound back into the house. It worked to a degree, but after he wolfed down my lunch, he just came back out, wanting more. But there was no more. Only a packet of crisps left and I wasn't about to give him that. There are limits you know. However, Plan C quickly materialised when a neighbour started throwing frozen fishcakes over the fence. They were heavier and more aerodynamic than my floppy sandwiches. Damn, why didn't I think of that? I'm not too sure about the morality involved here of feeding a dog frozen food, but if it got our four legged friend out of the way so we could treat our victim, I wasn't about to complain.

She was targeting them right at the back door – and was a pretty good shot, too. They were just landing in the doorway though and our canine was just popping his head in to grab the cake and not going right inside. I told her we needed deeper intrusion, which, in hindsight, sounded quite rude. She must have known what I meant though, as she quickly disappeared back into her house and then just as quickly reappeared armed with a tennis racquet. Damn, why didn't I think of that? She threw a fishcake up into the air and smashed the breaded potato snack through her neighbour's open door. From the way she served that frozen snack I'm sure that – unlike Cliff Richard – she had more than a touch of Sue Barker about her. With that direct hit the dog scampered into the house to retrieve another fishcake (and possibly turn the oven on, I don't actually know for sure). Ron pulled the door shut with a broom that he had hooked over the handle and then I quickly ran in and shut the door, until the obvious suddenly dawned on us.

"Is there anyone else in the house mate?" we asked.

"No."

Phew!

"Ambulance is on its way, let's have a look at the hand." As he held it up for us to see, we could clearly see it was sans pollex.

"No more thumb wars for him," whispered Ron.

"So what happened?"

I'm not sure if I completely believe what was then said to me. Our patient stated that he had been grooming the offending dog. All was happy in their world until someone down the street had turned on a jet wash. The noise of the jet apparently shocked our furry friend, and he span around and bit down hard on the owner's thumb, taking it clean off.

I say that I'm not completely sure if I believe what he then said to me on the basis that this guy had his trousers around his ankles. In all the time I've groomed Barney, I've never felt the need to do this trouserless. I just have the mildest of hunches that maybe he wasn't grooming the hound in that sense after all, and that maybe our friend was lucky to get away with just his thumb being bitten off.

The ambulance arrived on scene soon after.

"Was he trying to give him a bone or something?" the paramedic asked.

"Aye, something like that," I replied.

I explained that I had done a bit of First Aid, but that our alleged victim had not been overly complimentary about my attempts. When he complained about my bandaging, I'd informed him that I was doing it to the best of my abilities. His less than polite response had been something along the lines of 'I'd rather have someone who knew what he was doing, but not trying very hard, rather than someone who didn't know what he was doing and trying his best'. Lovely.

I think he came from the bluff and bluster school of thought; those who proudly boast, 'I speak my mind, me. I say what I think and I think what I say'. I say 'school of thought', but I don't think 'thought' ever comes into it. When did a bit of tact and diplomacy become such bad qualities to possess? I have feelings, too, you know. He was about as charming as a dented tin of custard.

Any sympathy that I might have had for the dubious dog lover evaporated after that point.

Still, I don't think we'll ever know the full facts of what happened between man and beast that fateful day, and it's only a hunch I've got, but it certainly brings a whole new meaning to the question 'What's your pet hate?'

CHAPTER EIGHTEEN:

Jumper

The school secretary was on the line.

"The Headmaster has lost his testees. Can you help?"

No, it wasn't that naughty dog at it again. The local Headmaster was helping out by invigilating the exams for some children from the nearby correctional facility and they had evidently gone AWOL. Could I assist in locating them?

Its official title is the Young Offenders Institute, but down at the station we tend to call it the 'Centre of Excellence'. The offenders enter at one end as a minor felon, however, once inside, they pool all their knowledge together and then exit the other end as master criminals – Convict University PLC.

I duly got in my panda car and started scouring the streets for a handful of delinquents. After half an hour, I had located three of them and was heading back to the school with them squeezed into the back of the vehicle.

Then I saw him. I say him, but at this distance it could just have easily been a her. No ...it's a him alright, I can see him scratching himself now. He certainly wasn't missing his testees.

He was balancing on the side barrier of the disused railway bridge that spanned one of the main routes through Sandford. He stood, arms akimbo, as if he was preparing to dive head first onto the road below. He looked as if he was just one stage away from adopting the pose of the plastic man in the game of *Mousetrap*, and two stages away from spoiling the day of the town's street sweepers.

There was a poster on the bridge next to him. This is what it said:

HAPPY 40th DAVE.

Either this was Dave ...not happy with his presents, or some ying yang thing. Where some Dave is really happy, some non Dave is sad. Of the two choices, I'd guess that this was more likely to be the sad Dave ...looking as if he was planning to end it all ...on the main road running into Sandford ...during the morning rush hour ...on my shift.

I pulled over and got my passengers to sit by the side of the road.

"Stay here, boys. I'll just find out what the fella on the bridge is up to."

"Ecilop, I think he's trying to top himself," naughty Norman volunteered.

Naughty Norman was one of the testees, and notorious for his own botched suicide attempts. Whilst most of the youths at the centre had 'street cred' nicknames, Norman had the same nickname that he had been given when he had started misbehaving as a toddler. At seventeen, it didn't really seem to convey the seriousness of his current transgressions, but the name had stuck nonetheless. In turn Norman called us Ecilop because that was what was written on the bonnet of our cars.

"Well, let's hope he is as good at this as you are then, Norm," I replied.

Perhaps the only thing funnier than watching a dog scrape its bum along the ground, is the full list of Naughty Norman's failed attempts at ending it all.

Exhibit A.

Taking an overdose of antibiotics.

The ambulance staff said he wouldn't die, and probably wouldn't even get a cold for the next week or so.

Exhibit B.

Trying to hang himself from a tree.

Except he made the rope too long and when he jumped, he landed on the floor, breaking his ankles instead.

Exhibit C.

Trying to electrocute himself by putting a radio – plugged into the mains – in the bath with him.

Unfortunately for Norman (and us), as his mother went upstairs, she noticed that the hoover had been unplugged and usurped by another, unidentified plug. Taking it out of the socket, she traced the lead to the bathroom where she was unlucky enough to witness a naked Norman standing in the bath, shouting, "I hope you're happy now!" before throwing the radio into the soapy water. After a small fizzle and a couple of seconds contemplating, Norman realised he wasn't actually dead. On looking up and seeing his mum at the door, holding the plug in her hand, he realised he had only succeeded in showing her what a wet, pasty, naked, unfit, waster looked like.

Exhibit D.

Trying to get chopped in half by a speeding train.

The best time for this, however, is not during the train strike. Naughty Norman was found several hours later, suffering from the initial stages of hypothermia.

Exhibit E.

Trying to drown himself.

Norman had paid for a pedallo, and then pedalled to the middle of the town boating lake where he had proceeded to hold his nose and jump into the water, only to find it only came up to his knees (can anyone tell me why anyone who is really intent on drowning themselves would hold their nose before jumping in?).

Exhibit F.

Trying to set fire to himself.

Except he doused himself in diesel instead of petrol. Not the horrific end that he imagined for himself, although pretty horrific for his mum whose insurance premiums rose dramatically thereafter.

Finally, Exhibit H.

Trying to choke himself.

I had arrested Norman after he had pulled a knife on me when I had gone round to his mum's house following a report of some criminal damage. An hour later, a disgruntled Norman was stood in the inside of his cell, shouting that he was going to teach us all a lesson and do himself in, then we'd be in trouble, he told us. As a result, Geezer then found himself on suicide watch outside the cell. He called up on the radio half an hour later telling me that I had to see this, so I hurried down to custody. 'This' it transpired, was worth the journey. 'This' was a classic. 'This' was Norman clenching his two hands around his own throat, making gurgling noises and trying to choke off his own oxygen supply. As it started taking effect, he didn't have the energy to keep his arms in position and they dropped to his side, allowing him to breathe again. Clearly not a follower of the old maxim, *If at first you don't succeed, destroy all evidence that you have tried*, Norm did it again. And failed. And tried again. And failed. And so on, ad nauseum. Robert the Bruce would have been proud of the persistent failure, if not a little puzzled.

But I digress.

I scrambled up the embankment towards poster man.

When I eventually reached the bridge, I put my hands in my pockets and ambled over towards him, stopping near the edge.

"Is it your birthday then?" I asked.

"No," came the reply. I could see him clearer now ...and smell him. He smelt like a brewery. About thirty, dishevelled, bleary eyed and looking like he'd worn the same clothes for days. He didn't appear to be in the mood for a chat, but taking a hint has never been my forte, so I rudely continued nonetheless.

"Thought it wasn't. So what's going on here then, mate?" I asked.

He was standing on the wrong side of the safety barrier, one hand holding the rail, the other clutching a half empty bottle of whisky. He was shaking ...not through fear ...maybe due to the bleak, overcast November morning ...but the smart money was on the fact that it was alcohol induced.

"I'm going to kill myself. Happy now? Can't you just give me a patronising lecture and leave me alone to get on with it?" He seemed all angst and attitude, just like a Mike Leigh movie.

"No problems. I'll just have to get some details first, though. You know what it's like – paperwork and all that."

"So you're not going to try and talk me out of it then?"

"God, no. That's way out of my league. They've got highly paid Superintendents to do that. I've not got much on this morning though, and after you jump, I can keep you company until the ambulance arrives, if you like?"

"Really? You being serious?"

"Sure. Just got to take some kids to school, but they can wait. It'll be an adventure for them, anyway. When they see the mess you make, maybe it'll put them off from doing it themselves in the future."

"No, I mean serious about the not talking me down?"

"Well, it's a free world, but between you and me, I'd rather not have to fill out all the forms if I can help it, but if I must, I guess I'll have to. So what's the story then?"

Eventually, I managed to tease some more information from him. Our poster man was actually called Geoff, and Geoff was not having a good time at home.

"I didn't put it up!" he assured me, nodding towards the birthday banner, just to show that whilst he might be prepared to disrupt the town's traffic, he wouldn't dare flout council directives over unauthorised signage.

I discreetly got on the radio and told Comms that I had found a jumper on the bridge. I had to clarify that I wasn't actually reporting some lost property, and quickly the penny dropped and they started to action things at their end.

Soon, ambulance were on standby around the corner, the Force negotiator was travelling down from HQ, the community support officers were keeping the gathering crowd under control and officers had the road blocked off in both directions. Whilst Geoff might be perfectly happy to spoil his own day by diving off the bridge, I'm sure some passer-by in an open top sports car didn't want Geoffrey tossing himself off onto them.

In the meantime, I set about trying to develop some kind of dialogue with our friend who seemed intent on his own personal path to self-destruction. It's just that suicide seems such a tragic waste of a life and is never something that can be taken in isolation. It affects a myriad of people. It devastates whole families.

I was both perturbed and troubled, but at the same time intrigued. When did it get so hard just to take life as it comes? When did the world start winning? Why did he just decide to turn his back and walk away? More importantly, how could we help?

I say I tried to develop a dialogue, but when Geoff realised I was genuinely interested, it turned into a monologue as he poured forth his issues and problems. The marital difficulties, the financial issues, the depression, the drinking, the awkward incidents ...the only light he could see was the one at the end of a barrel. Geoff poured his heart out to me for about half an hour as we stood on the edge of that bridge. Crisis after crisis, all with such intensity.

I don't know if you have ever played the card game Trumps? How about Top Trumps? The idea of the game is that you have to trump your opponent by putting down a better card with a higher value. I don't know why I'm telling you this, you probably know it already.

I could empathise, but I could never really know the depth of his despair. I didn't have the answers. If I did, I'd have been sitting in a nice warm consulting room somewhere, earning considerably more than I do now, as opposed to freezing my knackers off on a precarious ledge on the outskirts of Sandford.

No, I didn't have the solution. I'm not sure if anyone really did, but at least if I could stop him killing himself now, I'd have a chance to get him to some of those overpaid professionals who just might. And I'd get back in the warmth. And save myself a fair wedge of paperwork to boot.

The only skill I did have, dubious as it may be, was a penchant for useless trivia ...and Top Trumps.

"So you have a black dog on your shoulder now and again? I have a black dog actually living with me. I have to clear up his shits too!" I told Geoff.

Trumped!

"Marital problems? Look, I know marriage is a good three-year commitment, but I'm divorced, and I have an ex-girlfriend who is stalking me."

Trumped!

"You say you're not sure if your wife still loves you? Well, I live with my dog and I'm pretty sure he's just with me because he's suffering from Stockholm Syndrome."

Trumped!

"You say you made a scene at your son's christening by turning up drunk? According to twelfth century historian, William of Malmesbury, King Ethelred the Unready had managed to crap on the font at his christening," I informed him.

Trumped and followed through!

It may not have been the official line in suicide negotiating – I wouldn't know, I'm not senior enough to go on the course – but it did manage to get Geoff laughing. Five minutes later, and with the promise of a hot chocolate back at the station, we both scrambled down the embankment.

We arrived at the station just as the harassed negotiator arrived. I briefed him, but thought it best to leave out the bit about the Saxon royal doing his business in the sink. Some of these senior officers can be a bit uptight about things like that.

After the promised hot beverage, I took Geoff down to the hospital to see the medical professionals. The doctor said he wasn't surprised that Geoff had tried to top himself as he hadn't been taking his antidepressants.

"I'm not surprised that Geoff has tried to top himself as he hasn't been taking his antidepressants," said the doctor.

See, I told you.

I then took him down to the psychiatric hospital on the edge of town where Geoffrey booked himself in for a month or so of relaxation and recuperation.

I'd give a wave to him each time I saw him there as, for various reasons, I become a regular visitor to the wards over the next few months.

A month later, I arrested the King of Finland. Why he lived in a flat in Ruth Reid House, near the town centre, instead of in a palace set amongst the stunning scenery and unspoiled wasteland, I really don't know. He *was* actually called the King of Finland, having changed his name by deed poll from Alan Jones.

His neighbours had first become concerned after he had sat out all the previous night on the balcony in a canoe, with radars made out of clothes hangers stuck on the back and front, apparently awaiting an invasion by the Germans. Later that day, bank staff had rung in when he had threatened to blow up their establishment. The reason given was that they wouldn't give him a loan to buy Africa. I think two hundred pounds is about my cash limit, so I could see his point. That wouldn't even get you a bit of Mozambique and it's a bugger if you have really set your heart on getting something. However, disappointment is one thing and laying waste with a big bomb is quite another.

When Geezer and I finally traced his Highness, he was dressed entirely in black, criss-crossing the town, running from shop entrance to shop entrance. He informed us that he was an undercover cop on a mission and that if we blew his cover, he'd have us executed.

At the risk of incurring his royal displeasure, we told him he had to come with us. His royal displeasure was consequently incurred, and he told us that if we tried to get him into our waiting police van, he would get snipers to shoot us in the head. Undeterred, we led the secret agent to the wagon.

He then started to stage whisper something into the cuff on his anorak. "Code Red. Unit 2 take out the police officer wearing glasses to my right. Head shot required."

I obviously didn't take it seriously, but checked nevertheless on which side of the King I was standing. Geezer was on the right. That's OK then.

"Unit 4, rocket propelled grenade needed. Shoot it into the officer on the left. Unit 3, several high velocity shots to rip his head apart. Do it now!"

Hang on a second! Why does Geezer just get a head shot and I get the Full Monty?

Yeah, yeah, I know it was all in his imagination, but I didn't fancy hanging around at the back of the van, if you don't mind. As we slammed the van door, I could hear him counting down from fifty. He broke off at forty to tell us that he'd set a bomb to blow up the whole world ...and then he'd buy Africa. I'm no expert, but I don't think he had thought this through somehow.

Gwen and I ended up searching his flat afterwards, just in case he did indeed possess any bomb-making paraphernalia. What we did find was an Aladdin's cave of electronics and militaria that appeared to have been bought from various car boot sales and army surplus stores. Most of it was useless but had been stuck together to resemble various technical looking apparatus. We also found his bemused girlfriend who was convinced that our charge *was* a spy and had been in the Special Forces, involved in covert ops in the Falklands, Ireland and Iraq, despite the fact that he was only twenty five.

We continued to catalogue the various items strewn about

the flat. One box contained his 'operations' medical kit and our attention was immediately brought to a bottle marked 'Rohypnol'.

"It's got a *Best Before Date*," said Gwen. "Oh no, hang on, it just says *Best Before Date.*"

We took it away regardless and did some analysis, but it just turned out to be salty water. I guess it was just going to have to be a case of *emission impossible* for our secret agent.

Tests proved that all his fancy gadgets were just junk. It seemed the King lived in his own fantasy land, a hero in his own mind, a legend in his own lunchtime.

It's just a shame that it all had to spill out into the real world and involve us. He wasn't a bad sort really.

My other visit to the mental hospital had been with Mrs Nation. Lucy had made a series of bizarre calls, including the memorable one where she informed me that she had lent her vacuum cleaner to Prince Charles, who hadn't returned it yet.

"Well, it's not theft then, if you lent it to him," I explained. "Give it a few weeks and I'm sure he'll get it back to you. Look, here it is anyway, in the cupboard."

"Well, he must have sneaked it back in. He's still got my frying pan though."

She was a nice old woman, and I didn't really mind going and having a chat with her about her various incidents but, unfortunately, she had started to become increasingly erratic and was becoming a danger to herself. In the end, Social Services took the decision to move her to the hospital, and had asked us to come along in case anything kicked off.

When I arrived, she was wearing a hat fashioned out of tinfoil. She told me that it was to protect her from the 'zaps' that her neighbours were sending. Apparently, they were sending electric shocks through the windows that caused her to yell out an expletive every time they hit her. To demonstrate, she removed her protective headgear, waited a few seconds, and then shouted 'Soapytitwank!' whilst simultaneously throwing her hands up in the air. I told her I thought it best that she put her hat back on if that's what happened when she removed it.

She told me that her neighbours apparently also sent another, more elaborate zap at six o'clock every morning, which caused her to hear birds chirping and singing. The bastards ...I think they must be zapping my house too!

I watched as the social worker explained to Lucy that she would be better off where they were going, and I tended to agree. It could have proved to be very embarrassing being zapped when the vicar was round for tea.

I often wonder what happened to Lucy, the King and Geoff.

The King, I guess, is probably quite happy. If you genuinely believe you rule Finland, things must be pretty sweet. We are the ones who are disturbed over his actions, think he's not all there, but if his Highness himself is actually convinced that he rules a vast swathe of beautiful countryside, he must be as happy as Larry. Now, if he can just control his imperialist tendencies, things will be even better.

Lucy? I admit that having your Dyson taken by the man who owns the Duchy of Cornwall Estate must be grating, particularly as he probably has someone in to do the cleaning for him, anyway. However, I'm sure that in the secure enviroment of the mental health unit, she'll feel a lot happier and contented. They probably have a cupboard with a lock on there for the cleaning stuff, too.

And, finally Geoff. Well, I don't need to wonder any more. I saw him in Tesco car park with a female in the passenger seat and his young son sitting in the back looking like he was doing some colouring. It appears that things must have turned around for him. There is a lot of satisfaction in doing a job which results in a wife still having her husband, and a little boy still having his dad.

I was about to pull out of the parking bay as Geoff

reversed in next to me. He gave me a grin as he finished reversing, just as I gave him a smile back and pulled forward. I'm not sure what exactly happened, and I don't know if it's ever happened to you, but the next thing I saw was Geoff flailing about and mouthing a rather unpleasant obscenity. I think that in that split second after he stopped, when he saw me moving slowly forward, he was convinced that he was still travelling backwards, hence the look of sheer panic on his face and the unsavoury language. I can't be sure, but I think I could see Mrs Geoff was on the phone – probably to the hospital, and probably asking if his room was still free.

CHAPTER NINETEEN:

Dracula

There are millions of calls made each year to the police, both on the emergency and non-emergency lines. When that phone rings, no one knows what may be on the other end of the line.

Some calls may trigger a number of potential incidents that need to be investigated. For example, a well meaning member of the public will ring in an incident, but are maybe not quite sure where they actually are.

"I saw someone who looks as if they are about to jump off a bridge."

"Where was that?"

"I'm not sure exactly, but we are travelling north on the motorway. It's somewhere between junction 59 and junction 60."

There may be five bridges between those junctions – cue five separate potential incidents that need to be checked out as a matter of urgency – or to put it another way, five separate vehicles that need to be dispatched for one possible jumper.

Or else it may be duplicate calls regarding the same job. A male might be seen brandishing a knife in Carisbrooke Way. He then runs down East Bridge Street and on into West Bridge Street. We could get a call regarding the male from each location. Can we make the assumption it's the same offender or are these three separate incidents unfolding? Can we afford to take the risk? Again, multiple units may be required to check each location to ensure that the public is kept safe.

However, as confusing as this may be, we'd rather have several calls rather than none at all. Believe it or not, sometimes a horrendous event can occur in front of crowds of people and nobody does anything at all – no one calls the police, assists the victim or requests an ambulance. Sometimes, it can be because the onlookers are afraid of reprisals, but other times, it's a result of what is called the 'bystander effect'.

In short, the term *bystander effect* refers to the phenomenon in which the greater the number of people present, the less likely people are to help a person in distress. It seems that bystanders monitor the reactions of other people in an emergency situation to see if others think that it is necessary to intervene. Since everyone is doing exactly the same thing (nothing), they all conclude from the inaction of others that help is not needed. From the studies carried out, it appears that when an emergency situation occurs, observers are more likely to take action if there are few or no other witnesses around.

Sometimes, calls are made in good faith but just turn out to be a bit pre-emptive.

"Kilo 1 mobile, this is Control, we have a report of a dead body in a front garden in Seal Street."

"Kilo 1 mobile en route," with blue lights flashing and sirens sounding as befits a cadaver being discovered by some poor member of the public innocently going about their daily business.

"Kilo 1 mobile, this is Control, we've just received an update. Kill the blues. Apparently the corpse has just got up and walked away."

"It's a miracle!"

But by far the favourites of the Comms room staff are the bizarre ones, and from the tales they tell, it appears that there are no shortage of crazy calls.

My tame Comms operator friend told me about a call that came in from an angry woman.

"I want to complain about the farmer across the road. Every morning at six a.m his cock wakes me up and it's getting on top of me now."

Was it a noise complaint or a sexual assault?

Sometimes, the call handlers will confide in me that they think they must have just misheard what's going on.

Caller: "I want to report that I'm trapped in my house."

Police: "Is someone holding you against your will in your home?"

Caller: "Yes. A frog."

Police: "A frog is holding you against your will?"

Caller: "Yes, there's a frog on my porch."

Police: "A frog?"

Caller: "Yes, I'm scared of frogs. I can't go out the front door. He might get me."

Police: "It's not really a police matter, but have you thought about going out the back door?"

Caller: "Good idea!"

Sometimes, it's worth questioning that little bit further.

Caller with heavy Geordie accent: "It's an emergency. They're shooting. Shooting through the windows."

Police: "Shooting?"

Caller: "Yes, shooting."

Police, whilst simultaneously getting the armed response unit scrambled: "What weapons are they using?"

Caller: "Weapons? What are you on about? They're shooting that me wife is a big, fat slag."

Other times, through no fault of their own, the Comms operator are made to feel as though they are in the wrong. I guess the police non-emergency number must be similar to a local clinic judging by the next conversation.

Police: "Police, how can we help?"

Caller: "I'd like to make an appointment for an X-ray please."

Police: "OK, so how can we help you? This is the police."

Caller: "The police? I was calling Dr Walder's office. How DARE you answer her phone!"

Sometimes though, the police themselves can be guilty of creating confusion by virtue of the way in which we report an incident.

Between Sandford and the neighbouring town in Kilo 3 is a small village. Hardly a village really, more a collection of houses clinging to either side of the grey ribbon that twists and turns in, and then just as quickly out of this conurbation. Some say that witches live there. Unfortunately, not hot witches like Tabitha or Sabrina. It does have a fine pub set back from the road, but apart from that, I'm sure to some drivers the village is just regarded as an annoyance, causing them to slow down to thirty before they can pick up their speed again. To others, it's no bother at all as they don't seem to feel the need to decelerate and adhere to the safety limits. I've often seen the skid marks across the road, or come out to a vehicle that has misjudged the bend into the village and careered through someone's garden fence. As I've blue lighted through the village from one job to another, I've almost been caught out once or twice myself, particularly when it's icy.

One frosty autumnal morning, for two speeding motorcyclists, 'almost' became reality when they lost control of their bikes and slammed into each other, sending the vehicles sliding down the road before they eventually collided with a stone wall thirty or so yards further down the village.

George was travelling to the morning briefing at Sandford from Kilo 3 when he turned into the corner and saw the carnage before him. His shouts into the radio got us all sitting up even before we could make sense of what he was saying. We all instinctively held our radios closer to our ears to catch what was happening, although at the volume George was operating, I'm sure the whole station could hear him.

"Urgent! I've just come across a collision between two motorcyclists. I'm going to need some help closing off the road – there are body parts everywhere!"

Shit! All of us ran out to our cars, put our sirens on and started to drive through the deserted streets at breakneck speed to the scene. Comms, meanwhile, had put the emergency call out to Fire and Ambulance and their sirens soon joined ours, drowning out the morning chorus with a cacophony of urgent yelps and wails.

I should at this stage, perhaps, explain that George does have a tendency to overreact sometimes. I don't know whether he sees himself as a frustrated thespian, but some of his radio commentaries are legendary.

At one assault we both attended, his commentary on the radio was a classic.

"The signs are decidedly foreboding. The body of the victim is now lying motionless on the bare stretcher, a limp arm hanging loosely down, fingers outstretched, gently touching the damp tarmac of the road. A solitary paramedic checks the pulse before gently lifting the limb back into position and pushing the ensemble into the safety of the ambulance. The Spartan blue light clears the highway as the vehicle moves off towards the infirmary."

Usually a quick, "He's off to hospital," would have done just as well.

In this instance, the convoy of emergency vehicles raced through the streets only to be greeted by the two riders sitting happily on the verge, exchanging biker tales. A rather sheepish George had to then explain to the gathered throng of emergency personnel that when he said 'body parts', he actually meant motorcycle body parts. By the look on the faces of Pugh, Pugh, Barney McGrew, Cuthbert and Dibble (Grubb must have been sitting back in the fire engine), I'd definitely say that's one less wave for George from now on.

Sometimes though, it's the different accents that can cause confusion.

I've never really had much inclination to transfer to CID, mainly because I haven't got much of a dress sense. However, I don't think that this detective lark can be too difficult. I base this groundless assumption on the fact that I deduced five pieces of information from a prisoner in custody without even asking him one question.

Firstly, secondly and indeed thirdly, I correctly guessed that the gent sitting on the wooden bench was called Paul, that he was drunk and that he also had military links.

These three nuggets of information were gleaned when I peered through the bars of the gate to custody.

"Let us in please, Sarge."

Daisy then pressed a button under the custody counter, releasing the magnetic door contacts.

"PULL!" she shouted to me.

Simultaneously, as I opened the gate, the male jumped up from the bench, came to attention, saluted and slurred, "Yeshsssir!"

I think we can safely say military links, inebriated and called Paul, don't you?

In custody, as part of getting all the details from the prisoner, we need to establish occupation. When I usually ask one of our frequent flyers if they have a job, you'd think that I had just asked them if they have herpes.

"You what? Of course I don't have a job!" they reply most indignantly. Most of our repeat offenders are unemployed – a job would get in the way of their burgling and other various criminal activities. Maybe 'removals' could fit as an occupation but even that would be pushing it. Often, although obviously fit enough to go out burgling and robbing, they'll inform me that they are off on the sick or disabled. They are what we would term 'DSS disabled' as opposed to 'actually disabled'.

However, today was different. A black cat had run across my path on the way to work. I couldn't remember if that was supposed to herald good luck or bad luck ...I just knew something special was going to happen today ...and it did. We got an offender who actually worked!

Paul had responded with a, "Why aye, man!" when Daisy asked him the question. A North Eastener my delicate ears would lead me to believe. Fact number four in the bag.

I had only one more piece of information to go to establish my superior investigative skills. For my next trick, I would determine how old our prisoner was just from his occupation.

When Daisy asked what he did, Paul mumbled that he was now in the transport business, but when she selected 'driver' from the drop down list of occupations on the screen, he shook his head vigorously and indicated, by pretending to write in the air, that he worked in the office. At this point, as poor Daisy seemed rushed off her feet with a multiplicity of other tasks demanding her attention, I gallantly decided to help out, and after consulting the list, I selected another transport related occupation.

"Haulier?" I asked Daisy.

Paul, who obviously thought I was talking to him, jumped to his feet and shouted out, "Thirty seven." Fact number five. Sherlock Donoghue reporting for duty. Does this tie go with this deerstalker?

All that was left was for me to ask Daisy what the difference was between a kangaroo and a kangaroot.

Answer: one is a marsupial and the other is what Geordie Paul says when he's stuck in a cell. She didn't laugh either.

Other times though, even the basics can be hard to establish.

I had gone to a house with Lloyd to take a crime report for a case of criminal damage. It was a nice house, in a nice part of town, owned in turn, by a nice couple. The type of place where the TV was turned off, a cup of tea offered and you were one hundred per cent certain that the rim would be smeg free. After ten at night, we are usually double crewed in a vehicle. When we were, we usually took it in turns to complete the paperwork. I had fronted the last job, this one was Lloyd's turn.

I sat on the sofa, playing with their pet dog, whilst my partner opened up his note book.

"Can I take your name please?"

"Lesley," replied the wife.

"Do you spell that with an 'ey' or an 'ie' at the end?" queried Lloyd, his pen hovering above the paper.

"It's a different spelling for men and women," she replied, rolling her eyes in a sort of 'how silly is that' type of way.

"I can never remember which is which," my colleague added, pen still poised.

"Women are the ones with boobs," clarified the husband.

Sometimes, it's not even a case of misunderstandings. Some callers just blatantly exaggerate to get a quicker police response. We call them 'not as reported' which is an important thing to say to Comms when you attend, otherwise they will expect you to provide a logical sequel to the erroneous call that initially came in.

"There are twenty people fighting in the street," came the report over the radio.

Gwen and I responded, racing our vehicle through the dusky Sandford streets.

When we arrived, there were a couple of kids kicking a football about.

"I want to report thirty males scrapping," was the next call into Comms about thirty minutes later.

Another rapid response and this time just a deserted street.

Half an hour later, another report of youths fighting, this time the number had increased to fifty. Another blue light run, and another empty road. Despite the pattern to these calls, you can't just not bother turning up because the one time you don't, that will be the time it's for real. Mind you, I'd also found that I didn't bother becoming nervous or wound up anymore about going to calls of mass carnage, or of dubious males running around the streets with machetes, hacking at innocent bystanders. Don't get me wrong, I hadn't suddenly become complacent – or super brave for that matter – I was just trying to look after my health.

It's the old 'fight or flight' response we had as cavemen whenever we happened across a Sabre-tooth tiger. Your brain suddenly goes into emergency mode. Adrenalin starts to flood through your body, your heart starts pumping at two to three times its normal speed, sending nutrient-rich blood to your arms and legs, your eyes dilate so you can see better and non-vital functions close down – even your immune system is temporarily turned off. Within seconds you can run faster, see and hear better, hit harder and think more rapidly than you could moments before. Your super-charged body has now evened the odds of either fighting or fleeing from your attacker.

Task completed, emergency over, and you then need to rest up and let your body slowly recover.

Flash forward to the present day, and we still have the same internal working parts of our caveman. Instead of the tiger though, it's the boss calling you into his office ...what's going to happen? What have I done wrong? Has he finally found me out? What can I expect? The same old fight or flight responses are triggered. In my case, it's the radio call about a violent domestic, the ongoing pub fight, the maniac with the knife. Cue the pumping heart, adrenalin shot and bionic vision.

The automatic responses are great if they are really needed, but each time it's a false alarm, all that pent-up energy in your body has no place to go – and it plays havoc with your internal systems. Too many false alarms can lead to stress-related disorders like heart disease, high blood pressure, immune system disorders, insomnia, migraines and, worst of all, sexual dysfunction – and none of us want that!

And, as most of our calls are either false, 'not as reported', or at best, exaggerated, I was getting all set to fight my Sabre-tooth tiger several times a day, but he never showed – the big pussy!

Don't get me wrong, I'd still blue light posthaste, that's the fun part of the job – but I'd save my body the ordeal of being put through the stress and worry of what I was going to do until I actually arrived and found out what was *really* happening.

Eleven o'clock at night and another call, this time the number had increased to a hundred youths brawling. Males and females, all fighting outside The Bush Inn across town. Yawn.

You can end up doing this all night sometimes. Call and response, call and response. Sometimes villains will even make a false call to get all available units to the other side of town, while they commit a burglary free from our prying eyes. Come to think of it, The Bush was about the furthest pub there was from the industrial estate. They had been having a rough time with break-ins recently. We'd quickly check this job out and then head back over there for a general float around the business units.

A quick four minute run and we turned into the offending street where The Bush was situated ...and there in front of us were about a hundred drunk persons, scrapping and carrying on.

"Assistance required. Things are definitely a bit hairy at The Bush."

In situations like this, despite there seeming to be few officers on duty, a call for a big pub fight generally gets police from all over converging to assist. After a liberal amount of assault and pepper, order was once again restored. Once a few of the ringleaders are taken out of the picture, calm generally returns pretty quickly. Whilst caged vehicles and panda cars pulled away with their new occupants to various custody suites, most of the antagonists wandered off homeward bound, and soon all that was left in the street were a few diehards, wondering whether to have another drink or go for a kebab. Five minutes on and everything was peaceful once more. Just a solitary, young male in his early twenties, was standing in the road, chatting amicably to myself and Gwen along with Ron and Bob who were still on scene. A dishevelled woman with hair modelled on Medusa then emerged from the nearby pub, clearly the worse for wear.

"I'll sort him out!" she yelled. "Is he bothering you, officers? Come here, you radgie, off home with you, now!"

"Is that your mother?" queried Ron.

"What you trying to say, like?" the male responded indignantly. "That's me lass!"

The embarrassment indicator then leapt from zero to ten as Ron started to quickly back peddle ...badly. To be honest, I think we *all* thought the woman was his mother. She was quite a distance away when we first saw her, but to be honest, as the distance closed, we all still held onto the same opinion. She must have had one rough paper round. Not wishing to be tarred with the same brush – insulting the poor bloke's girlfriend – we all thought we would help the situation by chorusing, "Yeah Ron, what were you trying to say about the young lady?"

Ron might be handy in a physical, confrontational situation, but trying to extricate himself from a social faux pas, was an altogether different matter.

This was his problem now. After a few feeble excuses about the lack of street lighting, the distance that he first saw her, and how it could be interpreted as a compliment about her perceived maturity (how can that possibly be a compliment?), he did what all quick thinking coppers do in such a situation when they no longer wish to speak to a member of the public: he touched his earpiece, and leant his head to one side as if listening to something intently and then, in an over exaggerated way, pretended to speak into his radio.

"Yes, yes, I'll be there shortly."

Then, turning to the rest of us, informed us in a loud

voice that a job in Kilo 2 had just come in and he had to rush. "But I'm sure that these officers would be only too pleased to give you and your lovely wife a lift home" ...before he sped off to the non-existent detail with his tail between his legs.

So, even we get things wrong from time to time.

One of the other types of call that is almost never 'as reported' are MISPERS – or, to put it in terms that people can understand – missing persons. When I first heard about mispers, I envisaged abductions and kidnappings, and whilst it can turn out that way, 99.9% of the time it's something quite different.

Generally, it is children who are reported missing, but who aren't *actually* missing – just not back by their bedtime. However, because we live in a society where we need to blame someone if something goes wrong, each naughty child is given the full misper treatment. A comprehensive booklet is completed on every aspect of the person (which takes so long to complete that the child often walks in just as you finish the last line), and the priority of the shift is then to search for the wayward urchin. It's a bum covering exercise, but just like those spurious reports of fights, it's the one time that we don't investigate that something, no doubt, really will have happened. Thankfully, the hundreds of reports I've completed have all been false alarms.

I always find the attitude of the parents fascinating. Some, like you, dear reader, will be responsible guardians who will already have been ringing around friends and out combing the streets. Others, like those who use this book to prop up a wobbly table (the infidels!), will be sitting with a beer, watching the telly.

"So what have you done already to locate your daughter?" I'll ask.

"Nowt. It's your job, copper," will come back the reply.

Adult mispers are a different kettle of fish. Often, when they go missing, they just don't want to be found.

"We don't want to be found," they'll say.

It's their right, too. Anyone can go missing if they want to. Except me, on bin day. I'll get in trouble if I miss that.

However, we will dutifully track our adult misper down, ascertain if they are ok, and then carefully release them back into the wild again.

Sometimes, they will be surprised that anyone has missed them at all, sometimes they will come back home of their own accord, or sometimes, as happened to me the first time I found someone who was classified as a vulnerable missing person, when you find them, they will punch you hard in the face as a thank you for your concerns. Mispers can be classified as 'vulnerable' for a variety of reasons.

Cherie Knowles was reported as missing, and as a regular self-harmer, she was consequently categorised as vulnerable. She was well-known in the town, so the first thing we did was let the local supermarkets know she was up to her old tricks, and asked them to let us know if they saw her. And it worked! Well, not exactly as I would have hoped, I grant you that, but it worked nonetheless. The security officer from the shop rang a couple of hours later to say that Miss Knowles had just been in, that her arms were a bit of a mess, being covered in blood, and that she had bought a packet of razor blades. I thought about enquiring why they didn't stop her buying the razors if she was in that state and they knew that she was suicidal, but hey, it's a cut-throat world out there, profits are profits, and every little helps.

David Nyle was another such vulnerable missing from home. David was a twenty-something male, classified as a high risk as he had left a note saying he was going to end it all which, consequently, meant that even more resources were poured into the search for him. On a cold, November night, I was one of those resources.

He was a Goth who had met up with his partner at a Marilyn Manson concert. As all neo-romantic Goths do, he had swapped spells and morbid musings with her and no doubt hoped that one day they'd be happily miserable together in hell. However, she had lately discovered the twenty-first century, Phil Spectre-ish sound of the Pipettes, and had swapped her dyed black hair, heavy, black medieval gowns and panda eyes for a short blonde bob, a polka dot dress and ...well, panda eyes. He just couldn't accept she would prefer the upbeat, cheery, cherry tones of joy and happiness to the ambient sounds of the ethereal darkwave. He was naturally devastated, as any self-respecting lugubrious batcaver would be. Cue suicidal scribblings.

Like the mascara running down his sad, white face, he had run away from home, only stopping to pick up a bottle of black nail paint en route. A full blown missing person investigation had then started, and on that unforgiving November night, all the evidence pointed to our man being in the lovely North Yorkshire town of Whitby.

It seems that many people enjoyed lovely holidays there as children, and, bizarrely, choose that same place, with so many happy memories, to end it all. David Nyle chose Whitby for an altogether different reason.

With its quaint, cobbled streets and picturesque houses standing on the steep slopes of the River Esk, Whitby is dominated by the ruins of the old Abbey on the cliff top. Dracula is supposed to have landed at Whitby disguised as a black dog and then run up the 199 steps to the old St Mary's church that stands next to these ruins. This is where Dracula is supposed to be buried, and because of that, this is where I was heading at midnight.

North Yorkshire officers were tied up with their own incidents, and so I was tasked, along with Geezer from my shift, and the lovely Charlotte and old Whitey from the previous shift, to travel into a different Force area, to search the town for Mr Nyle. As he had a morbid fascination with all things Dracula, we were tasked to search the Abbey ruins and, in particular, find Dracula's grave where our lonely Goth might well be.

We drove through the night and eventually arrived in

Yorkshire, the county where they name towns after cakes. Another hour later and we arrived in Whitby itself and slowly drove up the hill to the ruined Abbey, parking in the deserted car park. It was a cold, still, full moon night and we were looking for a miserable Gothic type. I think that description covers about ninety five percent of this unique subculture. Hopefully, there shouldn't be too many about on a windswept headland, in the silent hours, on a freezing, dark night in late autumn. A few monkeys with welding gear perhaps, but hopefully not too many suicidal, shoe-gazing, 'Fields of the Nephilim' fans.

Charlotte confided in us all that she was a bit wary about all of this which, in hindsight, was a basic schoolgirl error. Never tell a group of fellow coppers what you are scared of as they will only use that information to further unnerve you. Or, ideally, petrify you. Her fears were deep-rooted. Firstly, she has a thing about dogs, ever since she was viciously bitten by one when she was on duty one day ...and I do concede, it was a nasty bite as, despite my protestations, she insisted on defiantly showing me her gash. Secondly, she had a thing about Dracula ...and not a good thing ...ever since watching Coppola's film of the same name.

There was a slight fret that night which seemed to hang over the Abbey, making things even more atmospheric. Dracula can shape shift and at various times, as well as a bat, dog, wolf or a rodent, he has also manifested himself as vapour or fog. Uncharacteristically, instead of trying to put the willies up her as I would have liked to have done, I gently reassured her, telling her that she was perfectly safe as he only went for young, beautiful virgins.

Unfortunately, both the café and souvenir shop were closed at two in the morning ...as were the gates to the Abbey. We solved this rather cleverly by breaking into the Abbey ...or scaling the wall at least. Halfway over the wall, Charlotte got cramp and suddenly went rigid, rocking back and forth like a human see-saw. We all seized the opportunity, after having calmed her initial worries, by hiding amongst the ancient relics, ready to scare the living daylights out of her when she finished her see-sawing.

We then proceeded to search every inch of the remains by moonlight, not wanting to frighten away our misper with the flash of a torch. During our forage, we did find a tomb that had the top missing. As we all gathered around looking into the vacated space, Geezer suggested the corpse had maybe got up in the middle of the night. Whitey confessed to us that if the cadaver was anything like him, he'd probably get up at least twice in the night.

Having reassured ourselves that there was no top-hatted, velvet pantalooned Goth, festooned with a black cape and wearing twelve hole Docs, hiding amongst the ruins, we broke out of the priory the same way we got in. No Whitby see-saw this time though.

Then, it was gravestone by gravestone in the churchyard. A cold sea breeze, a full moon, the silhouettes of seagulls that looked like giant vampire bats, combined with the occasional shriek of an unidentified beast, all added to the eeriness of it all. It was as if the whole place was filled with ghosts and ghouls. Charlotte didn't want to be caught by the ghosties and the rest of us didn't want to be caught out by an old joke.

As Whitey checked behind the final crooked headstone, a small dog jumped out and let out a shrill bark.

"FUCK!" echoed in the still night air. We all came running over, zig-zagging through the tombstones, just in time to see our hero pick himself up off the ground. The offending dog, a small Bedlington terrier, was sat nearby, scratching his head with his leg. Unless there had been severe budget cuts, I doubt that this was Dracula. Whitey stood there with all the grace and poise of a person who had been chatting to someone in a school yard and just had a football bounce hard off his ear.

We then drove down into the town, searching street by street for our misper's abandoned car, but with no success.

As dawn broke and daylight started to creep into the town, we decided to call it a day when, suddenly, Charlotte spotted a figure on the pier on the other side of the estuary who had climbed over the barrier and was walking along the old, wooden slats – along the dangerous part, off limits to the public.

We jumped back into our vehicle and started to drive round. Damn! The swing bridge was open, letting a fishing trawler through, so we sat at the traffic lights, helpless, wondering if our figure would still be there when we got round, or whether they would have jumped into the briny. The bridge finally swung back again and we raced over and along the front, slowing to a halt before leaping out and running along the pier.

The figure looked over towards us and quickly moved back and forth as if they were panicking. Suddenly, a leg went over the external handrail. Shit! All this effort just for the misper to jump into the cold water right in front of us? We slowed to a walk, two of us moving on, two staying put. As we closed in, I could see the figure had something in its hands. A Bible? Bram Stoker's Dracula? The 'Pull Shapes' CD?

We climbed over the barrier that closed off the dangerous end of the pier from pedestrian access, feeling exposed as the waves crashed beneath us. We stumbled over the uneven planks and edged closer to the figure who appeared to be staring intently at the Abbey ruins on the cliff top. They then raised something to their face. A camera?

It was a camera. And this wasn't our misper.

"Ciao Polizia!"

It was a photographer …and an Italian photographer at that. We tried to explain that we thought he was trying to jump into the sea. He gave us a quizzical look in return. He responded in pidgin English that he was just taking pictures of the Abbey. Apparently, in the clear, dawn light, it looked 'bellissimo' or some such thing. He asked if he was allowed on this end of the pier – at least that's what I thought he was asking. I had been on duty for twenty hours by now. I was tired, cold, hungry, hadn't found the misper, and just wanted to go to bed. I couldn't think what the Italian was for 'I don't give a monkey's chuff', so I left it to Whitey to explain as I wandered back to the car.

"What was he doing?" asked Charlotte.

"You'll only laugh," I told her.

"I didn't laugh when you gave me a copy of your last book, did I?"

Fair point. So I told her. She didn't know what the Italian for monkey's chuff was either ...or even if monkeys have chuffs.

The tale had a happy ending, by the way. Our misper was found the next day (as most normally are), and didn't know what all the fuss was about. He had been to the Abbey, but when the café was open which seems a lot more sensible if you ask me. He seemed happy that he was a missing person that someone actually missed. Not *too* happy, though, he's got appearances to keep up after all. Still, he never got to see the Whitby see-saw ...or heard Charlotte's scream as we had all jumped out from behind the old tomb.

And at least I didn't have to think up some funny line for the Abbey's visitors' book.

CHAPTER TWENTY:

Monday's Experts

I've discovered that there are certain tell tale signs that you are getting older.

When I switch on the TV in the morning, instead of finding the cartoons, I switch on the news channel to 'catch up with what's going on in the world' – or maybe the history channel – to catch up on what was going on in the world a thousand years ago. I'm not exactly sure when this disturbing phenomenon started ...around about the same time that I realised I could spell 'phenomenon' without using the spell checker. I also now find myself involuntarily groaning when I bend over. I don't need to groan ...I just do. Again, start date unknown. I also over prepare for long journeys, find myself leaving funerals before the end 'to beat the rush', and perceive women on pushbikes as attractive.

One of the things that I have not yet fallen foul of is spending more time than is socially acceptable walking naked around the gym changing room as, Chad pointed out, old blokes are oft to do. No, I follow the unwritten, age-old protocol regarding use of a gymnasium changing amenities to the age-old, unwritten letter.

When showering in communal facilities I ensure that I do not face outward (exhibitionist), I do not face the wall (something to hide?), I do not face the person showering next to me (over friendly), nor do I face away from the person showering next to me (over friendly again, but in a different way). Instead, after standing for several seconds with my hand in the water stream and finally realising that the temperature is not going to change, I enter and stand at the regulation forty five degree angle, keeping the soaping of the undercarriage to a bare minimum, and I am also fully prepared to count the soap as 'missing in action' should I accidentally drop it.

When sitting in the sauna, I also like to keep myself to myself. I go in there to enjoy the dubious, exaggerated benefits that the nice girl on the main desk says that I'll get from the experience, not to take part in someone's personal Q&A session. By this I am referring to the time when a guy I barely know to say hello to, decided to quiz me on what he referred to as 'a delicate legal matter'.

"You're a policeman. You can tell me what to do."

"Can I?"

He then proceeded to tell me the sorry tale of his 'friend' who had gone to an all male sauna in town – the sort where it's sans Speedos (I stick to a pair of knee length bathers, I'll have you know). His 'friend' had sat down, enjoying the heat and humidity and after a while gently dozed off, whilst unbeknown to him, his dangling balls had fallen betwixt the wooden seating slats. No real problem there ...that is until someone else entered the cubicle and tossed some menthol onto the heated rocks. Our narrator's 'friend' had then instinctively shot up as the overpowering odour filled the room, whilst his unfortunate nutsack remained in situ.

"Can I make a claim?"

"I thought you said it was your friend?"

...and I didn't want to see the collateral damage either.

I've also discovered that in the gym changing rooms, old guys seem to want to engage you in long conversations as they dry themselves off. They'll stand facing you, legs akimbo, one foot on the floor, the other up on a bench, leaving the last turkey in the shop dangling back and forth as they vigorously towel their back. I prefer to keep any social intercourse in this sort of establishment to a minimum ...whilst keeping my boxers on ...not that I have anything to be ashamed of ...and if any woman tells you otherwise, she's a bloody liar!

Nor do I do that thing that old folks do – complain about the number of e-mails I have received whilst I've been away on holiday. I cannot, as I have too often chastised an old person who has bemoaned the large volume of correspondence with the riposte, 'Yes matey, I've received exactly the same number as you, but I've had to answer them over the last two weeks, whilst you, you grumbling old codger, have been sunning your wrinkly hide in the Algarve.'

Whilst I am on the subject, and I am pre-warning you now, do not come up to me on a freezing cold winter's evening and tell me that you have just flown back from your holiday and expect me to feel sorry for you, "because when we left, it was blazing sunshine and ninety degrees!" You may be offended by my response.

But I digress.

I am also pleased to say that I have also not yet fallen foul of buying the *Mail on Sunday* just for the free DVD, started to think tank tops are fashionable again, nor indeed, have I started to judge women non-visually either.

The other thing I have yet to do is admit when I'm wrong – even if I am, which I'm not.

Don't get me wrong, I'm not saying that I never make mistakes. Indeed, some recent mistakes have been:

Walking upstairs and my legs thought there was one more step than there really was ...and sometimes my legs think there is one more step on the way down too ...my legs are really stupid.

Taking Barney to the park to try and chat up that nice girl I've seen there – nothing gets a woman more in the mood than seeing a bloke holding a Tesco carrier bag full of dog turd.

Whilst taking a ride on the tube on a recent trip to London, making eye contact and trying to start up a conversation with a stranger. I found out later that not only is this a heinous mistake, but also possibly a criminal offence down there.

However, these, I hope you will agree, are minor boo boos – understandable misunderstandings – everyday errors. The type of thing everybody does.

Other people's mistakes I reckon are worse than mine.

On a recent nightshift, I called into the all-night Tesco in the town, in company with Ron. As we left, we were collared by the security guy wanting a chat.

"We see a lot of police coming in here in the early hours. I was thinking, you know, since we started opening 24 hours a day, I'd say that between midnight and six in the morning about 65% of our customers are police. The other 10% are just people from the town."

Who are the rest? Aliens?

Sometimes, the mistakes are a lot worse.

My friend from Cardiff rang me the other day to tell me that he had received an invitation to a wedding reception in Leeds Castle. He told me he had thought that he'd drive up to Leeds, and then stop and ask for directions when he got there (for those of you who don't know, Leeds Castle is actually in Kent, which is, by sheer coincidence, what his posh girlfriend called him when she realised they were almost 250 miles from the party). He confessed that he eventually arrived at the wedding five hours late ...and single.

I have another friend who is a complementary therapist. So far so good. He wanted to get some business cards made to add a bit of professionalism to his activities. Still good. He mocked up the design and ordered the cards, along with a thousand leaflets for a mail drop to drum up more business. Still positive. He was delighted when he got the package through his door a week later. Quick service! He then looked a bit more closely at the finished goods and took them into the back garden and burned them all to a cinder. You see, as much as a space doesn't normally mean much to most people, it can mean a lot if you accidentally type a space where a space shouldn't normally be. My friend told me he didn't really fancy a thousand people locally having a leaflet dropping through their letterbox proclaiming:

Feeling stressed? You need my special treatment!
Give me a call today for something altogether different.
Don Kiddick (The rapist)

My personal favourite, though, involves a mistake attributed to the former Conservative MP, Geoffrey Dickens as told by television producer John Lloyd. It transpires that Geoffrey had been invited to a summer fête in his constituency, where he had been followed around the stalls by a devoted, smiling woman of the most indescribable ugliness. Try as he might, he just couldn't get away from her. A few days passed and he received a letter from a constituent saying that she admired him greatly, had met him at a recent fête and asked if she could have a signed photograph. In brackets, after her name, was written the apt description, 'Horse Face'. Geoffrey realised he had misjudged this woman. Not only had she come to terms with her repulsiveness, she had turned it to her advantage. Filled with admiration for her, he decided to enter into the spirit of things, bought a frame for the photograph, and wrote on it with a flourish, 'To Horse Face, love and best wishes, Geoffrey Dickens'. It was only when it was safely in the post to his courageous constituent that he was accosted by his secretary.

"Did you get the letter from that woman at the fête? I wrote 'Horse Face' on it just so you'd remember who she was."

Still, what I'm referring to when I'm talking about not admitting my mistakes is when the Monday's experts tell me I'm wrong. You come across Monday's experts in all walks of life. Those people who are not there when the decision has to be made, but who still pontificate – telling you what you did wrong and what you should have done. You often meet Monday's experts in the pub. There are a lot of Monday's experts when it comes to football. Who should have won, who they should have fielded in the team, who should have passed, who should have taken the penalty and so on. Unfortunately, you can't put a bet on at the finish of a race.

These are some of my disputes with the Monday's experts ...who, when the alleged mistake happens at work, are also known as the Complaints and Discipline Department (whose unofficial motto is, I do believe, *'we're not happy, until you're not happy'*).

Case 1.

A call had come over the radio about a theft from Blockbusters. Description of the suspect: white male, about six foot, stocky build, bald, wearing a black leather jacket and blue jeans.

It was only three o'clock, but already getting dark as I headed towards the town, when I spotted a shifty-looking bloke standing in a cut leading from the town centre to the nearby housing estate. Description of this shifty looking bloke: white male, about six foot, stocky build, bald, wearing a black leather jacket and blue jeans.

I stopped the panda, got out and started to walk over to the male. As he saw me, he turned away and pretended to talk on his mobile phone. You're not fooling anyone, shifty guy!

"Can I have a word please?" I shouted over.

"No," came the response and he started to walk away.

I closed in on him and asked him where he had just been.

"Nothing to do with you," was the reply.

I asked him what he was up to.

"I don't have to tell you," he answered.

"I'm going to have to search you, there's been a..."

Before I could finish my spiel, the giant had countered with, "You're not searching me, copper."

Here I was, in a small cut, with a six foot, stocky bloke who matched the description of the offender and who was acting in a shifty manner and was refusing to cooperate with me. Admittedly, this wasn't the most comprehensive of investigations since 'Who Shot JR?', but everything pointed to this being our man. Bingo!

I hadn't acted quickly enough when I had my run in with Peacock and he had put me in hospital. Eager not to repeat the same events (although I do concede that I did like the couple of weeks at the convalescence home), I grabbed one arm and applied a cuff to it and twisted it behind his back. I didn't fancy this hefty bloke hammering me into the ground like ...well, like some hammering machine. "You're under arrest on suspicion of theft."

He was a big fella and he twisted away from me so I couldn't get hold of his other hand. Luckily enough, Chad had pulled up in his car and now sprang to my aid. I started to apply some knee strikes to the suspect's outer thigh to try and get the monster to the floor and make it easier to control him. Grabbing his other arm, Chad forced it up his back. Our fella was a strong one, I'll give him that. Eventually, amongst shouts of, 'Stop Struggling!', we managed to get the suspect contained, face down on the floor amongst the dirty puddles of water and crisp wrappers. I picked up the phone he had dropped in the fracas, to hear a female voice.

"Garth, are you there? What's happening?"

I hung up.

We searched Garth. Nothing. I got on the radio to my colleagues. Lloyd went and retraced Garth's possible route from Blockbusters to here. Nothing abandoned along the route. Ron went into the store to check if there was any CCTV available. There wasn't, but he was provided with a better description of the thief.

Male. Check.

White. Check.

Six foot. Check.

Stocky build. Check.

Bald. Check.

Wearing black leather jacket. Check.

Blue jeans. Check.

Aged about twenty. Shit. This guy was about forty if he was a day.

Nothing for it but to let him go.

I did a few more jobs and then went back to the station. Garth had beaten me there and informed the Sergeant that I had beaten him here ...or there ...in the cut anyway.

"He's demanded a formal, unconditional apology," Barry informed me.

Now, this is where I'm showing my age. If I felt I had done something wrong, I'd happily have given an unconditional apology but I didn't feel I had done anything wrong. I'd acted in good faith. If Garth had cooperated, we wouldn't have had this unfortunate turn of events.

"But he doesn't have to answer your questions if he doesn't want to," Barry reminded me.

I'd be happy to say that I was sorry about the way the situation had turned out, but not to say that I was sorry full stop. I would do the same again in the same circumstances. Instead, Barry organised a 'love in' for the following day. Well, a meeting with Garth, me and someone from personnel anyway, where no doubt we would all sit around, join hands and chant *'Love in – hate out – love in – hate out'*.

As it was, I couldn't attend the love-fest as I was out and about, busy notching up my second incident for Monday's experts.

Case 2.

A call had come over the radio about a sighting of a well-known armed robber and heroin addict who was cycling around Tesco car park with a knife and what looked like a police radio. The whole station emptied as marked and unmarked cars sped off in all directions to try and locate the violent felon. He was last reported entering the maze of streets to the west of the supermarket.

I took my panda straight to a local parade of shops. It was school closing time and the area would be swarming with young kids and their mums. I parked up and listened to the radio traffic. There would be a sighting, and then he'd disappear from view up a cut where a vehicle couldn't follow. Officers were on foot now, running through the streets trying to cut him off. He was leading us all a merry dance. Then ...a confirmed sighting – he was cycling down Porter Way. That was near here! I took the vehicle and drove to the end of the road so I could see up the street. There he was, cycling like a thing possessed, being chased by Barry and the Inspector on foot.

If he managed to get to the shops, goodness knows what he would do. The last thing I wanted was one of the children or young mums being attacked or taken hostage. I needed to think fast. I could get out and try and stop the bike but he could just as easily avoid me when he saw me coming. I needed to stop him getting to the innocent public.

I reversed around the corner out of view and pulled the vehicle across the pavement, blocking access that way. I then started to get out, ready to intercept our knifeman, when I heard an almighty BANG!

I looked up and there was an ugly face pressed up against my windscreen. His bike must have crashed into the side of the vehicle, sending him flying into the glass. I jumped out as he staggered upright, and then grabbed his arm, taking him to the floor and applied the cuffs. I just had time to whisper, "You're nicked," in his ear before Sarge and the Inspector came panting around the corner. Within seconds other units arrived to see me there, kneeling above our prize, saviour of the public, crime buster extraordinaire. Maybe one day they will erect a small plaque here, reminding people how I saved the citizens of Sandford from a fate worse than death ...or just maybe death. Maybe, but just not today.

I thought at least maybe I'd get a thanks. But you know what thought did...

No. No thanks today and no plaque tomorrow. The cyclist was searched and nothing was found on him. He'd obviously thrown the knife and radio away while he was on the run. Instead of being congratulated, I was suspended from driving pending a breath test, and a comprehensive report was drawn up, the scene photographed and I had to write a statement – under caution – explaining my actions.

"So, we have an innocent member of the public out on a bike ride when a police officer drives his police vehicle into the path of the innocent rider, causing him to smash his face off the windscreen of the panda car ...and to add insult to injury, the cyclist is then wrestled to the ground by that same police officer. Is that about right, Donoghue?"

"Well, no, Sir. It wasn't like that at all."

"But that's what the papers will say. And that's what our cyclist's solicitor will say when he sues the Force for unlawful arrest and sues you for assault."

I just looked down at my boots. I felt embarrassed. Like when you open up a packet of tablets and find it's the instruction leaflet end.

"Luckily for you, I've smoothed over the incident so none of that is going to happen now. And I've sorted out the debacle when you beat up the innocent member of the public yesterday."

"Thank you, Sir." Maybe he wasn't so bad after all.

"Now get out of my sight, you idiot." Yes, he was.

"But before you go – just one last thing."

"Yes, Sir?"

"I'm like an elephant." Oh my God, he wasn't going to pull his trouser pockets out was he?

There was an uncomfortable silence as he stood up from the chair. I averted my gaze. I find staring at my boots is always a good thing to do in these sorts of circumstances. I gave it a few seconds and then looked up, but he was still drawing out the overdramatic pause. I felt like I was on *Who Wants To Be A Millionaire?* Finally, he spoke again.

"I never forget."

Phew!

CHAPTER TWENTY ONE:

Christmas

Christmas can mean different things to different people.

To some in Sandford, it means wholeheartedly embracing the services offered by the National Grid. One day it will be a plain old council house on the Yellow Estate, and the next, when they perceive it to be the start of the Christmas festive period, sometime around the middle of October, that same plain old council house will suddenly be visible from the moon.

At the front, articulated reindeer made of neon tubes will jerkily move their heads as if to munch grass, whilst on the roof, colourful, inflatable Santas will pretend to break into the house via the chimney. All points in between will be filled with glowing snowmen, flashing signs and blinking lights. Inside, you could probably sharpen your knife on the electricity meter as it spins around at a rate of knots.

The owners usually leave their curtains open so they can glimpse the majesty of their light pollution. In return, anyone wandering by outside looking in is rewarded with the sight of a fat bloke in a grubby vest, holding a can of Carlsberg and watching telly.

For Lloyd, Christmas meant finding out that going into a fast food restaurant whilst doing his last minute shopping wasn't such a good idea. He described to us what unfolded thusly:

"The place was heaving with people; it was dirty, the food

was rubbish and to top it all off, there was no paper when I went to the toilet." Then, very matter of factly ...in fact, too matter of factly in my opinion, he added, "So, I had to use my sock instead."

His sock! A sweaty sock? It would have never occurred to me in a million years to use my sock. Waddle back into the restaurant maybe and grab a pile of napkins, ring the place from my phone and get them to send someone in with some loo roll, use the wrapping paper from the presents ...but a sock?

There were so many questions I had to ask: did he turn it inside out, did he use it like a sock puppet, did he flush it away afterwards, left sock or right? So many questions, but I was unable to ask any.

Instead, I was curled up, crying, the tears running down my face, my belly hurting from laughing so much. By the time I had recovered, he was gone. At least he has big feet or who knows what item of apparel would have been sacrificed next. In fact, maybe the Chavs are onto something in wearing two pairs of socks. They are fast food regulars. Perhaps they've learnt by past experience and are just carrying around their equivalent of spare paper? Meanwhile, we were just hoping that poor Lloyd doesn't contract Athletes Arse as a result.

Elsewhere, Christmas for Geezer meant him learning a valuable lesson, whilst Christmas for Ron meant him teaching Geezer a valuable lesson.

The lesson being: don't drop off to sleep in the passenger seat at three in the morning when crewed up with Ron. Shifts play havoc with your body clock at the best of times, add to this the cries of his newborn baby robbing him of what precious sleep he could snatch at home, and the result is one Southerner coming onto night shift more weary than normal. At three in the morning, as Ron and Geezer were driving around the industrial estate looking for the non-existent crooks who had, sensibly, already gone to bed, Geezer nodded off. It's understandable. There is a reason why they called it Z Cars. It's an unnatural time to be awake. If anyone asks you what the point of a sleepless night is, this is it. When you are racing from job to job, arresting felons, being awake all night seems a vital necessity in the prevention of crime, but other times, like now, when all you are doing is dodging the rabbits running around the business park, it can all seem pretty pointless.

However, as Ron was still awake and still driving, he wasn't really in such a forgiving mood. Instead, he slowed to about three or four miles per hour, drove into the truck stop, and when he was about six feet from the rear of a particularly large articulated lorry, slammed the brakes on whilst simultaneously shouting, 'AAAAAGH!!!!'.

Cue Geezer, our sleeping beauty, or as Ron prefers to call him, sleeping ugly, waking up suddenly, and flailing about, convinced that he was about to plough into the rear of a sixteen wheeler at high speed. It takes Ron about five minutes to stop belly laughing when this happens, gasping for breath as he does so, and Geezer a further ten to get his heart rate back to normal.

If Geezer falls asleep in the station, the opportunity is not lost either – we just play Buckeroo with him, loading him up like that little mule, with staplers, hole punches and used milk cartons.

For me, Christmas reminds me of my first ever experience of the police. I was about ten years old and playing at our local park. There had been some heavy snowfall over the proceeding few days and we had all got up to snow related activities. Well, throwing snowballs and building snowmen. As I was ambling home for tea, I saw two policemen talking to a couple of my friends – Hicksy and PJ – next to their snowman. It was only when I got closer that I saw that their snowman had a massive phallus made of snow, accompanied by equally big snowballs. They were being gently encouraged to remove the said appendages before some women came by and were offended. I thought the coppers were killjoys.

However, thirty years later, I came across my own snowman with a big cock. Snow had been falling on the town for a few days and everything had a bright dusting of the white stuff, making the whole area look clean and fresh. It was one of those days when you marvel at the beauty of nature, when you are pleased to be alive to enjoy the majesty of it all. Even the shit parts of the town seemed beguiling with their snowy veneer.

I was on foot patrol walking past the primary school when I saw him ...and it was definitely a him. Big and white, with bulging eyes made from empty Carlsberg cans, a big nose crafted from a hardened dog turd, a smile consisting of an array of bottle tops and sporting the most impressively massive erection you have ever seen, made by the look of it, from the shank of an old broom. What happened to the good old days when they just had a pipe?

Amongst all this beauty, this snow cock man was a thing of evil perpetrated by people with minds as pure as the driven slush. I couldn't let the little children from the school see this and let it soil their tiny minds. *Walking In The Air* would never have the same ring to it after seeing this abomination. It would be the stuff of nightmares for them. I had a responsibility ...nay, a duty to rid the streets of Sandford of such an outrageous monstrosity. Something had to be done to protect the innocent, young minds of this town ...even if it did look quite funny. There was no-one else around so the heavy burden of snowman censorship was down to me. I had reluctantly become a PC PC. I had to kill the abominable snowman and turn it back into a snow person with a wave of my magic asp.

I had decided to knock the cock off with my baton rather than just pull it off as I didn't want any passer-by thinking I was giving this creature a hand job. He had a big enough smile on his face as it was. This was to be a punishment beating, not a reward after all. I gave him a few whacks but, alas, apart from knocking it down slightly, I only succeeded in changing him from a rampant snowman to one with brewer's droop. By the look of it, it was a whole broom they had used. I changed tactics and stood directly in front, facing the offending snowman and lifted my leg back in an effort to kick the tip of his cock with the heel of my boot and so send the broom shooting out through his arse. Two kicks and it shot out the rear! I was now making contact with the fat snowman's belly, caving his snowy pelvis in. Take that you rude fucker!

I was feeling pretty pleased with myself when I looked over at the school. About fifty small faces were pressed up against the windows of their classrooms. Most looked frightened, some were crying, and the teacher just looked annoyed. I tried to mouth to the teacher a conciliatory *I was only trying to kick his cock off* but to no avail. I picked up the broom and tried to show how obscene it had been, pushing it back and forth like a huge phallus in front of me, but it only seemed to make things worse. Miss Jones was there. She just rolled her eyes. I could see the kids being shepherded away from the window and the blinds being pulled down. Shit!

Elsewhere, Christmas for Ben and George meant telling off some of the naughtier kids from the local comp for whom Christmas meant trying to roll a fat lass down the hill, hoping she would develop into a massive snowball before she reached the bottom.

Whilst some are celebrating Christmas with praises to the Lord, others are celebrating with strong lager. For many police officers, the season of peace and goodwill starts with Black Eye Friday – aka the Night of the Living Arseholes. This is the last working Friday for most of the general public before the Christmas holidays. The combination of Christmas parties, a Friday night out, and general festivity, normally results in one of our busiest nights of the year, giving New Year's Eve a close run for its money. Many police officers will start the festivities racing from drunken fight to drunken fight, carting people off to the cells, quickly swilling out the sick from the back of the cage before racing off to another drunken brawl. What a great start to your Crimbo holiday.

The festive period also means answering at least twice, if not more, the question: *if you wake up at midnight at Christmas and found someone dressed as Santa in your bedroom, would you be justified in beating him to death?*

I don't quite know if I was being tested by certain members of the populace of Sandford on my knowledge of law, or whether something more sinister was afoot. Maybe they were trying to persuade their mother-in-law that it would be fun for the grandkids if she were to don a red suit and beard to dole out the presents this year, luring her into receiving a sound (and legitimate – PC Donoghue said) beating. Maybe they were planning a Christmas Eve burgling frenzy and just wanted to make sure that they weren't putting themselves at undue risk.

I would reply in a vague manner, suggesting it depended on the quality of presents he was bringing you. They normally seemed happy with that.

To most, including me, it means spending too much and starting off the new year in debt. *Get thee behind me Santa!*

For others, the dark nights herald a season of sharing. That is; thieves sharing the presents you bought for your family with their family ...or, anyone down the pub who wants to buy a new Playstation. Burglaries usually see an increase during these darker nights.

To some, it means finding your teenage daughter's boyfriend has written his name in yellow snow over the front lawn, having a little laugh about it, remembering when you used to write your own name in wee in the snow, and then suddenly realising that whilst it may be *his* pee, it's in *her* handwriting.

For one lady along with Chad, Andy, Bob and myself, it

meant standing in the cold watching a snake. She had made the call to Comms, alerting us to the fact that she had spotted a snake loose on the street as she had walked back home with a takeaway. It wasn't your run of the mill call, so an audience had begun congregating to view our wayward reptile. Initially, I was on scene, then Bob arrived, soon joined by Chad and Andy who wisely observed from the safety of their vehicle. No one wanted to miss this.

"How long has he been there?" I enquired of the informant.

"I've been here about half an hour and he hasn't moved," she replied, still staring at the scaly specimen which was laid quietly under a lamppost.

It was a cold, December evening and the condensation on everyone's breath hung in the still air.

"Maybe he's escaped?" she volunteered.

We've all seen the wide variety of bizarre and exotic pets in various aquarium and glass fronted boxes in the houses on the estates – from tarantulas to stick insects, so anything was possible. He could have made his slithery way from his home on the estates to the posh end of town in a bid to compare graffiti.

"You're from Africa, what sort's that then?" Andy asked our Zimbabwean.

"A snake," came Bob's reply. Very helpful.

"Chad, you've got a degree. Is it venomous?" I queried.

"It's a law degree," he responded curtly.

"He hasn't moved for a while," our informant continued. "Maybe he's conserving his energy and getting warmth from the light?"

"Poke 'im!" shouted Chad from the safety of his car.

"Aye, aye, good idea," everyone chorused. "Good idea," and then all stood back waiting for someone else to make the first move.

Eventually, when it was clear that no one else was going to volunteer, I racked my asp (no pun intended) and tentatively poked the thing. Slowly, it rolled onto its back, still and lifeless.

"Is it dead?" enquired the female caller.

"I'm afraid it is," I replied.

"Do you think it was the cold that killed it?" She asked. Clearly, she now felt some tenuous link with our dead vertebrate.

"Either that," I answered, "Or when they stamped '*Made in China*' on his little rubber belly."

"Oh dear," she said, sounding disappointed that her adventure had turned into a mini farce. "You mean it was only a toy?"

"It was just a toy," I confirmed.

"Oh dear," she repeated. "You must think I'm terribly silly, standing watching a pretend snake for thirty minutes and then calling the police out?" she quietly queried.

This was the first time I really noticed her face. She was in her forties, smartly dressed and clearly took pride in her appearance. She reminded me of comely dairymaid made good. She was evidently well-intentioned and was now obviously deeply embarrassed. Her kindly face had turned a deep shade of violet. I could almost feel the heat coming from her cheeks. Her head was bowed slightly as if hung in shame and she looked up at me shyly, as if wanting some kind of reassurance that she had done the right thing, despite the sorry outcome.

"Do I think you are silly?" I asked, clarifying her question.

She nodded. That was what she wanted to know. Or rather be assured that she wasn't.

"Silly, for standing in the cold, watching a little rubber snake for half an hour?" She nodded again.

I thought about it for a second before placing a comforting hand on her shoulder.

"Yes, my friend. Yes I do," I replied, as I smiled and mentally added her onto my waving list.

Elsewhere, Christmas to Gwen and Barry, who had gate-crashed the Special Branch Christmas party, was a revelation. Not much singing or dancing there, they told me, but it's certainly the quickest game of pass the parcel that you'll ever see.

For Nancy in Comms, Christmas meant listening to some of the grumpier adults from Sandford ringing in and complaining about kids throwing snowballs in the street. *"What? You mean there are kids out there having fun? We'll get a patrol out there immediately and put a stop to it straight away!"*

Two other particular calls of note, she told me, represented two sides of the same coin.

Firstly, a call to the emergency services from a child, weeping so heavily on the phone that he could hardly catch his breath, reporting between sobs that his father was being 'mean to him'. Child abuse? Domestic violence? Neglect? Cue two officers despatched, racing with blue lights flashing through the deserted streets on a peaceful Christmas morn. On arrival, however, they soon confirmed that it was nothing of the sort. No brutality, no mistreatment, no crime. Sadly though, it transpired it was something just as bad – in fact, one of the seven deadly sins was in play – greed. It seems that despite sitting amongst a veritable mountain of presents, this spoilt child had felt it necessary to summon the forces of law and order to his home on Christmas Day purely to inform officers that his dad hadn't got him *all* the presents he had asked Santa for. However, what seemed to upset the brat most though was that his malevolent and cruel father had had the brazen audacity to buy him a book. Yes, a book! The monster!

Secondly, an incomplete 999 call from an hysterical adult. Shouting and swearing had been heard before the phone was smashed down onto the receiver. All attempts to re-contact the caller had proved unsuccessful, so the whole of the shift had turned out, racing twenty minutes through the snow blizzard that had suddenly descended, to make sure that all was in order. Now, I don't know if your parents ever told you that you shouldn't give in order to receive, but it is sage advice. However, someone had clearly forgotten this old adage; it turned out that the object of this male's frustration was the fact that he had sent a present to his children in London and they had failed to ring and thank him. I didn't think it was prudent to enquire whether it was a paperback sized gift he had sent, as that may have answered a lot.

All in all, another excellent example of the misuse of the Great British emergency services. Someone should really start charging these morons hard cash for wasting police time because I'm sure that the one time that you, dear reader, actually need us, we'll probably be tied up over the other side of town, caught up in a similar pointless escapade with one of these idiots.

But I digress.

For my dog Barney, Christmas means getting drunk. I was on duty over the festive period which meant no booze at all for me. However, I was in receipt of a lovely, rich, alcohol sodden Christmas cake donated by Nancy. I was really looking forward to tucking into it after my run of shifts had ended, maybe accompanied by a nice piece of Stilton and a glass of port or, preferably, in the company of a nice, young lady, a piece of Stilton and a bottle of port. However, due to the pure selfishness of my hound, I wasn't able to do either. Barney had obviously declined to acknowledge that it was the season of peace and goodwill *to all men*. I've written that in italics because it's not the time of peace and goodwill to all selfish dogs – I think that's in February sometime. No, this was definitely supposed to be the season of peace and goodwill to men.

I don't know the full sorry detail of this betrayal of trust by Barney, but the end result was the aforementioned cake being removed from the big Quality Street tin in which it was originally housed to keep in the moistness and flavour, and ending up in the extended belly of a sheepish looking Labrador.

This heinous act was discovered at five in the morning as I came downstairs to get ready for work. I don't know if you are aware, but raisins and alcohol are actually poisonous for our canine friends. As much as I wasn't feeling particularly friendly towards him at that moment, he was still my responsibility. He ended up being bundled into the back of the car and being taken to the emergency vets where he spent all Boxing Day on a drip in the surgery ...being fawned over by the young female veterinary assistants ...which he loved. So there is going to be no lesson learnt there for him. In case you are concerned (and you really shouldn't be), he was diagnosed as being fine ...just suffering from acute alcohol poisoning. A pissed dog ...what is the world coming to?

I also know what the season of peace and joy means to an unnamed Chief Constable, who, in order for me to keep my job, shall remain nameless.

The story goes that the Chief was flattered to be asked by the local TV station to appear on a pre-recorded programme entitled *What Would I Like For Christmas?*

Eager to be noticed in the circles that Chief Constables like to move in, he was even more delighted when he saw the list of fellow dignitaries who were involved with the venture.

On Christmas morning, after ringing around the other top brass to tell them to tune in, he sat down in front of the telly with his family, excited at the prospect of appearing on the box.

The Bishop was the first to appear, saying that what he wanted for Christmas was greater understanding between the different faiths, and a lasting peace on earth.

The Mayor then said that what he wanted for Christmas was more prosperity for the town, and for more industry to invest in the area.

The local MP said that what he wanted for Christmas was stronger trading contracts for the region with our European neighbours, to enable the town to develop to its full potential.

Finally, it was the turn of the Chief Constable. His family, the top brass and the local population all heard him, to his lasting shame and embarrassment, say in clear, bold tones, that what he really wanted for Christmas ...was a new golf putter.

For me though, in addition to beating up a snowman, Christmas also meant the end of my first full year on 999 response at Sandford.

It was the early hours of Boxing Day night. Technically, we were now into a sort of white space, that limbo period between Christmas and New Year when you are never quite sure what day it is or whether you should have taken annual leave or not.

The incidents and enquiries of the day were all complete. There was no-one left in the cells and all was quiet in the town. I finally had time on my own to sit in quiet reflection.

There's no doubt that being a police officer changes you.

Roughly translated, the philosopher Friedrich Nietzsche once said something along the lines of 'Battle not with monsters lest ye become a monster'. Repellent as they may be, I don't really classify the likes of Drew Peacock and Hugh Janus as out and out monsters. I hadn't yet reached the stage where I stared into the abyss and the abyss stared back at me and then looked away in shame. However, in some way I felt I'd lost what was left of my innocence – that in some ways life had maybe lost a bit of its mystery. Dealing with the worst that society can offer certainly makes you more cynical. To a certain degree, I also felt that I had become de-sensitised to life. Dead bodies, cruelty, neglect – whereas they may have given me sleepless nights in the past – they were now just jobs that had to be dealt with.

On the other hand, I'd fitted a lifetime of new adventure into just one year, and had so many good laughs that my sides ached, had real job satisfaction and felt some genuine camaraderie again. Some experiences were good, some were bad, but all taught me a lesson one way or another. They say that what doesn't kill you makes you stronger, except for polio, of course.

To me, the pros vastly outweighed the cons (insert your own punch line here). The office of Constable is certainly the best position I'd ever held.

I'd even got a couple of romantic opportunities bubbling under. Who knows where they could lead? And I'd remember not to do any comedy sofa jumps this time.

I wondered if the Chief had noticed anything that had happened down here in this small corner of the Constabulary. Hopefully, he may have heard about me saving that suicidal chap on the bridge. Had updates about tackling the mad axe man filtered up to him? Maybe the news of unmasking the Sandford bomber had come to his attention? With any luck though, he hadn't heard of those disciplinary matters.

Not without a small degree of trepidation, I ventured down to the cell area and flicked the switch that turned his computer screen on. I gave it five minutes to warm up and then went back into the parade room, put my password into my computer and logged into my email to see if there was a personal Christmas message from him.

I searched and searched. Nothing. Zero. Not a bean. Zilch.

As I went to turn off the machine, I noticed an email pop into my inbox. It was from the Superintendent. Surely he wouldn't be working at this time and on Boxing Day too? I sat back in my seat, looked behind me to see if I was alone, swallowed hard and then pressed the button to open it. There was just one single word.

Baboon.